Seven Studies
in Medieval English History
and Other Historical Essays

Seven Studies in Medieval English History and Other Historical Essays

Presented to
Harold S. Snellgrove

Richard H. Bowers
Editor

UNIVERSITY PRESS OF MISSISSIPPI
Jackson

This book has been sponsored by
Mississippi State University

Library of Congress Cataloging in Publication Data
Main entry under title:

Seven Studies in Medieval English history and other
   historical essays.

   Includes index.
   Contents: Demographic aspects of the Norman invasions /
by Josiah C. Russell — English merchants and the Anglo-
Flemish economic war of 1270–1274 / by Richard H. Bowers
— Canonists and law clerks in the household of Archbishop
Hubert Walter / by Charles E. Lewis — [etc.]
   1. Great Britain — History — Medieval period, 1066–
1485 — Addresses, essays, lectures. I. Snellgrove, Harold
Sinclair, 1913–   . II. Bowers, Richard (Richard H.)
DA175. S48 1983   942.03   83-3530
ISBN 0-87805-183-X

CONTENTS

PREFACE

Several years ago the late Charles E. Lewis proposed that friends and students of Professor Harold S. Snellgrove prepare a collection of essays which would be presented to Dr. Snellgrove upon his retirement from active teaching. Had it not been for a tragic and fatal automobile accident, Professor Lewis surely would have edited this presentation volume. Unfortunately, this task fell to another.

Those who do not know Harold Snellgrove will have the opportunity to become acquainted with this patrician mentor in the biographical note written by his long-time friend and colleague, Professor Glover Moore. For those who have studied or worked with Professor Snellgrove, Moore's comments will rouse old memories of polished and thoughtful lectures, personal encouragements, informal study sessions devoted to Latin and paleography, and firm but patient guidance for those engaged in research and writing.

Many of Professor Snellgrove's students caught his infectious enthusiasm for the colorful and turbulent history of England in the reign of King Henry III. However, during the years that he presided over the Department of History at Mississippi State University, the faculty was not large, and he was often called upon to direct graduate studies in fields other than medieval history. In planning this volume it was decided to invite contributions from all his friends and students who wished to submit essays even though this made it impossible to give the collection a unifying theme.

I thank Professor Glover Moore and Mississippi State University for the financial support that made possible the publication of this book. I shall always appreciate the help and encouragement Dr. Moore gave me throughout the preparation of the manuscript. I am also grateful to Dr. Barbara Moorman who helped me unknot a number of problems I encountered in transcribing the Anglo-Norman text in the appendix. Finally I want to thank our typists, Cindy, Cheryl, Kathy, and my wife, Janet, for their excellent work.

Richard H. Bowers

FOREWORD

Harold Snellgrove

Classicist and Medievalist

In September 1947, Harold Snellgrove arrived at Mississippi State College to assume the position of instructor in European history. Immediately ahead of him lay much hard work. He not only had a heavy teaching load but, in addition, had set himself the task of completing, by the end of the year, the dissertation which would entitle him to a doctorate at the University of New Mexico. A prodigious worker, well versed in his subject, he had indeed finished the dissertation by the time the Christmas holidays were over. In the same period he accomplished two other feats: he acquired a reputation for being a dynamic teacher, and he began to assemble, in the library of Mississippi State College, a collection of medieval and Renaissance source material which today has reached impressive proportions.

Harold Sinclair Snellgrove was born on May 18, 1913, at Meridian, Mississippi, the son of Edwin Doty and Laura Sinclair Snellgrove. The Snellgroves, who formerly spelled their name Snelgrove, were of English origin. Coming to America in colonial times, they gradually moved westward from Virginia and South Carolina to Mississippi. They were people of strong convictions who appreciated the value of an education and felt an urge to serve the Lord, many of them being Methodist ministers.

Harold Snellgrove began his formal education in the public schools of Meridian, where he was fortunate in having competent and dedicated teachers. When it was time for him to enter college in 1932, the nation was in the grip of the Great Depression. However, with the aid of his uncle, Olin Carman Snellgrove of Montgomery, Alabama, Harold entered Duke University to begin a lifetime of labor in the service of Clio and the classics. The beautiful Gothic campus of Duke was in itself enough to evoke interest in the past. Then there was the influence of the faculty. It was an inspiration to study under such scholars as Allan H. Gilbert, John Tate Lanning, Dorothy Mackay Quynn, and E. Malcolm Carroll. The Duke library affected Snellgrove in the same manner in which it influenced countless others. Working there as an assistant, to help pay college expenses, he came to realize that in the liberal arts the library is the most important thing about a university.

In 1936 Snellgrove was graduated from Duke University, with a major in Greek and English and a minor in Latin. In 1940 he received a master's degree at Duke, with a major in history and a minor in French. Pushing on toward a doctorate, he held a teaching fellowship at the University of North Carolina in 1941-42. In the meantime, he had served as an instructor at Gulf Coast Military Academy in Gulfport, Mississippi, between 1936 and 1941.

As was true of so many young Americans, World War II was to be a watershed in the life of Harold Snellgrove. Entering the armed forces at Camp Shelby, Mississippi, in 1942, he did not return to civilian life until 1946. During the intervening years, he was a personnel technician in the Adjutant General's Department, being stationed first at Camp Shelby and later in New Caledonia and the Philippines. At the time of his discharge, he had attained the rank of technical sergeant.

After leaving military service at the close of the war, Snellgrove continued his studies for the doctorate. His major professor at the University of North Carolina, Josiah Cox Russell, left Chapel Hill in 1946 to become chairman of the History Department at the University of New Mexico. Professor Russell's love for medieval history and culture is of that contagious quality that affects students, and it is not surprising that Snellgrove followed him to New Mexico in 1946.

By this time Snellgrove's aptitude for historical research had been clearly demonstrated. The bibliography in his master's thesis—a study of Robert de Sorbon's *De consciencia*—was described by Father Astrik Gabriel, a distinguished medievalist, as the most comprehensive one that had been assembled on the subject. Snellgrove's doctoral dissertation, a study of the Lusignan family in thirteenth-century England, was so outstanding that the University of New Mexico selected it as the second monograph to be published (1950) in its *Publications in History* series. This book was favorably received by scholars both in the United States and in Europe, where it was reviewed in such prestigious journals as *Le Moyen Age* and the *English Historical Review*. Faith Thompson, writing in the *American Historical Review*, called it a "scholarly" monograph which amassed "impressive evidence." Sir Frederick Maurice Powicke, one of the leading medievalists of Great Britain, declared in reviewing *The Lusignans in England* for the *English Historical Review* that this was a "clear and critical survey [that] gives body to the generalizations which appear in contemporary chronicles and later histories."

There are two main ingredients in the historical writing of Snellgrove: exhaustive research and literary polish. An uncompromising Rankean, he is interested in ferreting out facts and drawing conclusions from them, not in formulating a hypothesis to be defended with a lawyer's brief. His sentences are meticulously constructed, his quotations selected with great care. Thus, in *The Lusignans in England*, the Douai Bible rather than the King James version is used to describe the plight of King Henry III: "Now there was not such another as Achab, who was sold to do evil in the sight of the Lord: for his wife Jezabel set him on." Contemptuous of verbosity, Snellgrove can summarize a situation with minimal words, as when he noted in a book review that John V, duke of Brittany, "was involved in a web of diplomatic intrigue that must have been as frustrating to him as to those who read about him."

Almost as soon as he arrived on the campus of Mississippi State College, Snellgrove set about to instill in his students the affection and admiration which he himself felt for medieval and Renaissance culture. It was not until 1951 that he directed a master's thesis in one of these fields, but in the meantime enthusiastic undergraduates were crowding into his medieval and Renaissance lecture courses and into European history survey classes where the importance of this area was not overlooked. Freshmen began to learn from upperclassmen that an education was not complete without a course under the colorful and forceful Professor Snellgrove.

Enlarging the library holdings of Mississippi State was a consuming passion with Snellgrove. According to Miss Nannie Rice, who was the head librarian when he became a member of the faculty, he had the distinction of being the first professor in the history of the college who requested that the library buy a long list of books even before he appeared on the campus in person. Thereafter his demands for new acquisitions seemed to the librarians to be insatiable. To complicate matters, Mississippi State was traditionally an agricultural and mechanical college. It was generally assumed that library funds should be spent with this in mind and that liberal arts teachers should not expect too much.

In 1948 Professor Alfred W. Garner, a conscientious scholar who had held the History Department together during the lean years of depression and war, retired from the headship and was succeeded by John K. Bettersworth, under whose vigorous administration the department grew rapidly. New courses and new staff members were added, with special emphasis on the expansion of graduate studies. The department awarded its first master's degree (an M.S.) in 1942; in 1957 it was authorized to grant both the M.A. and Ph.D. degrees. Significantly, too, in 1958 Mississippi State changed the word "College" in its title to "University."

Attracted by Snellgrove's increasing stature as a medievalist as well as his enthusiasm for the Middle Ages, a number of talented students entered his graduate courses. Placing these in suitable academic positions, once they received their doctorates, turned out to be no problem. A Ph.D. in the medieval field was a rare specialty in the 1960s, and Snellgrove had wide contacts in his discipline. He presided and spoke at national sessions of professional meetings; his reviews of books appeared in *Speculum*, the *Historian*, and the *American Historical Review*. Students who received doctorates under his direction soon held teaching positions in widely scattered universities.

In 1961 Snellgrove became head of the Department of History—a position which he continued to hold until his retirement in May of 1978. Since the department did not grant its first Ph.D. until 1961, the organization and implementation of its doctoral program largely devolved upon Snellgrove. Into this task he plunged with characteristic energy. Every effort was made to secure a cosmopolitan staff, and each member of the department was expected to specialize in a clearly delineated field.

Several factors account for Snellgrove's success as an administrator. One is his ability to distinguish between sham and pomposity as opposed to competence and scholarly potential. Many of the young Ph.D.'s whom he added to the staff of the department have since written nationally acclaimed monographs and studies. Those who wished to pursue research were encouraged to do so by promotions, reduced teaching hours, and extra funds for travel and clerical assistance. For all members of the staff, adequate wages and reasonable teaching loads were provided.

Although the statistics for the improvement of the History Department under his headship are impressive, Snellgrove has always thought of himself as primarily a teacher rather than an administrator, and so he has been regarded by others. In the classroom he was fair but not permissive. He made his high expectations known to students and challenged them to strive for excellence. Endowed with charisma, he could make almost any topic interesting. Former students have remarked that his lectures were clear and well organized, and often delivered from memory without the aid of notes.

When students presented Snellgrove with shoddy work, he did not hesitate to label it as such. Nevertheless, he generally acted on the principle that constructive criticism is a more effective weapon than ridicule. For graduate students suffering with thesis "blues," he nearly always had a word of encouragement. He was equally concerned with students who were unable to remain in college because of financial problems. He secured scholarships and part-time jobs for some of these; to others he made generous gifts. A bachelor, without children of his own, he helped several young relatives to secure a college education.

Actually, Snellgrove had far more contact with students than do most administrators. Before assuming the headship of the department, he had directed the writing of seventeen master's theses. After becoming head, he supervised thirteen master's theses and thirteen doctoral dissertations. His field of medieval history made it necessary to work with several languages, and his direction of theses and dissertations required him to tutor students in such highly specialized skills as medieval Latin and paleography, which Mississippi State did not offer as courses. At the same time, he devoted particular attention to students who needed courses designated as Special Problems. These were usually "hardship" cases requiring a few additional hours for graduation or accreditation. Often they came from a great distance to meet class once a week. Since most members of the department did not wish to be saddled with such a burden—for which there was no extra remuneration—Snellgrove himself handled many of the Special Problems.

Snellgrove was involved in extracurricular activities at Mississippi State University. He was the first president, and one of the founders, of the local chapter of Phi Kappa Phi, the national scholastic honorary fraternity. He also served as president of the local chapter of the American Association of University Professors. He was faculty adviser for Phi Alpha Theta, the national history fraternity, and was a member of the Graduate Council of the university. For many years he served as faculty secretary of Omicron Delta Kappa, an organization of students and faculty members which stresses both scholarship and campus service.

Snellgrove's interest in Renaissance history is second only to his love of the Middle Ages. Indeed, in the 1950s, he helped to inspire a minor renaissance at Mississippi State by reintroducing the teaching of Latin and stimulating student interest in art and music. An avid connoisseur, he accumulated one of the largest classical record collections in Mississippi. In teaching cultural history, he utilized his records in class by playing the compositions of the musicians being studied. In like manner, with slides which he brought home from Europe, he illustrated his lectures on painting, sculpture, and architecture.

Snellgrove looks the part which in life he has actually played. He is commanding in bearing, with an impressive face which a Spanish artist compared to that of a Florentine aristocrat. Students who went to his office to discuss business matters beheld an affable and gracious countenance, but those who went there for the purpose of boasting or wasting time might find themselves in confrontation with what one student ruefully called "the Great Stone Face."

Described by the late Dean Herbert Drennon of Mississippi State University as "Mr. Liberal Arts," Harold Snellgrove epitomizes the educated man. As a classicist, linguist, teacher, historian, philosopher, connoisseur of the arts, litterateur, collector of antiques, gourmet cook, and lavish dispenser of hospitality in his home, he indeed bears comparison with the many-faceted men of the Renaissance whom he so greatly admires.

Glover Moore

Medieval Social
and Economic History

Demographic Aspects
of the Norman Conquest

JOSIAH C. RUSSELL

In 1066 three able leaders with three strong armies fought for control of England. When Harold Hardrada of Norway and Harold Godwinson of England fell in battle, their causes died with them.[1] The cause of William of Normandy would have suffered a similar fate if the Conqueror had been killed or even defeated at Hastings. On the other hand had Harold Godwinson survived the English defeat at Hastings and escaped from his Norman enemies, his cause might still have been successful because the English had the spirit and the means to resist William's advance into the interior of the island. As it was, the arrow that killed Harold sealed the fate of England. The Conquest established a Norman aristocracy and Norman policies in England. It is significant, however, that the Norman invaders, who preferred the countryside to the towns, never filled the void created by the loss of military and economic leadership in the boroughs that had played such an important role in late Anglo-Saxon history.

The impact of the Norman Conquest on the English population has hardly been touched on.[2] Certainly the Normans replaced the English as a ruling class, but what happened to the English thegns? Somehow or other as an influential group they disappeared for a couple of centuries only to reappear with language and influences so strong that they helped shape the society and culture of England after that time. However, the subject of this study is not only the demography of the leaders of the country, but also the demography of the cities and countryside in the post-Conquest years.[3]

To establish bases for comparison and contrast, it is necessary to look back at the late Anglo-Saxon period. As is well known,

King Alfred (871-899) and his son Edward the Elder (899-924) reorganized and set up burhs to defend the countryside of England from the Danes. The nature of this settlement has demographic connotations which are seldom considered.

English demographic conditions made the development of the burh system possible with little difficulty. Before the plagues of A. D. 542-700 there had generally been a male surplus that had provided manpower for the bands of Germanic adventurers that forced their way into the western Roman provinces.[4] By the late seventh century the reduced male surplus must have lessened the need for these warrior clubs. The low point of population was reached about A.D. 700. From then on the male surplus rose again, creating an ideal condition for setting up the garrison communities at the end of the ninth century. The population probably increased in the tenth century and there was a gradual transformation of burhs, or garrison communities, into commercial centers.[5]

A list of southern burhs, known as the Burghal Hidage, explains the system of settlement and defense.[6] Four men were to defend each pole (16¼ feet) of the walls of every burh and each of the defenders was to be supported by a hide of land (usually 120 acres) in the countryside. These hides were often miles away and were sometimes near other towns. The Burghal Hidage gives the number of hides for each burh and thus, in effect, the length of the walls since each hide provided defense for 1.257m of the burh's ramparts. In several cases the lengths of the walls have been measured and the results seem to conform to the lengths extrapolated from the Burghal Hidage.[7] One may assume then the approximate accuracy of the rest.

It is possible to estimate from wall length the area of a burh. If the burh was square, squaring one-fourth of the total length of the walls would provide the approximate area within the walls. If the burh was of another shape, this method would give more than the actual area but would not be too far wrong. Regardless of shape, the average burghal area represented by a hide varied greatly between the smaller and the larger burhs. Lyng, the smallest, would have only 10 square meters to each of its 100 hides, while Winchester, the largest, would have about 236 square meters to each of its 2400 hides. Obviously a hall could not be constructed on an area of 10 square meters. However a clue to the mystery of the housing is offered by the Domesday account of Lydford, to which the Burghal Hidage assigns 140 hides which would produce an area of about 12.8 square meters to each hide. According to the Domesday Book, Lydford had 28 burgesses inside the walls and 41 outside. Thus one burgess within the walls represented five hides and there was only one hall within the burh for each five hides.[8] Even then the land occupied by a burgess of Lydford would be only 69 square meters which is a very small city lot. Presumably the holders of the other four hides shared the hall in times of siege or wall repair, a situation which may explain references to half or quarter burgesses in Domesday Book.[9]

To estimate the population of the burh, one may use the "basic" concept of urban numbers. A basic factor is one which brings in money for support, usually from outside of the town or city. The basic factor is matched by a nonbasic factor of those who provide services and supplies to the city. Today a factory which employs a thousand men will add seven thousand persons or thereabouts to the city, half basic and half nonbasic.[10] Lydford had a basic garrison of 28; the others outside of the walls numbered 41, which assumes 28 nonbasic and a few others (both basic and nonbasic). If the burh had one family of permanent residence for each five hides, the total population should have been about seven-fifths of the number of hides. To this would have to be added whatever other existing basic factors, such as a monastery, provided. For example, Battle Abbey, a very large abbey of about 80-100 monks, had in its village about 115 tenants in the early twelfth century, or about one family for each monk.[11] The royal court and the mints at Winchester were other basic factors. Thus Winchester with its 2400 hides should have had a population of more than the 3360 to 4200 that its garrison suggests.

If one checks the density of the burhs as evidenced by the hides and areas, it is clear that the smallest burhs, like Lyng and

Tentative Estimates of Size of Larger English Boroughs, 1066

Rank	Name	Population Estimate	Hypo-thetical	Area in Hectares	Density to Hectare	Houses, Persons	Parishes	Farm
1	London	17,850	17,850	138	129	1,875–1,918	85(104)	
2	York	9,590	9,818	86–89	86–90	1,527	34	30
3	Norwich	7,635	6,783	58	132			
4	Winchester	6,500–7,000	5,230	70–80	90			
5	Lincoln	5,600	4,284	65	85	1,150		30
6	Oxford	5,350	4,284	74	72	1,070		30
7	Thetford	4,715	3,117	45–48	98–105	949		30
8	Gloucester	3,065	2,820	47	65		10	36
9	Dunwich	3,000	2,535			600	10(50+)	
10	Canterbury	2,995	2,321	40–50	60–75	599		51
11	Wallingford	2,760	2,142	48	58	517–55		30
12	Chester	2,645	1,981	44	66	529		
13	Stamford	2,575		30	86	515		15

Lydford, were just tightly packed fortresses. Only when the hidage reached 1000 was there really enough space in the burh for all to live within the walls. In a burh the size of Winchester with 2400 hides, the population density was less than 75 to the hectare, a modest density for medieval cities[12] (see table).

In short the forcing of countryside residents to live in the burhs produced a considerable urbanization in the tenth century. While the system of forced residence doubtless tended to break down in the course of time, many of those so forced must have adjusted to burh life and shared in the commercial and social aspects of the community.

In the late Anglo-Saxon period the burh played a vital role in English administration, defense, and commerce. Besides their association in royal armies, the burhs were capable of fighting on their own. In 896 the Londoners and others attacked the "army" (Danes on the Lea). In 918 the men of Hereford, Gloucester, and other towns put the "Amoricans" to flight.[13] In 921 the Danish army failed to break into Towcester. In the same year the men of Bedford routed the Danes. The burh men were naturally an integral part of the political life of the burhs, attending meetings of the burh, hundred, and shire courts, and they paid geld in the burghal halls.[14] The close association of the burh and countryside in legal and military matters tended to produce something like the ancient city-state. After all the *comitatus* (once just the company of a leader) could now mean the shire or county, the county court, or the area occupied by the old military groups. Moreover, the guilds of cnechts, retainers of the Anglo-Saxon lords, were perfectly reasonable expressions of the expected activity of burh thegns. And thegn-recht itself could be attained by commercial activity, that is, by three voyages overseas, presumably as shipmasters.

The commercial importance of the burhs in the tenth century is illustrated by the remarkable coinage of the period. Under Edgar (943-971) recoinage occurred at regular intervals, usually every three years, in about seventy mints scattered in burhs over the land.[15] At the same time Edgar built a powerful fleet to provide, at least in part, protection for England's maritime commerce. It is not surprising that English coinage circulated far outside the country and was especially popular in Scandinavia, or that English merchants were familiar figures on the continent. Some, together with English religious and political leaders, even made their way to Rome.[16]

Domesday Book compiled during the Conqueror's reign makes possible a better estimate of burh, or borough, population than can be determined from earlier data. Using information from the Domesday surveys many historical demographers have estimated sizes of English burhs, but with a usual focus on the year 1086.[17] Domesday Book exists in two volumes. The older of the two is a detailed account of East Anglia. The second is a more concise account of the rest of England. The latter volume is written in a single hand, probably that of William's chief clerk, Samson, or of Samson's subordinate.[18] Both volumes show signs of haste and the scribe of the second volume did not complete some of the descriptions of the boroughs: London, Winchester, and the Cinque Ports, among others. Since both volumes were built upon earlier documents, the compiler may have neglected to complete the borough accounts either because the information was available elsewhere, or because conditions in the boroughs had changed significantly since the survey.

From several types of information contained in the Domesday Book it is possible to estimate the size of English cities at the end of the Anglo-Saxon period. The primary source of population estimates is the number of houses or other habitations or number of persons. The number of parishes is given in several instances. Also the amount of the farm, or rent, due from the borough is available for many places, but burough farms are very rough clues. More important is information concerning the area covered by the borough, and the density of population to the hectare in the borough, since evidence exists elsewhere about borough density with which these late Anglo-Saxon figures may be compared. Finally one can use rank-size estimates to indicate population densities of cities for which data is nonexistent or insufficient, because, within regions, cities tend to conform to a rank-size pattern. Although the evidence one can glean from the

Domesday is not as good as one might wish, it is as good as much information accepted as useful by medievalists. The existence of several different approaches to determining population size is, of course, quite helpful.

When using the number of houses or other habitations to estimate population size, usually five is suggested as the number of persons to the dwelling. One thinks of a family as consisting of man, wife, and an average of three children, together with an occasional servant. However, if one considers the number of members to a family over the course of a marriage and subsequent life of a married survivor (if he or she lives alone), then a much lower estimate results. The family is usually only two at marriage and it is some years, often as long as seven years, until three children are reached. Then as the later children arrive, the older begin to leave. Eventually, only one or both of the married couple remain in the house or move to a cottage. Definite figures for Britain confirm this. The average number in murdered families was, for example, 3.5.[19] The hundred villages of 1377 from which returns for the poll tax are recorded show about 2.45 persons over the age of thirteen to a household, which again indicates a total family size of about 3.5.[20] Furthermore, a hypothetical life table for the period, assuming boys got their landholdings at about age twenty-two, would suggest about 3.5 members to a household. Against this evidence have been presented the lists of partial serf population from three villages, which are alleged to show higher numbers of persons to the household. Even here the interpretation of the evidence is subject to corrections which reduce the averages close to the 3.5 estimate.[21] A second argument is that, since households of the sixteenth century show more than the 3.5 figure, the medieval households should have been the same size. Yet the size of huts and even houses, well into the fourteenth century, suggests living space and arrangements for only the nuclear family.[22] In addition the large number of cottars, who often lived alone or in small numbers, can suggest, at least for this class, only a small household. It is true, however, that in other countries, with different living arrangements, larger households did exist in the Middle Ages.

Did these estimated household sizes hold true for the boroughs as well as for the countryside? Households in the cities as late as 1377 seem about the same as for the villages (except for a part of York). Urban houses were built of wood and must have been very close together since they burned so readily. The fire-minded chronicler, John of Worcester, recorded fires in 1122 for Gloucester, 1130 for Rochester, in 1133 for London and Worcester, in 1137 for Rochester and York, in 1138 two fires in Hereford and one in Oxford, in 1140 fire in Nottingham, and 1141 for Winchester.[23] Yet among the few instances in Domesday where the sizes of holdings are enumerated are entries indicating sizable lots which may have held more than one dwelling. At Guilford 175 burgesses were said to have held only 75 "haws." The term "haw" usually meant dwelling, but in this instance the scribe must have been referring to lots. If this was the case, then there must have been many lots with more than one dwelling in Guilford. There is also the distinction in many Domesday boroughs of greater and lesser burgesses. Even then the greater burgesses should have been men of some wealth with larger houses than others. Thus the household of the greater burgesses may have exceeded the 3.5 average in size. As seen in the table the density of borough populations to the hectare is not as high as one might have expected, even if the higher average of five is used to expand each enumerated person or holding. Probably Sawyer's higher estimate than 3.5 persons per household for the boroughs is justified.[24] Consequently, five has been used to arrive at the estimations in the table for the year 1066, with the understanding that there is considerable doubt in the matter. Furthermore the existence of suburbs outside the walls would in a number of instances add to the estimate. For example, London with its suburb of Southwark might add up to as many as 20,000 persons.

Of the other methods of estimating population, that of the size of parishes can be tested in three boroughs. Ipswich and Gloucester seem to show about sixty houses to the parish. Cambridge apparently had seven churches in 1066,[25] and, if its population was 2000 then, each parish would have had just under 300 persons. London had about 85 parishes and Norwich 34. Multiplied by 300 London would have had a population of 25,500 and Norwich 10,200, or a density of 185 to the hectare for London and 176 for Norwich. These figures seem much too high for England in 1066, probably because the parishes in the central areas of both boroughs had considerably fewer than 300 persons.

Finally, one must consider rank-size as a method of estimating civic populations within regions. Rank-size pattern tends to proceed from the largest on down in this order: 100, 55, 38, 30, 24, etc.[26] When deviations from this order occur, and they do frequently, they provide interesting indications about the conditions of cities within a region.

The farms of cities are indications of community wealth rather than population but are included for information.

By the use of the methods described above it is possible to secure an estimate of borough population in 1066 and the extent of the decline in the succeeding two decades. As mentioned earlier the most serious doubt is whether the household should be considered to have about five members or whether the somewhat smaller figure of 3.5 as in the countryside should be used.

In 1066 London, England's largest city, had a probable population of 17,850. The city's churches were apparently in the central area and were too closely located to allow 300 inhabitants to the parish. London's 85 parishes would yield a population of 17,850 if each parish had an average of 60 families with 3.5 members.[27] The city's population density then would have been 129 persons to the hectare, slightly above the average for medieval cities, but proper for London. Based on the larger figure of five for houses and burgesses, York would have had a population of about 9,590. Its area is hard to define but may well have been about 86-89 hectares, which produces a low density of 107-111 persons to the hectare. Unlike London, which probably suffered little between 1066 and 1086, York suffered terribly.[28] The third city in size was probably Norwich. It is said to have enclosed about 46 hectares in 1066, but the map of the parishes in the *Atlas of Historic Towns* suggests perhaps 70 hectares in 22 parishes. The list of parishes, including those which disappeared or were consolidated with others, suggests at least 12 more than the 22 parish figure, giving a total of 34. Many in the center of the city must have been very small, with populations much less than 300.[29] Norwich had at least 1,527 burgesses and may have had 1,600. At 58 hectares the average density would have been about 132 to the hectare, a reasonable figure. Winchester was probably the fourth city in size. It was the capital of the kingdom and probably lost little in size during the Conquest. The area within the Roman walls was about 57 hectares, but the inhabited area was probably 70-80 hectares. The presence of two large monasteries and royal buildings probably diluted the density of Winchester to perhaps 90 persons to the hectare with a total population of about 6,500-7,000. Southampton, only twenty miles away, may also have restrained the growth of Winchester's population.[30]

The next three boroughs in size were probably Lincoln, Oxford, and Thetford. Lincoln had about 1,150 burgesses and housing units which represent about 5,600 inhabitants.[31] Lincoln itself was about 31 hectares in size, but including adjacent Wigtown would bring its area to a total of 66 hectares, probably badly distributed over the area. Oxford may have had as many as 1070 units and thus a population of about 5,350. It was a fairly extensive city of about 74 hectares with a low average density of 72 persons to the hectare. This borough had apparently grown from its size in the Burghal Hidage.[32] Thetford was in the center of East Anglia, a heavily populated area. It seems to have had a strong basic industrial factor which explains why it was so large even though it was close to Norwich. It had about 943 burgesses and housing units in 1066 and thus an estimated total population of 4,715. Its 45-48 hectares gave it a population density of about 98-105 to the hectare.[33]

In the general population range 2,400-3,000 (and thus considerably less than the first seven cities) came another six boroughs: Gloucester,[34] Dunwich,[35] Wallingford,[36] Stamford,[37] Canterbury,[38] and Chester.[39] Their data appear in the table. It should be understood that at best these city population estimates are only approximate. The totals seem about what should be expected of medieval cities of the period, and the divergencies in density also seem reasonable for the particular sites. Further research should refine these estimates considerably. Nevertheless, for the purposes of this study, the data provide good working figures.

The total population for the first ten cities in 1066 would then have been about 160,400, or about 5.47 percent of England's entire population, which is estimated then to have been about 1,105,000.[40] Just before the Black Death broke out in 1348 the estimated population of England's ten largest cities was about 170,000, or about 4.5 percent of the country's estimated population of 3,757,000.[41] Thus the percentage of total population in 1348 of the first ten cities was less than it had been at the time of the Conquest. England was one of the few regions where the percentage of the leading cities with relation to the total population had actually declined. Since urbanization is normally regarded as a sign of progress in the Middle Ages, England would seem to have lost ground as a result of the Conquest, at least in comparison with other countries of western and southern Europe. The population of London was about 1.6 percent of the total population of England in both periods. This is about what might be expected of relatively primitive agricultural areas. However, between 1066 and 1348 population percentages of the second to the tenth largest cities declined.[42] This phenomenon raises the question of when the loss occurred and what happened to the people.

The problem of population changes in the years 1066-1086 has been largely neglected by historians and demographers. Recently it was estimated that 200,000 Normans and other Frenchmen had settled in England by 1087 and that perhaps twenty percent of the million and a half English inhabitants in 1066 were missing.[43] The million and a half figure is probably too high. A population of 1,100,000 in 1066 would be closer to actuality. Furthermore, no evidence was given to support estimates of Norman immigration and English losses.

Let us then first look at the immigrants. Domesday Book gives some figures for French residents in the boroughs: 145 for York,

124 for Norwich, and 65 for Southampton, and much smaller numbers for other places.[44] London, Winchester, and the Cinque Ports were, of course, not included in extant Domesday compilations, and there were probably many other French residents in the boroughs who simply were not included in the survey. Those known to have come to England with their families and settled in the boroughs number about 1200. Making allowance for those escaping numeration, no more than 4,000 Normans and their dependents should have settled in the boroughs. To these should be added probably a thousand military, administrative, and servile retainers of the royal court. In the countryside fewer than two hundred Norman families received the larger holdings of the late Anglo-Saxon aristocracy. It is hardly likely that these families brought over more than twenty members and household retainers each. Thus the Norman magnates, their families, and households perhaps totaled no more than 10,000 people. Also, perhaps a thousand clergy came over to fill bishoprics and lesser clerical positions. A larger number must have come in with the perhaps 5,000 knights and other soldiers who were given holdings of one or more manors in England.[45] The estimate of the number of the family members and retainers these men brought with them depends upon the multiple, or factor, assigned to this five thousand. A single man, who joined the army as a mercenary and was granted one or more manors by the king or one of the great lords, need not have brought more than a couple of followers with him. He could marry in England and find more servants there for his manor house. On the other hand, he might have been married and had a number of retainers already. Perhaps a multiple of about ten might be hazarded which would mean that the lesser Norman aristocracy, their families, and retainers were about 50,000 in number. This figure together with the others would place the Norman and French immigration after 1066 at some 65,000, and this is probably a high estimate.

English antagonism to William and his army may well have discouraged greater emigration from Normandy. Anglo-Saxon communities did not welcome Normans, and England was a rough country with a high homicide rate even in the thirteenth century. And the homicide rate was probably higher in the eleventh century.[46] The incidence of murder of Frenchmen was certainly high enough for the early Norman kings to order coroners to distinguish French murder victims from others, and to demand a higher murder fine for them.

The sexual composition of Norman immigration appears to have been overwhelmingly male. A recent study has suggested that women were given Norman names at only about half the frequency as men after the Conquest.[47] Thus, if immigration and the giving of names were proportionate, only half as many women came over as men.

Population losses in the boroughs from 1066 to 1086 are apparent in some of the accounts of Domesday Book and become even more certain as the volumes of the *Atlas of Historic Towns* appear. Professor Carl Stephenson in his *Borough and Town* estimated population losses during the Conquest for the following towns: Lincoln—20 percent; York—30 percent; Shrewsbury and Dorchester—40 percent; Wareham, Chester, and Oxford—50 percent; and Ipswich—80 percent.[48] At least part of the loss was caused by William's destruction of dwellings in the boroughs to build castles for his garrisons. Because of English hostility Norman immigrants tended to settle only in special locations such as those boroughs where the presence of a large friendly garrison provided security. To estimate the population loss in the boroughs is difficult, but probably an average of 10 percent, or 8,000 to 10,000 inhabitants, would not be too great.

The problem of what happened to the Anglo-Saxon thegns is also not an easy one. Some were killed at Hastings and in other battles. More fled from the country, while almost all of the rest either lost their holding or were reduced in social rank. Seldom was any ruling class treated so brutally as William and his Norman adherents treated the Anglo-Saxon aristocracy.[49] Medieval battles did not usually produce large numbers of casualties. Thus one can probably assume that no more than three or four thousand thegns actually perished in armed conflicts. However, the Normans' savage treatment of the vanquished surely forced many more thegns to leave England. Some idea of the number who fled can be deduced from their influence in the regions where they settled.

A recent study indicates that at least a thousand and probably more got as far as Constantinople in time to help Alexius Comnenus secure the imperial throne in 1081. For their aid the English warriors received Byzantine gratitude, and some were rewarded with higher rank than they had attained in England. Although the English had apparently gone east by sea, they did not make their reputation in the empire as mariners. They served in the imperial army and garrisoned the emperor's fortresses where they won renown for their prowess, bravery, and loyalty. Ironically, their path again crossed that of their old enemies, for they helped defend Byzantine territories against the attacks of the Normans of southern Italy.[50]

A second group of English thegns treked into southern Europe. In Italy it may have been their pleas that persuaded Pope Alexander II to impose a severe penance upon the Normans for the murders, rapes, and thefts they had committed in the period following the Battle of Hastings.[51]

Still others appear to have fled to Scandinavia. Here they encouraged Norse leaders to invade Norman England. While the invasions were only threatened, the once substantial trade between England and the Scandinavian countries dwindled badly in the early Norman period, as evidenced by the very few English coins from those years found in the northern area.

Probably many more English thegns fled to adjacent Scotland, Wales, and Ireland. The English immigration to these lands should have encouraged the growth of such cities as Glasgow, Edinburgh, Dublin, and others. How much of the hostile feeling that existed in these lands for the government of Norman England resulted from the presence of these Anglo-Saxon émigrés is difficult to ascertain. The presence of the rapacious and aggressive Norman "defenders" on the borders was enough to create difficulties, especially on the Welsh frontier that was to see the most violence.

The brutal Norman campaign of pacification after Hastings

must surely have forced Anglo-Saxon emigration across the northern and western borders. Studies have appeared that trace the progress of these campaigns by the damage to the countryside reported in the later Domesday surveys. One recent study has shown that damage to parts of Yorkshire was especially severe.[52] It is reasonable to assume that most Englishmen forced from their homes in Yorkshire would have fled to Scotland. Yet, unfortunately, again it is difficult to discover a direct correlation between the property losses reported in Domesday Book and actual Anglo-Saxon emigration from England.

The study of the flight of the English deserves much further study. Cursory consideration leads one to conclude that much of Anglo-Saxon England's shipping may have left permanently. Moreover, the decline in the quality of English money in the early Norman period suggests a flight of English mintmasters, or at least their replacement by Normans of inferior skill.[53] Those who fled may well have been among the ablest and most energetic of the race and may well have had considerable influence abroad. This was certainly true at least of those who made their way to the Byzantine Empire.

Can an estimate of the number of Anglo-Saxons who fled be made? Only the very roughest. Perhaps a thousand or so Anglo-Saxon thegns form the nucleus of ten thousand or so Englishmen who went to the Byzantine Empire. The second largest group probably went to Scotland to form the base for five hundred years of border warfare between the two nations. Perhaps this group was nearly as large as that that migrated east, that is, another ten thousand. The groups that went to Scandinavia, Ireland, Wales and the continent would have numbered only a few thousand each, perhaps another ten thousand. The total number of Anglo-Saxon refugees, one may guess, numbered only 30,000, but among them may have been a very large part of the skilled and able leaders of pre-Norman England. Nevertheless, England probably never saw as a result of the Conquest the 200,000 to 300,000 loss and gain in population that have been suggested.

Despite its smallness, the change in population affected English life profoundly, primarily because the Anglo-Norman nobility and gentry avoided cities, except London, and built their residences in the countryside. The boroughs, as we have seen, lost heavily in population and probably in leadership. The ships of the port towns sailed away, carrying merchants, money, and commerce that never returned. William, in one of his worst follies, built castles in most of his greater cities, wasting a tremendous amount of capital to protect cities which were never attacked.[54] In much of the rest of Europe at this time feudal families lived in or moved to the cities where, in many cases, they assumed leadership in commerce and politics while their retinues increased civic populations. In England London did play a more dominant role as royalty settled there and drew nobles and gentry into the city for the season of politics, law, and finance. On the other hand, York, Norwich, and Lincoln never became the outstanding centers of commerce and culture that Toulouse and Lyon were in France or that other cities were in Germany and Italy. In most of Europe, and even in Scotland, universities appeared in the great cities, but in England they grew up in parishes under royal patronage in two minor cities, Cambridge and Oxford.[55]

The great Norman families' preference for the countryside in many cases actually detracted from the old Anglo-Saxon boroughs. In Yorkshire, for instance, the earls of Northumberland, the Nevilles, the De Lucys, and other families built castles which enhanced such places as Alnwick, Richmond, Ogle, and Langley rather than York.[56] Along the Welsh border castles were built, but they did little to aid Hereford, Worcester, or other western cities, except for Bristol. Even the religious foundations of the great Norman families favored country sites rather than the cities.

There were exceptions to the indifference of the Normans toward urbanization, if we may call it that. Bristol profited by the change. It was a favorite of the Conqueror. As Professor E. M. Carus-Wilson has shown, the city's fine position for commerce and trade with Ireland, especially as the Normans expanded their "interests" there, made Bristol's growth and influence inevitable. Then Robert, earl of Gloucester, made it his principal residence, which the crown permitted because he was a member of the royal family and therefore less dangerous than other great nobles. The earl's presence alone should have brought hundreds into the city. Moreover he founded and funded the Priory of St. James and probably St. Michael's Church, and contributed to the Templar's establishment as well. Likewise the Fitz Hardings, a merchant family of great wealth, founded the house of he Austin Canons in Bristol and made other generous benefactions.[57]

Nevertheless, events in Bristol were an aberration, for the Normans were not urban minded and what few efforts they did make along this line were rather anemic.[58] At Rhuddlan, Earl Hugh of Chester built a castle on the waste. Domesday Book shows only eighteen burgesses there, in addition to the family, the garrison, and several other houses. William Fitz Osbern built Wigmore Castle also on waste, but by 1086 it was valued at only £7. Under the circumstances it is difficult to agree with those who see "the security afforded by a Norman castle"[59] and extension of privileges and immunities patterned after the rights of the Norman town of Breteuil contributing to an increase in trade. Indeed, the larger boroughs benefited little from the rights of Breteuil, for in general they were given to the smaller towns not more imposing than Breteuil itself.[60]

What happened to the Anglo-Saxon thegns who remained in England? Professor Doris Stenton has written:

> So far as can be seen, most of the prominent Englishmen who survived the wars of the Conquest were deprived of the greater part of their estates, retaining no more than sufficient to maintain them in modest prosperity. Their fate was hard but in the circumstances of the time it was inevitable. They were the victims of a social revolution.[61]

The thegns, although reduced in numbers and affluence, retained their expertise in politics and their ideas about their role in the governance of the realm. They continued to participate in local government where they often identified the interests of the English masses as their own. They first revered and then clamored for canonization of such anti-royal leaders as Thomas Becket, Stephen Langton, Hugh of Lincoln, Robert Grosseteste, and Simon de Montfort.[62] Their language, English, eventually triumphed over that of their Norman conquerors. A parliament of two houses developed, Lords and Commons, with the division based upon dignity rather than on estates as on the continent.[63] And the customs of the local courts where the thegns had retained the most influence—seating by status, fixed agendas, and regular times of meeting—were eventually adopted by Parliament.[64]

The Anglo-Saxon boroughs proved less resilient. The Norman Conquest was accomplished by an army of perhaps five thousand to seven thousand men.[65] After the victory at Hastings perhaps sixty thousand persons—lords, retainers, clergy, merchants, wives, children, and others—came to England, but possibly an equal number of Anglo-Saxons died or fled. The boroughs definitely suffered heavy population losses during the period of the Conquest as did the northern countryside. While overall the change in numbers was not great, the changed character of the new ruling aristocracy was very significant. The invading families, especially the feudal element, settled primarily in the countryside and it was there that they built their castles and manor houses. Moreover, in many cases the Norman aristocrats maintained their interests and connections on the continent and spent little, if any, time in England. The extensive civic development encouraged by Alfred and Edward the Elder, which was as remarkable as any in northern Europe, deteriorated as the surviving thegns fled and were not replaced. Perhaps the most significant result was that cities smaller than London remained relatively weak during the Norman period and never became strong centers of local culture or enjoyed the political influence that secondary cities on the continent wielded.

English Merchants
and the Anglo-Flemish Economic War
of 1270-1274

RICHARD H. BOWERS

In the predawn hours of a late summer day in the year 1270 Philippe de Bourbourch, castellan of Bruges, led his men-at-arms out of the citadel into the deserted streets of the town. The castellan's men then divided into small detachments each of which trooped off to one of the inns or houses where English merchants resided when business brought them to Bruges. Once inside the houses and hostels, the soldiers placed all Englishmen under arrest and searched the storerooms and cellars for merchandise and money that belonged to the startled foreigners. Everything of value, sacks of wool, bales of cloths, bags of pepper, spices, and rice, blocks of wax, even blankets, clothing, lanterns, and harness they seized in the name of the countess of Flanders. Other men under Bourbourch's command boarded ships and lighters carrying English cargo and impounded the goods. Before the day was over, the few Englishmen who had left Bruges to trade in other Flemish towns were also in custody. Although Flemish officials soon released the merchants and ordered them to leave the countess's lands, they refused to return the property they had seized and instead gave the Englishmen only enough money to arrange passage home.[1]

The large number of English merchants caught in the Flemish snare makes it apparent that they had not been warned that Countess Margaret intended to move against them. Nevertheless, it is surprising that the Englishmen had remained so uncharacteristically insensitive to signs of new strains in the ever-tenuous relationship between the two countries. English merchants must have known that the countess and her people had not forgotten the abuse Flemings had suffered in London at the hands of rowdy urban partisans of the rebel leader Simon de

Montfort during the Barons' War of 1263–1265. Nor had the countess and her subjects forgotten the piratical outrages committed by English mariners who had seen in the anarchy of civil war an opportunity to prey on Flemish shipping. Even after the defeat of Earl Simon at Evesham in 1265 the men of the Cinque Ports had continued to wreak havoc at sea until royalist forces compelled them to submit in early 1266.[2]

King Henry III had moved quickly after the royalist victory at Evesham to normalize relations with Flanders. He had ordered those who had seized Flemish merchandise to return what they had taken, and the countess of Flanders had released the English property her subjects had seized in retaliation. It was unlikely, however, that either the English or the Flemish merchants ever recovered their full losses. If this was the case, then the Flemings were at a disadvantage since Flemish merchants had long enjoyed the preponderant share of the trade between the two countries and would have suffered the greater loss. While the Flemings could not reasonably blame King Henry for the excesses committed by the partisans of Simon de Montfort, they may well have felt that the king had not done enough to indemnify them for their losses, and they would not forget the manner in which the English had treated them during the war.

Had the Flemings been able to recover the share of English commerce they had held prior to the war, and had they not been confronted with new provocations, they probably would have been able to shrug off the ill feelings spawned in the baronial conflict. Unfortunately, however, by the summer of 1270 a series of incidents, whose impact was made more poignant by an acrimonious relationship between King Henry and the countess, doomed any possibility of an Anglo-Flemish reconciliation.

Enmity had not always existed between Henry and the countess. Margaret had sympathized with the king's plight during the baronial revolt, and when Henry was captured at Lewes in 1263, she had allowed Eleanor, the English queen, to assemble in Flanders an invasion force to rescue King Henry. Yet when the war ended, Margaret began to press him for the arrears of the 500-mark annuity that the counts of Flanders received from the kings of England for their all but meaningless oath of homage. Henry would probably have paid the debt had he been able, but all the impecunious king could give Margaret was promises. The Barons' War had made a shambles of English finances. When the fiscal machinery began to function again, Henry had diverted all available money to finance a military expedition his son Edward was to lead to relieve beleaguered Christian forces in the Holy Land. Henry urged the countess to be patient, but patience was not the countess's long suit, and, as the years passed and the debt mounted, she grew increasingly exasperated with Henry's procrastination and more perceptive and critical of English actions that adversely affected her subjects.[3]

By 1270 the countess and her merchants could recount to the English a litany of provocations and incidents that had begun as early as 1266. In that year King Henry had granted his eldest son and heir, the Lord Edward, custody of all foreign merchants trading in England. Edward expected from the foreigners, in return for his grace and protection, payment of an extraordinary duty on all goods they brought into or took out of the realm.[4] King Louis IX of France immediately protested the levy and obtained for his subjects special respite from the duties until a delegation of ten French merchants could discuss the matter with representatives of the English government.[5] While Flemish reaction to the new taxation is not documented, it is reasonable to assume that the Lord Edward's actions angered the Flemings no less than the French. Flemish clothmakers not only depended on English wool to keep their looms busy, but they also sent substantial quantities of cloth to England. This meant, of course, that the new duties had a unique doubling effect on Flemish merchants who paid when they took wool out of England and paid again when they brought it back as finished cloth.

The protests of foreign governments did not persuade the prince to repeal the new duties, but he did satisfy at least one of the complaints by requiring English merchants to pay the levy on imported and exported goods at the same rate as the aliens. However, if this concession mollified the Flemings, their gratification was short-lived because the English government soon began to insist on strict observance of the assize of cloth, a statute that prescribed the legal dimensions of cloths sold in the realm.[6] For many years the crown had exempted favored merchants from the strictures of the assize and had sold immunity to others.[7] However, in the late 1260s the king's financial embarrassment and perhaps nascent protectionist sentiment caused the government to announce that henceforth the restrictions of the assize would be rigorously enforced. It would be hard to imagine that this action was not motivated by a desire on the part of the crown to raise additional revenue through the sale of either new grants of immunity or special licenses permitting merchants to import and sell cloths that violated the assize. Royal letters addressed to merchants of the Flemish towns of Douai and Ypres drafted in April 1270 at least suggest that this was the government's intention. The king grudgingly promised his protection to merchants from the two Flemish towns who wished to import and sell cloths at the fair of St. Ives. Henry pointed out to the Flemings that he was making this concession in spite of the "contention which has arisen between them and the king on account of their cloths not being so long or so broad as such cloths ought and have been accustomed to be," and he went on to admonish them not to attempt to sell these cloths anywhere in England other than at the St. Ives fair without first obtaining his special license.[8] Clearly the Flemings were disturbed about the enforcement of the assize, and their concerns are understandable since most of the foreign cloth brought into England came from Flanders. Were the Flemings convinced that the cloth regulations, like the customs, made them the special butt of England's new commercial policy?

Perhaps the new duties and cloth restrictions would not have been as vexing to the Flemings if their commercial position in England had not already been eroding. During the first half of the thirteenth century Flemish merchants had enjoyed a virtual monopoly on the purchase and export of the finer grades of wool grown in northeastern England. At least as late as the middle of the thirteenth century, the quantity of Flemish wool exports probably exceeded the combined efforts of their Italian, French,

German, and English rivals. After 1250, however, Flemish wool exporters faced increasing competition in England from German and Italian merchants. The Germans gained a powerful advocate in Henry III's brother, Richard of Cornwall, who accepted the crown of Germany in 1257. At Richard's request Henry confirmed the ancient privileges of the Hanse of Cologne in 1260.[9] Then in 1266 the merchants of Lübeck and Hamburg both received royal consent to form hanses modeled on that of Cologne.[10] The concessions granted to the Germans in the 1260s imply, of course, that before the end of the decade the Flemings were being forced to compete for English business with an increasing number of Germans who possessed privileges at least equal to those enjoyed by the ephemeral Flemish hanse.

Yet, in the long run, the Italians rather than the Germans proved more successful in undermining the commercial hegemony the Flemings had long enjoyed in England's wool and cloth trade. Just before the middle of the century the Italians gained a foothold in England as collectors of papal taxes. Most of the Italians who came to England were members of large companies, or societies, that engaged in both banking and trading and that had the capability of maintaining permanent branch office in European economic centers like Paris, Bruges, Rome, and London. Of greatest importance was the fact that the superior organization and advanced business practices of the Italians enabled them to offer financial services that were beyond the means of most of their Flemish competitors. The Italians could not only play the old Flemish game of purchasing several years' future wool production from the larger monastic growers by lending the houses money to be repaid in wool, but also provide letters of credit for English ecclesiastics traveling to Rome, transfer funds, and through their branches in Rome, lend money to those pursuing business at the papal court. Understandably many English monasteries eventually found themselves indebted to their Italian bankers, and the Italians were always willing to accept wool in payment of these obligations.[11]

At the same time that Flemish merchants were being pressed by their Italian and German rivals, relations between King Henry and Countess Margaret had heated to the flash point. Henry continued to ignore the countess's requests for payment of the arrears of her 500–mark annuity, and he was equally indifferent to demands made by several Flemish merchants for payment of long overdue debts owed them.[12] Margaret's personal grievances against the king surely gave greater poignancy to the complaints of her merchants and intensified her concern for the welfare of her subjects who traded in England. Had it been otherwise, two incidents involving Flemish merchants in England in 1270 would not have been sufficiently serious in themselves to provoke a bitter confrontation.

In the spring of 1270 at the English fair of St. Ives Gottschalk of Almain, a merchant of German birth but denizen of the English town of Lynn, brought suit in the fair court against all Flemish merchants at St. Ives. Gottschalk claimed, in a plea of debt, that he had suffered grievous financial loss in 1265 when the countess of Flanders, reacting to reports that her merchants were being abused in England, seized his merchandise and the merchandise of all other Englishmen in Flanders. The fair court was sympathetic and awarded Gottschalk judgment against the Flemish merchants even though they were not personally responsible for his misfortune. The merchants then complained to their countess. Margaret immediately demanded that Henry respect a long-standing Anglo-Flemish agreement that no merchant, of either land, would be liable for any debt for which he was not the principal debtor or guarantor.[13]

Several months after the St. Ives incident, officials at the fair of Boston charged Flemish merchants with violating the assize of cloth and banned them from the fair. Although the Lord Edward intervened on behalf of the Flemish merchants, his letter reprieve dated August 21, 1270, came too late.[14] About September 1 the countess, her patience exhausted, lashed out and ordered the seizure of all English and Irish property in her lands and the expulsion of all of King Henry's subjects. Instead of merely impounding the money and goods confiscated by her officials, Margaret, in her anger, ordered the merchandise sold. She kept part of the money exacted from Henry's subjects to satisfy the debt Henry owed her, and the rest she divided among the king's Flemish creditors.

In England the king and his council professed surprise and proclaimed outrage when they heard news of the Flemish arrest. The Lord Edward was traveling through France on his way to the Holy Land when messengers reached him with news of the Flemish affront. He wrote immediately urging his father and the royal council to punish the Flemings. The reprisals drafted by the council included an order for the arrest of all Flemish merchants and the seizure of their money, merchandise, and accounts receivable.[15] Then the government prohibited all exports of wool from the realm, a measure that the countess had probably not anticipated. In those closing months of the year 1270 it was probably assumed on both sides of the narrow sea that the conflict would be quickly resolved. However, the struggle was to outlive both King Henry and Countess Margaret and would be the most important episode in the history of the wool trade and Anglo-Flemish relations prior to the outbreak of the Hundred Years War.[16]

At first the English merchants supported the government's policy of reprisal. They expected, even if the measures failed to extract restitution from the countess, to receive compensation from Flemish assets seized in England. However, the countess's recalcitrance and the decision of the king and the council to use the impounded Flemish property for bargaining leverage in the negotiations with Flanders delayed relief for the English merchants. Only in June 1271, after negotiations with Flanders collapsed, did the government summon English merchants to appear before the council to make sworn declarations of their losses in the Flemish arrest. The hearings, which were originally scheduled to begin in October, were later postponed until January of the following year.[17] Although no record of these depositions exists, they were probably all reiterated in an extant audited statement prepared in 1275. According to this document the total losses of English and Irish merchants amounted to £10,627 10s. 2 1/2d. The arrested merchandise included nearly 1400 sacks of wool valued at £7810 18s. 3d., substantial quantities of cloth, wax, spices, pepper, and raisins, and, of course, specie.[18]

Since the existing statement was not completed until 1275, it is impossible to be certain of the extent of English losses in the initial arrest. The English merchants probably sustained their greatest losses at the beginning of the conflict, but part of the losses cliamed in 1275 resulted from arrests made after the seizures in 1270. There were brief intervals during the prolonged struggle when anticipation of a negotiated settlement caused both countries to retreat from open belligerency. During these calmer interludes, some English merchants ignored the risks and attempted to resume trade with Flanders. A few of them paid a high price for their daring. For nearly four years every attempt to reestablish normal commercial relations between England and Flanders ended in failure, and each failure raised a new wave of retaliation.

Laurence de Aune of Winchester was one English merchant caught on these troubled waters. He prefaced the second of his two claims in the statement of 1275 with the startling admission that he had had "again" (encore) arrested in Flanders goods valued at £129 16s. 8d., which brought the total of his losses to nearly £300.[19] Although Martin of Lewisham, a London merchant, did not make, like De Aune, a tacit admission that he had violated the embargo, he did state in his declaration that he had lost in Flanders three sacks of wool "de croise roes." The wool Lewisham described was contained in sacks to which officials had affixed a red wax seal bearing the cruciform to attest that the exporter was bound by his oath neither to take the wool to Flanders nor to trade directly or indirectly with Flemings. Since the seal was not used before May 1272, Lewisham could not have lost the wool in the initial arrest.[20] It is also likely that the dozen or more English ships that fell into Flemish hands were captured after the first seizures in September 1270. During the initial arrests Flemish officials boarded English ships anchored in their waters and seized the cargoes aboard. They did not, however, hold the vessels and crews. But, later in the conflict English and Flemish mariners waged war against each other on the seas.

The Flemings stripped some of the ships they captured of their cargoes and equipment and then released them, but they held others and sold them as prizes. Unfortunately only two English shipowners mentioned dates in their claims. Nicholas Adele de la Pole said that he lost a ship and cargo to the Flemings at Calais on June 4, 1274, and Gerald de Elington claimed, no doubt with some embarrassment, that Catherine of Dammes took his ship off Normandy after the proclamation of peace on July 28, 1274.[21]

The author of the *Chronica Maiorum et Vicecomitum Londoniarum,* who was exceptionally well informed about this conflict, was probably very close to the mark with his assertion that the losses claimed in the depositions of 1272 amounted to £7,000. If, indeed, he was correct, then English merchants lost additional money, merchandise, and shipping valued at more than £2,600 before the audited depositions of 1274-1275.[22]

At the time the verification of the English claims was completed in 1275 they included depositions from at least eighty-two English merchants or shipowners and ten additional claims from Irish merchants. However, several other merchants who said that they had not been notified of the proceedings came forward to make claims against the Flemings as late as 1282. Eventually the number of claimants stood at at least ninety-six, and the total value of their claims amounted to more than £11,000.[23]

As far as can be determined from the depositions, the Flemings had seized most of the English and Irish property in the city of Bruges or aboard ships anchored in Flemish waters. However, at least five English merchants were arrested at Thorout, a small Flemish town about halfway between Bruges and Courtrai that was famous for its fairs. The great London merchant, Thomas of Basings, suffered his greatest losses at Bruges, but he lost an additional £67 in coin, silver plate, and wool in Ghent where officials arrested one of his apprentices.

The overwhelming majority of the English claimants came from towns in the southern part of England, and nearly half were citizens of three Hampshire towns, Winchester, Andover, and Southampton. Twenty-three claimants came from Winchester while only ten were citizens of London, England's largest and most important commercial center. Among the other English towns with several claimants were Andover with six, the ports of Sandwich and Southampton with five each, and the towns of Dunstable and Shrewsbury with four each.

The largest individual claim by far was that of the great Shropshire woolman, Nicholas of Ludlow, whose fine fortified manor house of Stokesay still stands as a monument to his wealth and influence. Ludlow claimed the loss of more than 330 sacks of wool valued at £1,928 11s. 5d. The only other English merchant whose losses exceeded £500 was Nicholas Adele de la Pole of Andover, who, with his partner Thomas de Aune of Dorchester, claimed from the Flemings £558 6s. 8d. for 100 sacks of wool seized at Bruges by Philippe de Bourbourch, and for £25 they had paid to Philippe to ransom cheeses he had taken from them. Nicholas also had a second claim in the amount of £112 for a ship, its equipment, and cargo of Poitevin grain seized at Calais. With the second claim Nicholas's losses totaled more than £670.

Four merchants, Thomas of Basings of London, Gilbert de Multon of Lynn, Laurence de Aune of Winchester, and Henry Chadde of Dunstable, made claims for amounts of more than £300, but less than £500, while nine merchants' losses ranged from £200 to £300, and eleven others had claims amounting to between £100 and £200. The rest of the English merchants claimed losses of less than £100, but it is important to realize that many of these men found it more difficult to absorb their losses than did greater merchants like Thomas of Basings or Nicholas of Ludlow. Consequently the lesser merchants were no less eager for a speedy settlement of the dispute than those men whose losses were more substantial.[24]

The merchants had their first opportunity to make their views known when King Henry convened his Michaelmas parliament at Westminster in October 1270.[25] They would not have come to Westminster en masse, but it is likely that some of the more important merchants had met, discussed their predicament, and chosen several of their colleagues to speak for them in the assemblage of lay and ecclesiastical magnates. Their probable representatives were Nicholas Adele and Alexander le Riche of Andover, and Roger of Dunstable, whom the government later recognized as spokesmen for all the merchants affected by the Flemish arrests. At the October assemblage the merchants surely pleaded for compensation and urged the king to lift the embargo on wool exports. At least in the matter of the embargo, the merchants probably had the support of the magnates since many of them would be adversely affected by depressed wool prices if exports continued to be prohibited. The most important outcome of the discussion was a decision by the government to permit wool exports to all foreign countries except Flanders. Clearly the effectiveness of such a scheme was questionable, but the more extreme measure of a total embargo would have been ruinous to wool merchants and intolerable to influential woolgrowers. The government's plan to discourage illegal traffic was to license exports of wool. Licenses were to be issued only to those exporters who would bind themselves by oath neither to ship the wool to Flanders nor to sell it anywhere to Flemings or their agents.[26]

As far as restitution was concerned, the king promised the merchants that if the countess remained adamant, then the claimants would shortly receive compensation from Flemish property confiscated in England. To that end the crown commissioned Nicholas Adele, Alexander le Riche, and Roger of Dunstable to act as receivers and gave them authority to take into their custody all Flemish-owned wool and other merchandise and to collect all loans and debts owed Flemings and all earnest money Flemish wool buyers had advanced for future delivery of wool. However, the commissioners were not authorized to disburse their collections to the English claimants, but rather were instructed to place the money and merchandise in the safekeeping of churches and monasteries and to secure these deposits with their personal seals.[27]

Nicholas Adele and his associates worked at their task for nearly two years. Undoubtedly the merchants' personal business interests made it impossible for them to devote their full time to collecting Flemish assets, but there is also reason to believe that they encountered serious obstacles. The sullen silence of those who owed the Flemings money, collusion between the Flemings and their English friends and agents, and even contemptuous defiance frustrated the commission's work. It is likely that in many instances Nicholas and his colleagues had to extract the information they needed from special panels of jurors assembled in localities where the Flemings had been most active, and judicial inquiries were always time-consuming and not always effective. Furthermore the government increased the commission's responsibilities in June 1271 by ordering Nicholas and the others to investigate embargo violations and to arrest Flemings who were trying to conceal their identity and remain in England. Even though the king gave them assistance by ordering Ponce de Mora, a prominent merchant from Cahors who had taken up residence in London, to impound Flemish assets and investigate embargo violations in the ports of Boston and Hull, the commission's progress was too slow to satisfy those merchants awaiting the promised compensation.[28]

Nicholas Adele's commission did not report to the king's council until October 1272. The three merchant commissioners had determined that Flemish assets in England were worth at least £8,000, if the king's debts to Flemish merchants were included in the total.[29] However, Nicholas and his colleagues had actually collected only about half of that amount because of the difficulty they encountered in getting Flemish debtors, the king notwithstanding, to pay their obligations. The nobles and ecclesiastics who were most likely to owe the largest debts to Flemings or to have been the recipients of substantial earnests from Flemish wool buyers had not been altogether cooperative. These haughty magnates, who would not even allow the sheriffs and other royal officials to enter their privileged estates, or liberties, certainly would have regarded a commission of merchants with indifference, if not contempt. One of the mighty, Gilbert de Clare, earl of Gloucester and Hertford, owed Flemish creditors more than £740. The earl never paid a penny of the debt to Nicholas and other merchants, and four years later was still resisting the king's efforts to collect it.[30]

Concerning the embargo itself, the commission had no more success persuading the great men of the realm to respect the sanctions against Flanders than it had had collecting Flemish assets. This resistance, together with the slow progress of the collections, caused the government to create a more formidable commission to deal with the Flemish problem in February 1272. The titular head of the new body was the lord chancellor of England, Walter de Merton; and Master William de la Corner, a royal justice and future bishop of Salisbury, and Thomas of Windsor, an exchequer clerk, were associated with him.[31] This commission assumed principal authority for enforcing the embargo and for appropriating of Flemish property while Nicholas Adele, Alexander le Riche, and Roger of Dunstable functioned primarily as receivers and custodians of the money Merton and Corner exacted from the Flemings and their debtors.[32]

The English victims of the Flemish arrests continued to await the promised compensation, but the government refused to release the impounded Flemish property as long as there was even the slightest possibility of negotiating a settlement of the dispute. There were influential men in England who wanted to see the conflict resolved quickly and who, on the basis of past incidents, believed that a settlement with Flanders could be most easily achieved by negotiating a quid pro quo. If the Countess would restore what she had taken from the English merchants, then King Henry would restore what he had seized from the Flemings and permit the resumption of normal commercial relations with Flanders. One of the men working behind the scene for a settlement was Walter Giffard, archbishop of York. In a letter to members of the royal council the archbishop expressed his fear that the sanctions against Flanders would endanger England's relationship with France. Giffard revealed that he had had discussions with John de Castello, a German knight, casual diplomat, and pensioner of the king of England. According to the archbishop, Castello, who was personally acquainted with members of the Flemish comital family, had a plan for resolving the dispute, and Giffard requested the council to give John an audience.[33]

Whether or not this personal diplomatic venture ever bore fruit is uncertain, but about two months later, on March 4, 1271, the council issued letters of safe-conduct for a delegation of Flemish envoys headed by John de Husya, dean of St. Peter's in Lille. This mission arrived in England the following June, but nothing came of the talks because the countess insisted on a resumption of normal trade as a precondition for substantive discussions. King Henry and his counselors were outraged at the impudence of the Flemings, and John de Husya's mission returned home before the end of June, having accomplished nothing.[34]

New overtures of peace came from Flanders in the spring of 1272 with the approach of a new wool season. Again optimism in the English court delayed a decision to give the English merchants the compensation promised them. It is hardly surprising that the patience of these merchants had worn thin, or that some of them had decided to take matters into their own hands. In London, Thomas of Basings and several other prominent merchants had moved to force their fellow citizens to share their misfortunes. Basings and his friends demanded contributions from the lesser merchants of the city as an indemnification for their losses in Flanders. The contributors apparently thought that the king would deduct whatever money they gave Thomas from their assessed share of the city's debt to the crown. When it was discovered that they would be allowed nothing, some of the unhappy contributors appealed to the king's council for redress; some got their money back, but others did not.[35]

The Basings incident was but another episode in the bitter perennial feud that raged between London's patrician families and the common people of the city, and it is not surprising that several years later, when the crown launched a sweeping investigation into usurpations and other wrongdoing in the realm, London jurors pointed accusing fingers at Thomas of Basings and the other great merchants. One embittered jury went so far as to claim that Basings and his friends had sought compensation for wool they had illegally exported to Flanders and lost after the imposition of the embargo.[36]

Flemish envoys came again to England after Easter 1272, but these discussions proved no more fruitful than those of the previous year. Before May 6 the government ordered the Flemish mission to leave England. After this only the most obdurate optimist could have believed that an imminent settlement of the dispute was possible. Finally King Henry authorized Nicholas Adele, Alexander le Riche, and Roger of Dunstable to sell the Flemish goods in their custody and to apportion the proceeds among the English claimants.[37]

The government must have assumed, on the basis of the information available to it, that the appropriated Flemish property was of sufficient value to compensate the English merchants for all their losses. However, even though Flemish assets had once been optimistically valued at £8,000, their realized value never exceeded £5,871 13s. The difference between the actual and estimated values was certainly due, at least in part, to the fact that wool made up a significant part of the confiscated Flemish property. When officials seized the wool, they then had to put it in storage where it deteriorated in quality and price.[38] Then some Flemish merchants had apparently attempted to minimize their losses by transferring ownership of their wool or other property to Englishmen or others whom the confiscation order did not affect.[39] Finally, as shown earlier, some men of power and influence successfully withheld money that should have been paid to the commissioners.[40]

The difference between the English claims and the receipts from confiscated Flemish property became the major obstacle to Anglo-Flemish rapprochement. The English government continued to demand, as it had insisted from the beginning, that it would allow the resumption of normal trade only when the English merchants received full compensation for their losses. After 1272 this meant that the countess of Flanders not only would have to renounce all Flemish claims arising from the English appropriations but also pay the English merchants an undetermined additional sum of money to complete the indemnification. These terms remained wholly unacceptable to the countess.

King Henry III died in October 1272. While personal differences between the late king and the countess of Flanders had loomed large among the causes of the dispute, his death changed little. Henry's son and heir, Edward, was still on crusade in the Holy Land and did not return to England until the late summer of 1274. A council of regents headed by the lord chancellor, Walter de Merton, governed in the absence of the uncrowned king, and chose to approach the Flemish problem along the line of least resistance. The council refused to lift the embargo but continued to mollify woolgrowers and exporters with various schemes that permitted licensed exportation of wool.

The lukewarm economic war waged by England seems to have had little effect on the Flemish cloth industry, the intended victim of the embargo. By allowing licensed exportation, the government only forced English wool to take circuitous routes to Flanders through the northern French or Brabantine ports. English wool exporters were pragmatists. Flanders was, and would continue to be, the main overseas market for English wool. If the Italians, French, and German merchants, who already controlled as much as two-thirds of England's wool export, refused to respect the sanctions, then the English merchants could not refuse to trade with the Flemish unless they desired to commit commercial suicide. And so they traded.

During the conflict, the English government made several modifications in its export licensing plan and even again temporarily suspended all wool exports. The first licensing scheme required applicants to swear, with hand on the Holy Gospels, that they would neither take wool to Flanders nor trade anywhere with Flemings or their agents. Licensees also had to provide the names of the English merchants, or foreign merchants known to the authorities, who were prepared to guarantee compliance with the restrictions. Most of these early licenses authorized the export of specific quantities of wool ranging from nine to as many as one hundred sixty sacks. However, in several licenses the quantity was left "open." the Knights Templar, the merchants of Amiens, the prominent German merchant, John de Briland, and astonishingly one Flemish merchant, Nicholas

Lyuns of Douai, were authorized to export all the wool in their possession.[41]

Before the end of July 1271 the government relaxed its requirement for guarantors, or pledges, and began issuing open licenses to all English merchants and to those foreign merchants who possessed the privileged status of "king's merchants."[42]

During the 1272 export season the government issued open licenses to all English and alien merchants, but halted this indulgent procedure in November of that year.[43] Beginning in December 1272 and continuing throughout the 1273 season, all foreign and domestic exporters had to obtain specific licenses. Virtually all the licenses issued during this period authorized the export of twenty, or some multiple of twenty, sacks of wool. Chancery clerks drafted the licenses in duplicate, attached to them the royal seal, and enrolled the authorization in the patent rolls. The exporter presumably delivered one copy of the license to the port authorities and retained the other. Exporters paid the usual chancery fees for drafting and sealing letters, and when they reached the port with their wool they paid the two-shilling export duty on each sack of wool and gave officials an additional half-pence per sack for attaching to each sarpler of wool a red cross seal attesting that the export was legal and that the duty had been paid.[44]

There is also sketchy evidence that the government toyed with the idea of establishing staple ports to better control payment of the custom and the destination of exported wool. Possibly for a brief period exporters were permitted to ship wool only through the port of London. There is a stronger case for a continental staple. If the government did indeed require a common destination for all wool shipped to the continent, then the staple ports were towns in northern France, first Abbeville and later St. Omer.[45] A continental staple would have discouraged direct exports to Flanders, but since neither Abbeville nor St. Omer was any great distance from Flanders, it is unlikely that the scheme could have prevented the Flemings from buying as much wool as they required through agents or French middlemen. However, the existence of a staple would have forced the Flemings to pay higher prices for English wool because of additional transportation costs, tolls, and commissions.

While the English government could not have been oblivious to the defects of the licensing system, it continued to license exports until the end of 1273 because there was no acceptable alternative. A negotiated settlement of the dispute had proved unattainable, and a lengthy embargo on all wool exports was still unthinkable. England's caretaker government was simply not prepared to assume responsibility for the adverse impact a total embargo would have on the country's economy and on relations with other countries, especially France. English policy makers also had to consider the government's precarious financial condition. The Lord Edward's crusade was financed at least in part by loans from foreign merchant-bankers made on security of revenues from the new aid, or customs.[46] This meant, of course, that the government could not impose a permanent total embargo on wool exports without breaching Edward's agreements with the foreign lenders, and there was no way the crown could have repaid these loans from its normal revenues.

The enrolled export authorizations for the year 1273 are in themselves significant because they have provided economic historians the first basis for quantitative study of England's wool exports. More than fifty years ago Adolph Schaube, a German historian, attempted to determine from the enrolled licenses England's total annual wool export and the share of that export handled by merchants of various nationality. Since then Schaube's work has drawn its share of criticism—criticism which has primarily served to point out the need for cautious use of the enrollments.

According to Schaube's figures, the wool export for 1273 totaled 32,743 sacks, and the English share amounted to 11,435 sacks, or 34.9 percent of the total.[47] However, more recent studies by E. von Roon-Basserman and T. H. Lloyd have raised serious questions about Schaube's calculations. They point out that if Schaube had really understood the licensing system he would not have assumed, as he did, that a perfect correlation existed between quantities enumerated and actual exports.

Almost all the licenses issued in 1273 authorized the export of twenty, or some multiple of twenty, sacks of wool, but the exporter could have shipped all or any part of his authorization. Therefore it is possible that the actual wool export for the 1273 season was considerably less than Schaube's figure of 32,743 sacks.[48]

Even though the large margin for error in Schaube's work justifies criticism of his methods, it does not necessarily follow that the wool export and the English share of the total were significantly smaller than he had calculated. If one compares Schaube's export totals for 1273 with figures taken from the earliest enrolled customs accounts, then his figures are not extraordinarily large. According to the customs accounts the average annual export for the years 1279–1290 was about 26,750 sacks with yearly totals ranging from a high of 31,000 sacks to a low of 24,000. Although Schuabe's totals for 1273 exceed by nearly 6,000 sacks the average annual export for the years 1279–1290, in the latter period a severe outbreak of scab ravaged English flocks and significantly reduced the wool crops of many growers, while in 1273 the sheep were still relatively disease-free.[49]

Furthermore, it would not have been necessary in 1273 for all merchants to export their full licensed authorization to attain an export total approaching 32,743 sacks, because some merchants shipped abroad more wool than was enumerated in their licenses and others exported wool without obtaining licenses.[50]

The only evidence of actual exports for the year 1273 is contained in several fragmentary returns from an inquest into violations of the embargo conducted in 1274 and 1275. All extant returns are from London and contain lists of Londoners, English merchants from the provinces, and foreigners who exported wool through the city. Beside each name is entered the quantity of wool the merchant exported during the 1273 season. The list of Londoners contains the names of thirty-four merchants, twenty-nine of whom obtained export licenses between Easter 1273 and January 1274. The total licensed authorization for the thirty-four was 1,849 sacks. Twenty-two of the twenty-nine merchants whose names are common to both lists exported less wool than specified in their licenses, but the remaining seven had larger exports than authorized. According to the London jurors twenty-nine merchants exported a total of 1,708 sacks, which was 92.4 percent of the quantity authorized in their licenses. Although the names of twenty-eight other London merchants, who obtained licenses for a total of 839 sacks in 1273, do not appear on the fragmentary return, they were probably listed on the missing part of the document, and there is no reason to conclude that these merchants exported a smaller percentage of their authorization than their fellow citizens. Furthermore, the London return contains the names of five London merchants said to have exported 79^1/$_2$ sacks of wool, but for whom no export licenses exist. If a comparable number of nonlicensed exporters were included in the missing fragment of the return, then the London merchants, as a group, would have actually exported nearly 97 percent of their licensed authorization, and this percentage would not include wool London merchants shipped from other ports.[51]

Although no returns pertaining to the special investigation of embargo violations begun in 1274 exist for ports other than London, the more comprehensive investigation into the state of the realm ordered in 1275 shows that during the conflict London merchants exported wool from Boston, Hull, and other ports north of London. Among these Londoners were some of the city's greater merchants including Thomas of Basings, Stephen Cornhull, Robert Botiller, William Fresenade, and Poncius de Mora.[52] Since London jurors could not have been reliably informed about activity in ports outside the city, it is unlikely that wool exported by London merchants from ports other than London are reflected in the city's returns to the 1274 inquest. If this was the case, and, if London merchants did export wool from ports other than London in 1273, then the quantities of wool actually exported by London merchants obviously would be greater than are reflected in the London inquest returns.

Smuggling was another unquantifiable factor that cannot be ignored in any analysis of export volumes. Lloyd argues that the two-shilling new aid and the half-pence cocket seal fee were not sufficiently burdensome to encourage smuggling, but it is possible that he underestimates contemporary resentment of new taxation however moderate it might be. While it is true that little evidence of smuggling is contained in the *Hundred Rolls,* the compilation of returns from the great inquest of 1274, these same returns suggest that the new aid was an irritant especially in the rich sheep farming regions of the northeast. Lincolnshire jurors who participated in the 1275 inquest boldly used the term "maletot," or unjust exaction, to describe Prince Edward's new aid, revealing regional resentment of the unprecedented tax just as the use of the same epithet in the next century reflected discontent with the more famous exactions of Edward III.[53] That some will attempt to avoid payment of an unpopular tax is inevitable, and some smugglers no doubt were successful because it was impossible for the government to police the countless small harbors and anchorages along the eastern coast where the diminutive vessels of that age could slip in and take aboard contraband wool.[54] And it is equally certain that the Flemings would have encouraged and assisted these clandestine activities.

Furthermore, the rapacity of some royal and private officials did little to discourage smuggling. There is evidence from later phases in the struggle that some officials demanded more of wool exporters than the authorized half-pence sealing fee to validate exports. Moreover, some sheriffs, undersheriffs, and private bailiffs sought to enrich themselves by extorting bribes from merchants who were carting wool to the ports. Even possession of a legitimate export license could not protect merchants from rapacious officials who could arrest them on mere suspicion of trafficking with Flemings.[55] Under these circumstances would not some merchants have decided that it was pointless to secure an export license, if they still had to bribe local officials to get their wool out of the country?

Doubtless when the government allowed exports under license, less wool left England concealed in wine casks or aboard small ships laden at night in secluded anchorages than when lawful export was totally prohibited. Nevertheless, many hundreds, possibly thousands, of sacks of wool were smuggled from England even when licensed exports were allowed in order to evade the customs or peculating officials.

England had lost, during the year 1272, whatever advantage it had gained from the economic sanctions arrayed against Flanders. At the beginning of summer the government discarded the trump it had held for nearly two years when it authorized the sale of the impounded Flemish property.[56] The sanctions were the only card left in the English hand, and they were good only if the government was prepared to impose and sustain a total embargo on wool exports, which it was not.

The English government might still have inflicted greater economic punishment on Flanders if it had resolutely chastised those merchants who had continued to trade with the Flemings and had barred Flemish merchants and Flemish goods from the realm. Yet enforcement of the limited embargo against exports to Flanders was generally lax, and treatment of Flemish merchants was indulgent or at least inconsistent. Several Flemish merchants were even able to get special royal exemption from expulsion.[57] Others soon discovered that local enforcement of the expulsion proclamation was so remiss that some Flemings remained in England while others, who had initially left in panic, returned. Thus the English government was in the ridiculous position of having to rebanish the Flemings every time diplomatic negotiations failed to resolve the dispute.[58]

Along the east coast, and especially in Lincolnshire, there was little enthusiasm among either royal or seignorial officials for excluding the Flemings. Flemish merchants allegedly compromised the sheriff of Lincolnshire and continued to buy wool in the region.[59] At the same time officials of Roger Bigod, earl of Norfolk, and Henry de Lacy, earl of Lincoln, appear to have been less than diligent in the suppression of smuggling and in closing their lords' ports to Flemish vessels.[60] Peter de Trois, steward of John of Brittany, earl of Richmond, was not only accused of welcoming Flemish merchants to the earl's fair of St. Botulph's, Boston, but also of exporting wool to Flanders in defiance of the embargo.[61] Along the coast of Kent a Flemish shipmaster was able to bribe local bailiffs and sail away with a cargo of good English oak timbers.[62] At Yarmouth in Norfolk Master William de la Corner, who was conducting hearings there into embargo violations, acted with the pragmatic flexibility that characterized the government's entire Flemish policy up to the end of 1273. When the men of Yarmouth complained to Master William that they were facing ruin because the Flemish fishermen were not able to bring their catches to the town's annual fish fair, he quickly allayed their concerns. The Flemings, he said, could come to the fair if they paid the traditional duties and an additional two shillings on each last of fish they sold, which the burgesses were to collect and deliver to his clerk "for the king's use."[63]

There is also reason to believe that the Flemings were able to buy wool in the northern shires by taking advantage of Scotland's neutrality in the dispute. Even though there were familial ties between the royal houses of England and Scotland, the Scots refused to be drawn into the Anglo-Flemish conflict and continued to welcome the presence of the Flemings. At Berwick in southeastern Scotland there was a thriving colony of Flemings, some of whom had no doubt become denizens of Scotland and as such would have enjoyed immunity from the sanctions invoked against other Flemings.[64] Presumably these Berwick Flemings could buy wool in England for export to Scotland where it could be sold to Flemish buyers or shipped directly to Flanders. There is, unfortunately, little documentary evidence to support this scenario. Jean Boinebroke, the famous Douai merchant, and his partners were active in Scotland during the period, and it appears as if Boinebroke continued to buy wool in northern England in defiance of the sanctions.[65] Also William de Fleye of Berwick reputedly bought as many as 1,000 sacks of wool in Yorkshire during this period.[66] While it is impossible to be certain that William de Fleye was either Fleming or a Flemish agent, it is still not unreasonable to assume that Flanders and not Scotland was the final destination of these large wool purchases. Perhaps, though, the strongest indication that there was a Scottish connection in the illicit wool trade between England and Flanders is the

English government's decision to ban exports to Scotland when it finally imposed a total embargo in September 1273.[67]

Even though enforcement of the sanctions from 1270 to 1273 was less than effective, Flemish merchants who came to England were still in some jeopardy. The greater than normal risk involved caused some Flemish merchants to rely on English agents to purchase and arrange shipment of wool for them. Before the conflict English woolmongers had bought wool from the smaller growers for Flemish exporters.[68] In addition, established relationships of mutual agency existed between English merchants who traded in Flanders and their Flemish hosts. When the English merchants made their return voyages to England they relied on their Flemish hosts to collect debts owed them and to dispose of unsold merchandise, and they, in turn, served as their hosts' agents in England.[69] Some English and Flemish merchants undoubtedly attempted to preserve these old relationships through the conflict.

One of the most interesting agency relationships involved the family of Baudin de Wafers, a Lincolnshire merchant. Baudin, before his death about 1270, had been an agent, or had had some other business involvement, with Jean Boinebroke.[70] During the conflict Baudin's widow, Marota, and her two sons, Jakemin and Amorett, bought wool in Lincolnshire for syndicates of Flemish merchants. The activities of Marota and her children probably centered on Boston where she enjoyed the friendship and support of Peter de Trois, the earl of Richmond's steward. In Yorkshire an English merchant named Richard Pontif worked as an agent for Jean Bonyn of Bruges.[72] Pontif purchased for the Flemish merchant twenty sacks of wool from the prior of Warter and another twenty sacks from other growers. According to Lincolnshire jurors, lesser merchants like the relict of Baudin de Wafers and Richard were not the only ones willing to enter into illegal compacts with the Flemings. Several of the kingdom's most prominent merchants, including William Fresenede and Thomas of Basings of London and Nicholas of Ludlow, were not above suspicion of acting in collusion with the Flemings.[73]

Everything suggests that well into 1273 the selective embargo against Flanders had more holes in it than a sieve and was at best only inconveniencing the Flemings. Only when King Edward reached France on his return journey from the Holy Land in 1273 did the situation change. Edward was at last in a position to inject his forceful personality into the smouldering dispute. Although another year passed before Edward returned to England, soon after his arrival in France he let his government in London know his displeasure with its handling of the Flemish affair and demanded that steps be taken immediately to humble the Flemings.[74] The chancellor, Walter de Merton, and the other members of the council of regency had been remiss, but they should not bear full blame for the situation in 1273. Merton and the others must have known that more drastic actions were necessary to reduce Flanders to submission, but they were not prepared, nor should they have been expected, to run the gauntlet of criticism that would have arisen if they had imposed and enforced a total embargo on wool exports without the king's personal support for such severe measures. On the other hand Edward's three-year absence from England had isolated him from the arguments and pleas of those who opposed the embargo, and he could press for a resolution to the conflict without having to listen to a litany of the disasters that would befall England if a total embargo were imposed.

Once the council knew Edward's feelings, it began to act vigorously. On August 21, 1273, the council ordered the constable of Dover to unleash the mariners of the Cinque Ports and authorized them to stop and search for contraband wool all ships on courses to Flemish ports. Soon these unruly privateers were sailing the narrow seas ready to seize all ships carrying wool to Flanders or elsewhere.[75] On September 7 the council ordered all Flemings, even those whom the late king had given license to remain, to settle their affairs and leave England before Christmas. But, the most important action was a proclamation from the council banning immediately all wool exports, a mandate that specifically prohibited shipments to Wales, Ireland, and Scotland.[76]

Meanwhile the attitude of royal officials throughout England underwent a dramatic transformation. With much laxness to atone for and the king's return imminent, these men suddenly became overzealous enforcers of the new measures.[77] They arrested formerly privileged Flemings before the Christmas deadline set for their departure, and English merchants complained that they could not even carry their wool from one town to another without fear of arrest at the hands of some sheriff or bailiff.

Edward, however, was still not satisfied that the noose was being slipped tightly enough around Flemish necks. In April 1274 the king gave responsibility for enforcement of the embargo in the maritime provinces to his Italian banker, Luke de Lucca, of the society of the Riccardi of Lucca.[78] This appointment may have astonished many, but it was an astute move. The Italian companies that did business in England, the Riccardi included, were all guilty of the most flagrant violations of the export restrictions.[79] Edward was undoubtedly aware of the shortcomings of Luke and his associates, but now that they were under his watchful eyes, he expected them to mend their ways and to use what they knew about the wool trade and the activities of the larger exporters in the interests of his government. Edward apparently believed that the commercially adroit Italians, with agents in both England and Flanders, could enforce the embargo more effectively than any commission of English bureaucrats and merchants. He was not disappointed.

Prospects for settling the dispute appeared the brightest ever by the early summer of 1274. The embargo, in spite of smugglers, was apparently effective, and the new wool crop was not reaching Flanders in sufficient quantity to meet the cloth industry's needs. Also the death of King Henry and the semiretirement of the countess of Flanders in favor of her son, Guy de Dampierre, made peace between the two countries less elusive. Guy and Edward had been together in the Holy Land, and they must have felt that, if they could fight side by side, then they could sit down together and settle a dispute that neither desired to perpetuate. Even though Edward was still in France, he was no longer isolated from English politics. Already a dejected delegation of English merchants had come to him to plead for a settlement of the dispute and an end to the embargo.

King Edward and Count Guy met at the coastal fortress of Montreuil-sur-mer in late June 1274.[80] After several days of discussion they agreed upon a general framework for peace, and then Edward sent for a delegation of English merchants to help work out the details of a settlement. When the merchants, led by Gregory de Rokesle of London, finally arrived, negotiations resumed, and on July 28, 1274, the terms of the Treaty of Montreuil-sur-mer were announced.[81]

The treaty ended hostilities and provided for resumption of normal trade between England and Flanders, but several details still remained to be settled. Count Guy and his mother were obligated to indemnify the English and Irish merchants for all losses they had suffered in the Flemish arrests, but the count could deduct the total value of Flemish goods seized in England from his obligation. The treaty did not specify the procedure for certifying the value of the goods lost by both sides, but the negotiators had apparently agreed that the auditing would be done in England under the supervision of two of King Edward's trusted ministers, Fulk Lovel, archdeacon of Colchester, and John Bek, clerk of the king's wardrobe. Four English merchants nominated by the Flemish towns of Ghent, Ypres, Lille, and Douai, and four Flemish merchants named by the English nominees would serve as the auditors.[82] According to the terms of the treaty, Count Guy and his mother were to pay any balance owed the English merchants within a fortnight after Easter, 1275, under penalty of forfeiting everything they possessed. As further security, a number of the count's noble friends were pledged to surrender themselves for imprisonment during Edward's pleasure if Guy failed to honor the terms of the treaty. In return the count and his mother received Edward's promise that he would protect all Flemish merchants who came to trade in England.[83]

King Edward arrived in England on August 2, 1274, and after all the festivities of his long-awaited coronation were over, he began to consider the fate of those who had violated the embargo. In the spring of 1274 Edward had ordered the arrest of embargo violators, but allowing the offenders to languish in prison seemed unreasonable now that the dispute had been settled.[84] It was better, decided the king and his advisers, that the guilty should pay, in a literal sense, for their offenses. The cost of royal forgiveness was set at ten shillings for every sack of wool illegally sold to the Flemings.[85]

In January 1275 the government created special judicial commissions to investigate embargo violations, to fine the guilty, and to "inquire what archbishops, bishops, abbots, priors, earls, barons or others . . . have permitted such traffic in wool to pass through their ports or districts, and to punish the same."[86] The council selected for this task four royal justices. Nicholas Stapleton of King's Bench and Ralph Broughton were to deal with offenders north of the river Trent, and John Lovetot and Geoffrey Neubald, who had just completed an investigation of foreign merchants accused of usury, were responsible for conducting hearings south of the river. While these hearings were underway additional information was gathered in the great inquest into the state of the realm that began in October 1274, and was completed the following year.[87] Among the approximately forty articles that were put to jurors in every hundred of every shire in England was one that required the jurors to name all those known to have violated the embargo and to identify those officials who had permitted the violations. The returns of this inquest known as the Hundred Rolls provide evidence not only of wholesale violations of the sanctions, but also of the corruptibility and ineptitude of local officials.[88]

The king's bankers, the Riccardi of Lucca, collected over several years most of the fines paid by foreign merchants, especially the Italians, for embargo violations. Eventually the Riccardi accounted at the exchequer for £13,321 15s. in fines from foreign merchants. All, or most, of this amount, which did not include a fine of £1,498 5s. imposed on the society of the Riccardi and subsequently pardoned by the king, represented exactions levied for illegally selling wool to the Flemings.[89] Unfortunately the rolls of fines assembled by the four judicial commissioners have not survived, and there are only a few references to the fines paid by English merchants in other existing documents. Yet existing evidence suggests that English violators did not escape lightly. The commissioners fined William Brise-launce, a minor London merchant, £111 4s. for illegal exports.[90] The king later pardoned the burgesses of Grantham in Lincoln-shire 20 marks John Lovetot had assessed against the town.[91] The king also pardoned sixteen men of the village of Louth Park, Lincolnshire, who had allegedly sold as many as 200 sacks of wool to the Flemings, but they may have paid all or part of their fine.[92] The burgesses of Bristol paid at least £36 13s. 4d., which the constable of Bristol Castle delivered to the king's wardrobe. The mayor of Chichester paid £15 6s. 8d. to the same depart-ment.[93] There is no evidence that the greater English merchants like Thomas of Basings, Nicholas of Ludlow, and William Fre-senede were fined for their transgressions, but they almost cer-tainly did not escape scot-free.

The merchants were not alone in seeking royal pardon for offenses committed during the dispute. John, duke of Brittany, whose officials had accepted bribes from Flemish merchants and permitted them to buy wool in the honor of Richmond and at the duke's fair of Boston, requested and received Edward's pardon for himself and his men. Also John, duke of Brabant, appealed to King Edward for forgiveness for Brabanters who had sold Eng-lish wool to Flemings in violation of the trade restrictions.[94]

There is little indication that royal or private officials who abetted, or at least ignored, violations of the embargo were systematically punished for their omissions. However, Poncius de Mora, the Cahorsin denizen of London who had enjoyed the privileged status of "king's merchant" and had served the late king in various official capacities, seems to have fallen from grace after the inquests of 1274 and 1275 revealed that he had violated his commission to enforce the embargo at Boston and Hull.[95] Yet while Poncius was never again taken into the king's service, there is still nothing that positively connects his eclipse with his failures at Boston. Great men like the earls of Lincoln and Norfolk, who were at least guilty of dalliance in the matter of the embargo, appear to have escaped the king's wrath and the clutches of his avenging commissioners.

While the investigations proceeded, the election of the four English and four Flemish merchants, who with John Bek and Fulk Lovel were to certify the losses of English merchants in Flanders, went forward. Lovel and Bek sat at St. Martin le Grand in London for months taking sworn statements from the English claimants.[96] They and the eight merchants soon discovered that a hasty conclusion of their work was impossible. Word of their hearings was slow reaching merchants in the provinces and in Ireland, and some merchants who had made declarations to the earlier commission may have had to be reminded that they would have to come to London to make new statements.[97] Moreover, Lovel and Bek were too conveniently situated in London for the government not to burden them with other work. They soon were adjudicating commercial disputes that had no direct connections with the problems arising from the embargo, and in May 1275, when the royal council imposed a new temporary embargo on wool exports, they were given the task of punishing violators. Moreover, the king gave them the arduous responsibility of collecting Flemish earnest money held by Englishmen.[98]

Understandably the date set for a settlement of claims, April 28, 1275, passed without a final report from the auditors. The certified audit was finally given to the king in early July, and on July 5 Edward informed Count Guy in a letter that English losses amounted to £10,672 20s. 2¹/₂d. against which he would credit Flemish losses in England that totaled £5,871 13s. 2¹/₂d. He requested the count to pay immediately the difference of £4,755 17s.[99]

The treaty of Montreuil-sur-mer obligated Count Guy personally to pay any indemnification owed the English merchants, but Guy and his mother had already informed the Flemish towns that they would have to bear the financial burden of a settlement. However, the count promised the Flemish merchants that he would reimburse them for any losses they had suffered in England. Regardless of the arrangements the count had made, and, in spite of the guarantees written into the Treaty of Montreuil, the count and the Flemish towns refused all demands for payment of the indemnity until November 1277.[100]

Normal trade between England and Flanders had resumed after proclamation of peace in July 1274, but before May 25, 1275, Edward and his council again banned all exports of wool from the realm. Since at this time the king could not have known that the Flemings would balk at paying the indemnity, it is unlikely that the new prohibition was directed at Flanders. Instead it appears as if the cessation of wool exports was part of a plan for implementing a new custom on wool. The new wool crop was beginning to reach the ports in May, and by embargoing its export the government would gain time to negotiate a new tax and to put the machinery for its collection in place. Discussions between the representatives of the merchants and the government had begun in late April or early May, and before May 10 the council announced that it had been agreed to replace the new aid of 1267 with the "new custom." Whereas the new aid had been levied on all imports and exports, the new custom was to be collected only on exports of wool, woolfells, and hides with rates established at a half mark (6s. 8d.) on each sack of wool or 300 woolfells, and one mark (13s. 4d.) on each last of hides. The king assigned the collection of the new custom to his bankers, the Riccardi of Lucca, and they continued to receive and account for the customs revenues until July 1294.[101]

When the government allowed wool exports to resume in the late spring or early summer of 1275, it made no effort to exclude the Flemings or to prohibit exports to Flanders. However, by May 1276, King Edward's patience was exhausted, and he decided that it was time to force the count of Flanders to observe the terms of the Treaty of Montreuil-sur-mer. On May 23 the king ordered the sheriffs and the bailiffs of the ports to permit no wool to leave England unless the exporting merchant could show a proper royal license bearing the seal of his chancery. He further instructed officials to prevent all commerce with Flemings and to make certain that no Flemish merchandise or other assets were sent out of the realm.[102] At the same time, Fulk Lovel and John Bek received a royal mandate to attach Flemish assets and to make certain that all efforts to conceal or transfer ownership of the property were unsuccessful.[103] In December 1276 Edward presumed that the Flemings were sufficiently chastened and sent Nicholas of Ludlow and Thomas of Basings to Flanders with demands that the count pay the indemnity.[104] If the two merchants reached Flanders, they came home empty-handed.

Flemish obstinacy caused the English government to continue the export restrictions through the 1277 export season. However, export licenses were somewhat easier to obtain in 1277 because both the chancery and the Riccardi agents at the ports had authority to issue them. Merchants applying for licenses had, as in the past, to swear that they would neither export wool to Flanders nor act as agents for the Flemings. Now the applicants also had to reveal the amount of their indebtedness to Flemings and to provide any information they might have about English and Italian merchants who violated the embargo. At the same time that the council instructed the Riccardi under what conditions they could issue licenses, it prudently admonished the Italian bankers not to demand any payment for licenses beyond the customs due.[105]

Flemish reticence to pay the indemnity was, at least in part, sustained by resentment of the wool customs, but during the summer of 1277 some of the Flemish towns began grudgingly to accept the inevitable and attempted to salvage what they could of the once profitable Anglo-Flemish commercial relationship. In England, meanwhile, practical considerations were moving the government toward a more flexible position in regard to payment of the indemnity. A letter from Baroncinus Gaulteri, a leading member of the Riccardi, pointing out to the government the difficulty they would have as bankers in financing loans for the king if merchants could not export wool and pay the customs, may have produced the first concessions from England.[106] In June 1277 King Edward announced that merchants would be permitted to ship wool abroad in Flemish vessels and ordered all Flemish ships seized by Englishmen turned over to the Riccardi.[107] In November of that year the Flemish towns of Ypres, Douai, Poperinghe, and Dixmude expressed their desire for a return to normalcy by paying their share of the indemnity that amounted to £2,002. In return the four towns received King Edward's protection and permission to trade in England.[108]

Although progress was made in 1277, two more years of negotiating and a chivalrous accommodation were required to obtain any more money from the Flemings. Finally in 1279 Count Guy agreed to pay £1,316 6d. to the Riccardi for delivery to the English merchants. Edward responded to this gesture by accepting the count's homage and granting him an annual money fief of 300 marks.[109] The following year, in another magnanimous gesture, King Edward ordered his exchequer to pay the English mechants £1,000 on the count's behalf.[110] This payment was probably a compromise settlement of the debts the Countess Margaret and her merchants claimed against the late King Henry. Regardless, Edward was obviously in a conciliatory mood and now believed amicable relations between England and Flanders were more important than the indemnity. Was this new approach part of an English diplomatic offensive intended to strengthen its position in the inevitable struggle with France for the continental remnants of the Angevin Empire?

After 1280 King Edward no longer pressed Count Guy for the balance of the indemnity, which still amounted to more than £1,100, and Guy was in no haste to settle the account. Finally, in 1286, Count Guy's envoy met with representatives of the English merchants to discuss once more payment of the indemnity. The merchants accepted the count's offer to pay the balance of £1,131 11s. 6$^{1}/_{2}$d. in four semiannual installments. Guy honored the arrangement and made the last payment in November 1287, seventeen years after Countess Margaret had made her first move against the English merchants in her lands.[111]

Although the economic war between England and Flanders had ended in 1279 with the restoration of normal commercial relations between the two countries, Flemish merchants were never able to regain the pre-eminent position in English trade they had enjoyed before the dispute. But, at least in the short run, English merchants gained little from the eclipse of the Flemings. During the remainder of the thirteenth century Italian merchant societies like the Riccardi of Lucca that enjoyed unrivaled organizations, enormous financial resources, and the privileged status of royal or papal bankers dominated the English wool trade. The lengthy conflict and intermittent embargoes had blunted opposition at home and abroad to duties on wool exports. Henceforth the great issue was not whether there would be a custom on exported wool, but rather what the rate of the exaction would be. Perhaps most importantly for future Anglo-Flemish relations the conflict had demonstrated that the Flemish economy was vulnerable to embargoes on English wool exports. In the next century, when Edward III decided to wean Flanders from her alliances with France, he knew that the soft white fleeces of English sheep were a persuasive cudgel to wield against the men of Flanders.

Medieval Administrative History

Canonists and Law Clerks in the Household of Archbishop Hubert Walter

CHARLES E. LEWIS

Study of the household of Hubert Walter, archbishop of Canterbury (1193-1205), reveals that a number of canon lawyers were united in the service of the prelate and of the English church. In light of the vast progress made in the field of canonistic studies in recent years, it seems appropriate to venture a preliminary report identifying Hubert's law clerks and their functions in his household, or *familia*. It is hoped that such investigations will serve to enlighten the growing literature of commentaries upon canonical writings and editions of canonical texts.[1]

In order to ferret out the canonists in Hubert Walter's service, it was necessary to make a collection of a large number of the archbishop's *acta*, concentrating on documents with witness lists. By using the procedures perfected by German episcopal diplomatists[2] and later employed to good effect by Professor Christopher Cheney[3] and Miss Kathleen Major[4] in England, a list of *familiares* was obtained. The list contains the names of forty-nine clerks, of whom twenty-nine are *magistri*.[5] To the last number may be added two officials of Canterbury and two archdeacons from other dioceses, all of whom were masters.[6]

There were, therefore, at least thirty-three members of the *familia* who were entitled to that academic distinction accorded both civil and canon lawyers. The witness lists from which the names of these men were drawn do not tell which of the lawyers were canonists, even as the biographical apparatus of the canonical literature reveals little of the canonists' careers as clerks and *curiales*. Yet when these two major sources are used in conjunc-

Charles Lewis's study appeared in *Colloquia Germanica* 2 (1970). It is reprinted here with the kind permission of the publishers, Francke Verlag of Bern, Switzerland.

tion, the relationshp of the ecclesiastical household and the schools of canon law is clarified somewhat. The effectiveness of such a procedure was demonstrated by A. B. Emden with respect to the Oxford School when he utilized Cheney's study of twelfth- and thirteenth-century households and the survey of Anglo-Norman canonists by Dr. Stephen Kuttner and Dr. Eleanor Rathbone.[7] These same studies were of great value in identifying the more important canonists in Hubert Walter's service.

Careful dating of the archbishop's witness lists and collation with other sources indicate that the prelate began to recruit canonists for his household staff in the latter part of his pontificate, beginning in 1198. Earlier, Hubert had exercised extraordinary powers in church and state as chief justiciar of England and papal legate for Celestine III.[8] His *familia* in that period was staffed mainly with royal servants, many of them civil lawyers, and lesser chancery clerks who handled their superior's ecclesiastical as well as his administrative correspondence.[9] Then, in 1198, the young and ambitious Innocent III ascended the papal throne, and Hubert Walter lost both his legateship and his justiceship.[10] Innocent's prompt action to put pressure on the king to remove Hubert from his secular office and the pontiff's support of the Canterbury monks in their quarrel with the archbishop[11] convinced the primate that he was in need of expert canon lawyers, men trained in the ways of Rome.[12] Such a group of canonists rose to prominence in the household during the period 1198-1202 and continued to be the dominant element until Hubert's death in 1205. Furthermore, it appears that many of the members of this group came from the academic community at Oxford. It was in 1198 or 1199 that Gerald du Barri, the Welsh archdeacon, went to Oxford to hire lawyers to conduct his case against Hubert, only to find that all the leading masters had just been recruited into the archbishop of Canterbury's employ.[13]

Master Simon of Southwell and Master John of Tynemouth have been shown to be the two Oxford lecturers whose opinions on the *Decretum* were recorded in the Caius and Gonville glosses and who were cited as authorities in the London *Quaestiones disputatae*.[14] Furthermore, one or both of these canonists may have been the author of other glosses bearing appropriate *sigla*.[15] The careers of Simon and John have been considered elsewhere,[16] but an outline and some additonal details concerning their duties in the household can be given.

Simon of Southwell[17] seems to have begun his career as a lecturer in canon law at Bologna or Paris, a distinction not shared by his colleague, John.[18] In Paris he had argued before Peter the Chanter a question concerning papal mandates and convinced that great divine of the validity of his position.[19] By about 1184 he had returned to England where he became a canon of Lincoln. It has been shown that he witnessed a number of the early *acta* of Bishop Hugh I (St. Hugh),[20] and the predominance of Oxford charters among these documents strengthens the case for believing that Simon was teaching there as early as 1188 or 1189. His tenure in the law school extended to 1198,[21] but in the same period he also served both the bishop of Lincoln and the archbishop of Canterbury.[22] His association with the latter's chancery began probably in 1195, and it may be more than a coincidence that Hubert Walter's legateship dated from the same year.[23] It is hardly surprising that the pope's representative would want to have on call a clerk knowledgeable of the ways of the Roman chancery and experienced in the lore of the Bolognese masters.

With the growth of litigation before the Roman court and the uncertainty which must have accompanied the elevation of Pope Innocent, the great Huguccio's pupil, Simon's value to the archbishop increased. It seems that he became a special advocate for the primate's cherished collegiate chapel at Lambeth. When messengers arrived from Rome with tidings of new developments, Hubert called together all his clerks and advisors to engage in "taedioso colloquio"; and in the discussion Master Simon of Southwell was spokesman for the college and canons of Lambeth.[24] The evidence, however, does not support Kuttner and Rathbone's assumption that Simon went to Rome to represent the Lambeth chapter, nor that he was sent to the Curia in the St. David's case.[25] The latter case must have been one of his assignments in the period 1198-1202; yet he also found time for other occupations. He completed work begun earlier as a papal judge-delegate,[26] and he spent some time at Lincoln, where he still held a canonry.[27] In 1202, however, it appears that he resigned from the Lincoln chapter to be promoted to the wealthy treasurership of Lichfield.[28] And this was not the only sign of favor from his patron, the archbishop. In the same year Gerald of Wales had dealings with Master Simon, whom he described as "then the principal clerk and official general left in England."[29] Gerald's narrative makes it clear that the canonists' role during the archbishop's absence was similar to that of vicars general in later years.[30]

It was probably in 1198 that Master John of Tynemouth joined Simon in the household.[31] By the next year he was unquestionably a *familiaris*, for he was present with Archbishop Hubert at the final arbitration of an important case between the abbey of Bec and the canons of Wells concerning the parish of Cleeve.[32] Once again, we find an Oxford canonist as counselor to the archbishop in a case in ecclesiastical law. John's association with Oxford has been traced back to 1188,[33] and it is possible that he was, like Simon of Southwell, a canon of Lincoln in the nineties.[34] The Oxford glosses and disputations gave Master John such a prominent place that Kuttner and Rathbone have referred to the whole group of canonists there as the "circle of John of Tynemouth."[35]

John was the amiable opponent of Simon of Southwell in the scholastic disputations,[36] and when both came to serve Hubert Walter, they were frequent companions. The two clerks attended the commission at Brackley in 1202 as proxies of the archbishop before the judges-delegate in the St. David's case.[37] In the final stages of this famous litigation Master John, whose name Gerald of Wales (a notorious punster) rendered "Osclaudens" in Latin, was the Welsh archdeacon's principal antagonist at the Curia and in England.[38] Gerald gave an engaging account of the famous episode of 1203, when the two learned masters played musical chairs in a French prison. Therein it is revealed that John had represented the archbishop at Gloucester and St. Alban's as well as at Rome. Furthermore, Gerald, in trying to convince his ransom-hungry jailer to release him and hold Tynemouth instead, claimed that the archbishop's clerk annually received upwards of one hundred marks in rents from his churches and prebends. An even more surprising revelation is the statement that John was a *consiliarius* of the English king. The remark, however, probably was added by Gerald for good effect, since he noted that King John was *hostis scilicet et inimici regis Franciae*.[39]

In 1202 or 1203, Simon and John were joined in the household by a former Oxford colleague, Master Honorius, archdeacon of Richmond, who had been in Rome fighting for his rights in his archdeaconry. The academic career of Honorius had ended in 1195, when he went to York to serve Archbishop Geoffrey.[40] The story of his long struggle for recognition as archdeacon (1198-1202), a part of the greater contest between the archbishop of York and Simon of Apulia, the dean, has been told.[41] It should be noted here, however, that Archbishop Hubert Walter was involved in the case as papal legate in 1198.[42] The prelate must have been well acquainted with the canonist's scholastic reputation, for he commissioned Honorius to transact certain cases for him at the Curia.[43] In 1203, the archdeacon was back in England, hard at work as a *familiaris*. Thomas of Marlborough, the Evesham chronicler, referred to him as "magistri mei in scholis, clerici archiepiscopi."[44] Of the three canonists, Honorius was the most noted author, for Dr. Kuttner has shown that he wrote a *Summa decretalium quaestionum,* one of the more important canonical treatises based on the *Summa omnis que juste.*[45]

Master Honorius, however, may not have been the most famous canonist to serve Archbishop Hubert. The name of Master Richard de Mores appears on one of the charter witness lists,[46] and this clerk surely must be the Richard de Mores who has recently been identified with the great Ricardus Anglicus, lecturer of Bologna and Paris, prior of Dunstable, and Dunstable annalist.[47] Significantly, Richard returned to England from the continent in or shortly before the year 1198, and nothing has been known of his activities from that time until he became prior in the fall of 1202, except that he held a canonry at the Austin house of Merton.[48]

While it is hazardous to adduce too much from one witness list, the exact similarity of the time of this *lacuna* in Master Richard's personal history and the time when the archbishop had several major cases pending in the Curia and was recruiting canonists to advise him should not be overlooked. The prelate who robbed Oxford of its legal faculty was not likely to have missed the chance to procure the services of a law master well known in legal circles for his *Apparatus*—called by Kuttner "the outstanding commentary in the first decade of the new decretalist teaching"—his *Generalia,* his *Distinctiones decretorum,* and his *Ordo iudiciarius.* [49] To buttress the theory that Ricardus Anglicus was a *familiaris* of the archbishop, there is a passage in the *Quaestiones Londinenses* where, according to Dr. Kuttner, Master Nicholas de l'Aigle quotes an opinion of "Master Richard." [50] Since the *Quaestiones* were written after 1196, and since most of the disputations were held at Oxford, it is likely that Ricardus Anglicus joined the Oxford law faculty before 1198-99 and was hired along with the other masters by Hubert Walter.

In addition to these outstanding law masters, several of the other *magistri* in the archbishop of Canterbury's household can be shown to have practiced canon law. Master Robert Balbus worked at the Roman Curia with John of Tynemouth, [51] and Master William of Calne was present with John and Simon of Southwell at a hearing, although in a lesser capacity. [52] Master William of Necton conducted an ecclesiastical inquisition for the archbishop at Dover. [53] Master Peter of Blois, archdeacon of Bath, who wrote a volume of canonical *distinctiones* as well as the more famous epistles, served Hubert as he had served Archbishops Richard of Dover and Baldwin. [54] Master John of Kent, a canonist who appears in the Caius glosses and who later was chancellor of St. Paul's, had been identified as one of the primate's clerks, [55] but the connection is highly questionable. The John of Kent who witnessed as a *familiaris* in the period 1202-1205 did not hold the magisterial degree, and his placement in the witness lists clearly indicates that he was one of the lesser clerks. [56]

This preliminary study of the canonists in Archbishop

Hubert's household can make no claims to completeness. Of the thirty-three masters known to have been in the primate's employ, we have identified five as canonists with academic reputations and three others as practitioners of the canon law. It may well be that still more deserve to be placed in these categories. How many of the masters active as royal judges were, like Peter of Blois, canonists as well as civilians? Was Master William of Milan, who witnessed several of the *acta*,[57] an Italian canonist? At the present state of research, these questions can not be answered. Furthermore, if the scope of the investigation is widened, additional questions arise. What was the effect of the association of the canonists with an archbishop who was such an important figure in the development of English customary law that a contemporary wrote of him, "Omnia regni novit jura?"[58] In consideration of the academic background of many of the clerks, did the archiepiscopal household serve as a kind of advanced law school?[59] And a possible link between the Anglo-Norman canonists and those of Cologne calls for more thorough investigation.[60]

Professor Cheney has posed the question, "Did [Hubert] surrender the Church's interests to the claims of the lay power?" This question, he added, "touches the root-problem of his career and the anomalous position of bishops in twelfth-century society."[61] The presence of a body of canonists in the archbishop's household should provide at least an indication of what the answer must be. May it not be said that, just as Hubert Walter, the justiciar and chancellor, hastened the progress of orderly administration of civil justice in England, Hubert Walter the primate gave the canon lawyers a chance to put their theories into practice at the very center of ecclesiastical administration? At the very least, it should be clear that the household of Archbishop Hubert included a legal staff equal to any in Europe: the church in England, it would seem, was in capable hands.

The Making of an Archbishop:
The Early Career of Walter de Gray
1205–1215

LEE WYATT

Little is known about Walter de Gray's life before he became chancellor of England in 1205. The date of his birth is uncertain and will probably remain so since no baptismal records exist for this early period and no chronicler mentioned his age at the time of his death in 1255. However, it seems reasonable to suggest that he was born c. 1180. If one assumes that he was at least thirty, the minimum age for canonical election to the episcopacy, when he was chosen bishop of Worcester in 1214, then he could not have been born later than 1184. And, unless he was over eighty years of age when he died, he could not have been born earlier than 1175.

There is also doubt about the identity of Walter's parents. The best guess seems to be that he was a younger son of John and Hawisia de Gray of Rothersfield in Oxfordshire.[1] However, Walter was more indebted for his early advancement to his uncle, John de Gray, bishop of Norwich, than to his parents whoever they were.

Walter apparently attended the university of Oxford where he became a disciple of the famous scholar and teacher, Edmund Rich.[2] Even though the chronicler Roger of Wendover believed that Walter did not possess great intellect, Gray did place a high value on education, and, in his later years, was an important benefactor of the university. He encouraged Edmund of Abingdon to devote himself to the study and teaching of theology at Oxford. (Edmund later became archbishop of Canterbury and was canonized shortly after his death.) It was with Gray's support that the university celebrated an annual mass to commemorate the translation of the saint. Furthermore, in 1242, when King Henry III left England to lead a military expedition against the forces of Louis IX of France, he placed the masters and scholars of Oxford under the personal protection of Walter de Gray.[3]

Walter literally burst onto the political scene in 1205. The prelude for his entrance was the funeral dirge for Hubert Walter, archbishop of Canterbury and chancellor of England, who died on July 13, 1205. Walter's uncle John de Gray, bishop of Norwich, was King John's choice to succeed Hubert Walter at Canterbury, and the bishop encouraged his nephew to seek the office of chancellor. John de Gray was one of the king's counselors and had faithfully served the crown as a royal justice, diplomat, and as justiciar of Ireland.[4] As Sidney Painter observed, "there was no man in England whom King John trusted so completely and so consistently as he did John de Gray."[5] It is not surprising that the king wanted his trusted favorite to hold the important see of Canterbury and that he exerted awesome pressure on the monks of Canterbury to secure John de Gray's election.

John de Gray was never to sit on the archiepiscopal throne of Canterbury. King John's interference in the election gave Pope Innocent III the opportunity to intervene and name his own candidate, Stephen Langton, to occupy the vacant see, beginning a bitter feud between King John and the papacy that lasted until 1214 and imperiled the aspirations of the Grays.[6]

Although John de Gray's ambitions were temporarily frustrated, the chancellor's office was the king's to confer, and he granted it to Walter for life in return for a payment of 5,000 marks.[7] Since he rarely performed the chancellor's duties in person, Walter was mainly interested in the prestige of the title and the financial profit he could make from the office. The chancellor received ten marks for every new royal charter drafted and sealed in his department, one mark for every confirmation of an existing charter, and two shillings for each letter of protection. Although the income from the office could vary greatly from year to year, in the early thirteenth century the chancellor's profits from fees probably did not exceed £340 a year in addition to the £33 he received annually in royal alms. At this rate of return, it would have taken more than eight years for Walter de Gray to have realized a profit on his investment. But a clever chancellor could always find other ways to make the office pay, and no one ever accused the Grays of being slow-witted. If a chancellor played his cards right, he could expect to have his choice of the bishoprics as they became vacant.[8]

Although Walter de Gray played an active role in the king's affairs, he left most of his duties as chancellor in the hands of his senior clerks. During his administration one of the senior chancery clerks had custody of the great seal and sealed all royal letters and charters. Hugh of Wells bore the seal until his elevation to the bishopric of Wells in 1209. Hugh was succeeded in the chancery by Richard Marsh, who had custody of the seal until October 1213, when Walter de Gray temporarily resigned as chancellor. From then until King John left for Poitou in February 1214, Peter de Roches, bishop of Winchester and one of the king's most trusted agents, bore the seal. During the campaign in Poitou the chancery was headed by Ralph de Neville, a future chancellor, who had custody of the seal until October 1214 when he resigned it to Richard Marsh.[9]

Walter de Gray did not wait long to begin his quest for ecclesiastical benefices. In 1206 the king granted him the prebend, or endowed income, of Malling in Rochester, a stall in Exeter Cathedral, the archdeaconry of Totnes in Devonshire, and half the vicarage of Holkham Church, Norfolk. John soon presented Walter to two other Norfolk churches, Stradbroke in 1208 and Cossey in 1212. In 1213 Walter received his first deanery when the king named him dean of St. Buryan in Cornwall, and in the same year granted him the church of Kirkham.[10]

Walter's first attempt to achieve episcopal office was frustrated by King John's quarrel with the papacy. Before the end of 1208 death had left vacant five dioceses in England. John would ordinarily have let the sees lie vacant as long as possible while he enjoyed their revenues. But Pope Innocent III had no intention of allowing him to get away with that without a fight. In January 1209 the pope wrote to the deans and chapters, or the priors and convents, of the vacant dioceses instructing them to hold their elections. If the vacancies were not filled immediately then he would fill them by appointment.[11] This letter forced John's hand. He decided that there would be elections and that the only candidates acceptable to him would be his trusted servants. John persuaded the dean and canons of Lichfield to elect Walter de Gray to succeed the late bishop, Geoffrey Muscamp, even though he knew that the monks of Coventry had already chosen their prior Josbert to preside over the then united dioceses of Lichfield, Coventry, and Chester.[12] The convent was powerless to resist the king demands, and sullenly the monks of Lichfield bent to his will. For the next several months Walter styled himself bishop-elect, but he would never be confirmed bishop of the associated dioceses.[13]

Pope Innocent was, in the meantime, increasing pressure to force John to accept Stephen Langton as archbishop of Canterbury. In June 1209 the pope ordered the bishop of Arras to assist the bishops of London, Ely, and Worcester, who had joined Langton in France, in publishing John's excommunication when the archbishop decided it was necessary. The ban was apparently published in November of that year,[14] and it proved fatal to Walter's aspirations in Lichfield, Coventry, and Chester. He decided to stand by the king after his excommunication and was censured. In 1211 Stephen Langton voided Walter de Gray's election, which may already have been annulled by the papal legate Pandulph.[15]

The loss of the bishopric diminished neither Gray's loyalty to the king nor his usefulness. During the summer of 1212 King John began preparations for his long-awaited military expedition against his bitter foe, Philip Augustus of France. While John was assembling his army at Portsmouth, he sent his illegitimate brother William, earl of Salisbury; John, the son of the notorious French soldier of fortune, Fawkes de Breauté; Hugh de Boves, his trusted Flemish captain; and Walter de Gray to Flanders. The envoys took with them 6,000 marks from the king's deposits in the New Temple, London, which undoubtedly was to be used to hire mercenaries and to encourage disaffections among Philip Augustus's vassals. The money was carried by cart with an escort of royal bowmen to the port of Sandwich and loaded aboard a ship requisitioned by the sheriff of Kent.[16] Walter and the other members of the mission sailed about the middle of October and returned to England before the end of January 1214.[17] King John and his army departed for Poitou in February.

Walter discovered upon his return that he had been elected bishop of Worcester. Although the news must have pleased him, he could not have been surprised at the change in his fortunes. The see of Worcester had been vacant since the death of Bishop Mauger in 1212, and, as had been the case at Lichfield, King John and the convent could not agree on a successor. John had nominated Walter, but the monks had chosen Ralph, their prior, to fill the vacancy. This time, however, the dispute had a different outcome. John had made his peace with the papacy and by doing so had won the support of Innocent III and of his legate, Pandulph. Pandulph voided Ralph's election, and, when the prior renounced all rights he might have to the bishopric, he received the abbacy of Evesham as consolation.[18] Stephen Langton, archbishop of Canterbury, consecrated Walter as bishop of Worcester on October 5, 1214, and he was enthroned in the cathedral on October 19.[19]

Walter de Gray occupied the episcopal throne at Worcester for barely a year. During this short time, however, he demonstrated that he possessed sound political instincts. To smooth any monkish cowls that were ruffled during the disputed election he appropriated the incomes of the churches of Cleeve Prior and St. Helen's, Worcester, for the use of the convent, leaving to their vicars a living he deemed adequate.[20] He and the convent were apparently reconciled, and in his later years he remembered Worcester with fondness. Shortly before his death in 1255 Walter endowed a chapel in Worcester Cathedral.[21]

Although Walter had resigned as chancellor before he departed for Flanders in October 1214, he resumed the office after his return, and seems to have held it until he left England in October 1215 to attend the Fourth Lateran Council in Rome.[22] During the turbulent year 1215 the bishop of Worcester's loyalty to King John never faltered. He openly sided with the king in the momentous confrontation with the rebellious barons at Runny-meade on June 15, 1215, and when John later decided to throw off the restraints of the Great Charter, Walter played an important part in his plan. The king sent Walter, Richard Marsh, Hugh Boves, and others to Flanders and Brabant to raise a strong force of mercenaries. The agents took the great seal with them so that they could provide royal promises of lands and money, and issue letters of safe conduct to recruits who were to be at Dover by September 29, 1215.[23] In late September King John was on the Kentish coast awaiting the arrival of a strong military force led by his mercenary captain Hugh Boves, but they never came. A savage storm caught the little fleet at sea, and Hugh Boves and many of his men were drowned.[24] However, between October 7 and October 9 other Flemish knights and men-at-arms under the command of Robert de Bethune began to arrive.[25] Walter de Gray fortunately had not sailed with Hugh Boves. He was still very much alive and was about to set forth on the most significant journey of his career.

The late archbishop of York, who was King John's half brother, Geoffrey Plantagenet, had died in exile in December 1212.[26] John was again in no hurry to see the vacancy filled, and for more than a year he refused to allow the dean and chapter of York to proceed with an election. The lucrative income he received from the vacant archdiocese was certainly attractive, but John's main concern at York was to obtain the election of someone acceptable to him. He had no desire to burden himself with another archbishop like Stephen Langton. However, on or shortly after December 23, 1213, Pope Innocent ordered the dean and chapter of York to hold a conclave and elect an archbishop with the advice of the legate Nicholas, bishop of Tusculum.[27]

On January 26, 1214, King John chose the abbots of St. Mary's, York, Selby, and Beaulieu; William Brewer; and the royal steward, William de Cantilupe, to represent him at the conclave, and sent by them his letters assenting to the election. The representatives had authority to give royal approval to the choice of the convent, but they also must have come to York with the name of the person the king considered most suitable for the office and with verbal instructions to accept only the election of the royal candidate.[28] In any event the dean and chapter must have decided that King John was infringing on their canonical rights and refused to proceed with the election, for nothing was accomplished. Later, however, John heard that the chapter intended to elect its prior, Simon of Apulia, and he warned the dean and canons that if they made this mistake they would never again enjoy his peace and goodwill.[29] Meanwhile, the king attempted unsuccessfully to gain papal consent for the translation of Peter des Roches from the bishopric of Winchester to the archdiocese of York. Then on May 13, 1215, the king informed the chapter at York that he had appealed to the pope, asking that the holy father reject the election of anyone who did not have his confidence.

Less than a month later, on June 18, 1215, King John again gave his assent for an election at York.[30] This time, however, he suggested that Walter de Gray, bishop of Worcester, was a deserving candidate. The obdurate dean and his canons defiantly dismissed Gray as an unlearned prelate unworthy of the office, and elected Simon Langton, the brother of the archbishop of Canterbury.[31]

Master Simon Langton was not without impressive credentials. He had studied at the University of Paris and was a canon of Notre Dame and of York. Having been the agent of his brother Stephen at the court of Innocent III, Simon was familiar with the politics of the Roman curia.[32] Unfortunately, Simon neglected to tell the chapter at York that he had taken the opportunity of a meeting with Innocent to offer himself as a candidate for the archbishopric of York. The pope had not only rejected the suggestion, but also asked Simon to swear that he would never seek the office.[33]

Incensed when he heard of Simon's election, King John immediately asked the pope to deny Langton confirmation. John's arguments were straightforward and forceful. He pointed out that the election at York was one more defiant act of a rebellious English clergy led by his avowed enemy Stephen Langton. Simon was the younger brother of the man who had conspired with the English barons and brought the realm to the brink of war. If the provinces of York and Canterbury were united in a blood alliance, then "the peace of the king and kingdom could not be of long duration."[34]

Since John's reconciliation with the papacy, the Langtons and others who had differences with the king could no longer count on Innocent's support. Stephen Langton's continued opposition to the king was beginning to appear to the pope as the malicious troublemaking of an embittered and vengeful man.[35] John, on the other hand, by his submission had recast himself in the role of legitimate sovereign entitled, at least Innocent believed, to the loyalty, counsel, and cooperation of his bishops. Innocent therefore wrote to the dean and chapter of York on September 13, 1215, informing them that he was setting aside the election of Simon Langton. His reasons were that he had strictly forbidden Simon to seek the office of archbishop of York and that he feared, should he give his consent, "the last error in England should thereby be worse than the first." The pope further ordered the chapter to send representatives to the council that would soon convene in Rome. Its proctors were to appear before him no later than December 1 when, with his advice, they would elect a suitable archbishop for the province of York. Should the representatives fail to appear, the pope declared, then he himself would appoint a prelate for them. Finally the pope said that if Simon Langton had consented to his election, then he was ineligible for election to the episcopacy without special papal dispensation.[36]

In November 1215 the canons representing the chapter at York appeared before the Fourth Lateran Council. There they were confronted by Walter de Gray and by King John's proctors who had come to appeal for ecclesiastical sanctions against Stephen Langton.[37] The canons, with bold indiscretion, made one more plea to Innocent for confirmation of Simon Langton's election. It was a futile gesture. The pope had just suspended Stephen Langton from the archbishopric of Canterbury, and he had no intention of elevating his brother to the archbishopric of

York. Instead, as he had threatened, Innocent declared Simon Langton ineligible for election to any ecclesiastical dignity without papal dispensation. The pope then ordered the canons to proceed with the election, and he almost certainly pointed out to the delegation that there was a candidate already in Rome who deserved their consideration—the bishop of Worcester, Walter de Gray. The canons had no intention of defying the pope, but they were momentarily perplexed. How, in good conscience, could they elect a man they had once rejected as uneducated? Their problem was solved when they told Innocent that their choice was Walter de Gray because he had remained a virgin since the day he left his mother's womb. The pope agreed that virginity was a great virtue and confirmed Walter's election to the archbishopric of York on November 10, 1215. This, according to Roger of Wendover, cost Walter £10,000.[38] The amount is probably exaggerated, but papal confirmation of his election must have cost the new archbishop of York at least £3,000.[39]

Walter de Gray received the pallium from the hands of the pope before leaving Rome. On February 19, 1216, King John restored all the temporalities pertaining to the archbishopric that he had seized in 1207 when Geoffrey Plantagenet had denied the king's right to tax tenants of lands held by the church. Gray's formal translation from Worcester was celebrated at York on March 27, 1216.[40]

The high price Walter de Gray paid for his election and confirmation left him burdened with debt. To pay his obligations the archbishop had to scrimp and save for years, a frugality seen by some as avarice. Although Walter had his detractors, he brought to York a wealth of administrative ability and experience which he used to bring order to a province that had been thrown into confusion by years of strife between his predecessors and the clergy. Even though Walter de Gray had come from an administrative family and had spent his early career in the royal household, he, like several other former servants of King John, rose above his former loyalties. After 1215 he played a leading role in the reorganization of the church and stood by the principles of the Great Charter.

Peter Chaceporc
and the Wardrobe of Henry III

JOHN E. DAVIS

Peter Chaceporc was born in Poitou and came to England before 1241. His meteoric rise from obscurity to personal treasurer of King Henry III (1216-1272) in 1241 can be attributed, at least in part, to personal connections with the royal family. Peter's brother, Hugh Chaceporc, was married to one of the king's relatives, possibly an illegitimate daughter of Peter of Aubusson, a member of the Poitevin house of Lusignan.[1] In addition, by 1241, Peter's uncle, Hugh de Vivonne, was already numbered among the king's favorites.[2] Although Peter served as treasurer, or keeper, of the king's wardrobe and held other positions of trust from 1241 until his death in 1254, the only published study of his career is one limited to his administration of the wardrobe.[3]

Peter presided over the wardrobe longer than any other keeper who held office during Henry's reign. During his administration and that of his Poitevin predecessor, Peter de Rivaux, the wardrobe evolved from an appendage of the chamber, charged with the storage and transport of the king's clothing, toiletries, and valuables into a major household department with an important role in managing royal finances. It was during Peter de Rivaux's second keepership from 1232 to 1234 that the wardrobe began to receive frequent and large money payments from the exchequer and that the keeper began to account regularly at the exchequer for his expenditures.[4] Although Peter Chaceporc lacked the innovative genius and personal influence of Rivaux, he was an able administrator and an astute financier. During Chaceporc's administration the wardrobe demonstrated a flexibility and adaptability that the exchequer, burdened with hereditary officials and arthritic with age, could not match. In times of crisis the staff and authority of the wardrobe could easily be expanded, and in time of peace it could just as easily be reduced to its former size and function. Furthermore, since the wardrobe traveled with the king while the exchequer normally remained at Westminster, the new department was more accessible to the king and more amenable to the royal will. For these reasons King Henry used the wardrobe extensively for managing his financial affairs during his military campaigns and visits abroad, and he came to rely on it, rather than the older exchequer, during periods of crisis.[5]

Peter's main responsibility as keeper of the wardrobe was to have sufficient money available to pay all the expenses of the royal household and to cover any other disbursements the king might order. The wardrobe's yearly receipts under Chaceporc's administration increased to an average annual figure that was at least £1,000 greater than the average yearly receipts of the other keepers between 1232 and the end of Henry's reign in 1272. More importantly, he managed to spend less than he received—an accomplishment that evaded most of Henry's other keepers.[6]

Under Chaceporc's administration the wardrobe continued to draw most of its monetary resources from the exchequer. But it also collected revenues, equal to nearly three-fourths of its normal receipts from the exchequer, directly from the sheriffs, the church, the towns, manors, escheats, wardships, royal castles, fines and debts, the monetary exchanges, and the mints.[7] But Peter also augmented the income of the wardrobe by diverting directly to his department, through royal mandate, crown revenues normally paid to the exchequer, and by borrowing from merchants and bankers.[8] Of course Peter had to account at the exchequer for all his receipts. This task, considering the inevitable resentment the exchequer had for the upstart wardrobe, must have require Chaceporc not only to produce accurate and detailed records but also to conduct himself with tact and discretion.

Peter Chaceporc discovered during his years of service in the royal household that King Henry demanded a great deal of his favorites, and was capable of working a competent and loyal clerk to an early death. Not having a corps of professional diplomats at his disposal, the king often selected his emissaries from his household, and he frequently turned to Peter when the mission was particularly sensitive or of personal interest to the royal family. In 1241 Henry sent Peter and one of the household knights, Nicholas de Molis, to conclude an agreement between the king and his mother, Isabella of Angoulême, and her husband, Hugh de Lusignan, count of La March, calling for joint military operations against Louis IX of France.[9] During Henry's futile campaign to drive the king of France from Poitou in 1242 and 1243, Peter and his uncle, Hugh de Vivonne, were twice called upon to arbitrate disputes between Henry's Gascon subjects.[10] Peter also played an important role in negotiating a truce between the kings of England and France in 1243. He was one of the royal proctors sent to King Louis with power to pledge Henry's observance of the truce, and he personally received at Bordeaux letters from Louis announcing his acceptance of the truce.[11]

Other diplomatic missions took Peter to the court of James I of Aragon in 1246, to the papal court in Rome in 1249, and to Lyons where the pope was residing in 1250. The mission to Aragon very likely involved discussions of the impact the death of Henry's mother, Isabella of Angoulême, would have on territorial claims in southern France.[12] On his first mission to the Roman curia, Peter probably conveyed Henry's intention to respond to the crusade preached by Pope Innocent IV, and discussed the conditions under which the king would take the cross.[13] He undertook his second journey to inform the holy father that the monks of Winchester had elected Henry's half brother, Aymer de Lusignan, their bishop.[14]

Peter received his last diplomatic assignment in 1252 while King Henry was preparing to depart for Gascony, which was in a state of insurrection. Henry was a timid sailor and hoped to make a short Channel crossing and then to lead his entourage through France to his Gascon possessions. His plan, of course, required French consent, and it was Peter's task to obtain it. However, the French regent, the aged queen mother, Blanche of Castile, testily refused to help Henry pull his chestnuts out of the

Gascon fire.[15] Thus Chaceporc returned to England without the letters of safe conduct he had sought, and Henry had to steel himself for the rough sea voyage to Gascony.

King Henry also made use of Peter's diplomatic finesse to resolve difficult problems at home. In 1250, when Henry heard that William de Raleigh, bishop of Winchester, had died at Tours, he decided that the monks of St. Swithun's should elect his youngest half brother Aymer de Lusignan to fill that vacancy. He sent Peter and John Maunsel, his favorite clerks, who were both "most clever in all kinds of arguments," to Winchester to prepare the way for Aymer's election.[16] Henry followed them and preached a sermon laced with threats to the assembled monks, who retired and reluctantly cast their votes for the king's half brother. Peter was also a member of the powerful commission of prelates and barons King Henry appointed in January 1252 to study the claims of his querulous brother-in-law, Simon de Montfort, who was demanding payment for expenses he incurred as the king's seneschal in Gascony.[17]

Henry exploited Peter's talent for administration as well as his diplomatic facility. In 1248 and 1249 the Poitevin clerk served as coguardian of the vacant bishopric of Durham, and during 1250-1251 he assumed the same responsibility for the vacancy of Winchester.[18] It is doubtful that Peter's burdensome duties in the wardrobe would have permitted him to attend personally to the tasks of guardianship, which were probably left to the care of his coguardians, Thomas of Newark at Durham and Gerard de la Grue at Winchester. It is more likely that King Henry made the appointments, perhaps at Peter's suggestion, to facilitate the channeling of the revenues of the vacant bishoprics directly into the wardrobe. It may also be significant that both Durham and Winchester figured in Henry's designs to obtain a bishopric for his half brother Aymer. Although the monks of Durham boldly rejected the king's nominee in favor of Walter of Kirkham, Henry, as we have seen, succeeded at Winchester.[19] If Henry thought that, by appointing Peter Chaceporc guardian of the vacant sees, his clever clerk might somehow promote Aymer's candidacy, then he was not twice disappointed.

Like all medieval rulers King Henry always used caution and discretion when selecting constables for his castles. He preferred, whenever possible, to commit royal fortresses to the custody of his relatives, who were numerous, or to his household knights and officials whose loyalty was sustained if, for no other reason, than by their dependence on his goodwill and generosity. Thus it is not surprising that sometime before May 1245 the king found yet another way in which the faithful Peter could serve him. He gave to Peter the custody of the strategic border castle St. Briavel's and the adjacent royal forest of Dean in Gloucestershire to hold during pleasure because, as Henry pointed out, of the services his clerk had rendered the crown and because of the high esteem in which he held him.[20] But there may have been another reason for the appointment other than securing the castle in safe hands or rewarding a trusted servant. St. Briavel's was the main royal factory for the manufacture of crossbow bolts, and if the wardrobe was to play an increasingly important role in Henry's military endeavors, was it not logical that its keeper should manage the production and distribution of the instruments of death?

King Henry expected a great deal from those who served him, but he rewarded generously those who served him well. Peter received from the king not only the usual gifts of robes, venison, wine, and oak from the royal forests given to the household faithful,[21] but also more substantial remunerations, most of which were at the expense of the church. Medieval kings were expected to live off their own, that is to say, under normal circumstances they were expected to pay both their personal expenses and the costs of government from the income derived from the royal estates, customary feudal dues, the profits of justice, and taxation established by ancient right. In Henry's reign the size and cost of government increased significantly, but there were not corresponding increases in crown revenues. One solution to the problem was, as it had been for centuries, to place as much of the financial burden of administration on the church as possible. Many royal administrators in the thirteenth century were clerics and therefore eligible for ecclesiastical offices and livings. Through the legitimate use of advowsons, the right to nominate priests to parishes in the royal demesne or to other churches founded or patronized by the king or his ancestors, Henry was able to provide many of his clerks with ecclesiastical livings. In fact it was not unusual for clerks taken into royal service to receive monetary stipends from the exchequer only until such time as the king could obtain for them a position in the church.[22]

Peter Chaceporc is a classic example of a royal administrator who drew his sustenance from the church. In 1241, the year that he assumed the office of keeper of the wardrobe, King Henry presented him to the churches of Aldham in Essex, Ivinghoe in Berkshire, and Croyden in Surrey, and in 1242 to a prebend, or endowed living, at St. Paul's in London.[23] The following year Henry decided to obtain for Peter the vacant bishopric of Bath, but subsequently withdrew the nomination.[24] Perhaps to make amends, Henry ordered prebends in the cathedrals of Chichester in 1244 and Exeter in 1245 assigned to his Poitevin clerk.[25] Peter also received in 1245 the deanery of Tattenhall in Somerset and, in 1250, the wardenship of the hospital of St. Cross at Winchester.[26] Even in the last years of his life Peter continued to accumulate benefices, receiving in 1253 the churches of Stoke Godington in Buckinghamshire, Ramsey in Huntingdon, and a prebend at Banbury in Lincolnshire. Shortly before his death in 1254, he was chosen treasurer of Lincoln cathedral.[27]

Peter accompanied King Henry on the Gascon expedition of 1253-1254.[28] He worked arduously for more than a year to raise adequate money to support the venture, deploy arms, and settle disputes among the factious Gascons. Exhausted by his labors he died at Boulogne on December 24, 1254, while King Henry and his entourage were awaiting favorable winds for a Channel crossing. He was buried in the church of St. Mary at Boulogne.[29] In a gesture of magnanimity that was rare for Henry when money was involved, he immediately pardoned Peter, his heirs, and executors of any debts the late keeper might owe the crown.[30] Perhaps there could be no more eloquent testimony of the king's respect and affection for Peter than this.

Peter bequeathed in his will all the lands he had bought from Saer de Wahull including the advowson of the church of Ravenston to his brother Hugh Chaceporc. Hugh gave the lands and advowson to King Henry, who, for the security of his soul and the souls of Peter Chaceporc and Hugh de Vivonne, presented them to the order of St. Augustine to finance construction of a monastery at Ravenston dedicated to the Blessed Virgin. Shortly after Peter's death the priory of Ravenston was built "out of the lands" of the Poitevin.[31]

Medieval Cultural History

Henry III, Westminster Abbey, and the Court School of Illumination

R. KENT LANCASTER

The depth of Henry III's interest in the arts and the breadth of his activities in art patronage have earned him a place among the great patrons of history. The close and liberate rolls of his reign contain the fullest account of the activities, interests, and expenses of any art patron prior to very recent times. These rolls document hundreds of practical examples of his patronage in almost every possible area of artistic production; they show, too, that the king was no dilettante when it came to problems of design, color, or structure. He knew the arts and the artists, and he knew what he wanted.[1] The very richness and breadth of the evidence of Henry's activities as patron, however, have led some to fill in, more perfectly than the records allow, the lacunae in his aesthetic interests. A Court School of illumination, which has become almost a formal part of the history of his patronage, is the case in point.

It would be difficult to deny that the Court School of builders and artists, whom Henry attracted by his benevolent patronage, dominated their fields in the last half of the thirteenth century and led their fellow artists in England into the synthesis of a sophisticated and international style. There has been, however, an unfortunate tendency—a centripetal sort of urge—to attribute any excellence at all to that school, to center it at Westminster Abbey, and to crown Henry III with more patronal laurels than the evidence can support.

This tendency to draw everything into the center has perhaps reached its fullest expression in a pair of recent articles on thirteenth-century manuscripts.[2] In this two-part study, the major extant illuminated manuscripts from the century are divided into roughly two groups, those from provincial ateliers and those of metropolitan origin, from the Court School and Westminster. Matthew Paris falls within the "provincial" category, and the reader is cautioned against uncritical acceptance of the inflated image of Paris the artist as recorded by the fourteenth-century St. Albans chronicler, Thomas of Walsingham, and against "feeding that image" the choicest works of the time. Another image, however, that of a Court School of illuminators, is substituted for Paris.[3]

On stylistic grounds alone (and grounds which deny, by implication at least, any mobility to men and ideas), the new image is fed a veritable who's who of extant illuminated excellence from the middle decades of the thirteenth century. *La Estoire de Seint Aedward le Rei* (Cambridge University Library, Ed.3.59) is derived from Paris and St. Albans, but is a Westminster edition. The Morgan Apocalypse (Pierpont Morgan Library, 524) is probably from a workshop near the court, and the Trinity College Apocalypse (Cambridge, Trinity College, R.16.2) is the result of a "pooling of talent such as Henry III might command." The Douce Apocalypse (Oxford, Bodleian Library, Douce 180) seems attributable to the workshop of the Westminster Painted Chamber and, to close the circle, the Dyson Perrins Apocalypse (now in a private collection) is from the same workshop that produced *La Estoire*. Even the illustrations in the Manchester Chetham Hospital *Flores Historiarum* are tied to Westminster by the suggestions that the writing of the text might have been interrupted at St. Albans, the book sent to Westminster for the drawings to be added, the work returned to St. Albans for completion of the text, and the completed history despatched again to Westminster Abbey because it was from the beginning a commission for that house.[4] This is an unusually circuitous path, even for something as mobile as a medieval manuscript, and one might well wonder at the St. Albans scriptorium humbly acknowledging its provinciality and passing a book on, midway in production, for decoration by metropolitan artists. At any rate, this remarkable clustering of important manuscripts around Westminster demands that more attention be given to the basis of evidence, other than the purely stylistic, on which a Court School of illumination can stand.

A thorough search of the extensive records of Henry's reign yields almost nothing to suggest that illumination or the production of books had any real place among his interests. Although it might be tempting to blame medieval record keeping for this failure of the rolls to reveal royal interest in this area, such blame should be leveled with caution. These are the rolls that record in careful detail Henry's orders, such as the one in 1238 for two gold boxes topped with crowns of silver-gilt which could be removed when the king wished, or another in 1244 for a dragon banner of red samite decorated with gold, with a tongue that seemed to move and burn with fire, and with eyes of sapphire.[5] The rolls are incomplete in some aspects to be sure; edges have decayed and isolated rolls have been lost, but the extant documents contain such abundant and detailed evidence of Henry's patronal interest in other artistic areas that it is improbable that the missing fragments have concealed a similar personal interest in books and illumination.

The rolls show that Henry had occasional contact with books. Probably the most significant incidents recorded were the repairing of the cover of his "Great Book of Romances" in 1237 and the borrowing from the London Templars of a "Gesta Antiochie" in 1247. These books were probably illustrated, but we know nothing whatever of them.[6] Throughout the reign there are notes in the rolls concerning the procurement of service books for royal chapels. In none of these entries, however, is the king's personal interest revealed as it is when he ordered the procurement of liturgical utensils or vestments or when he planned the architectural details of these chapels and of the castles or manors to which they were attached. Rather, sheriffs and custodians were told in a perfunctory manner "to buy service books," and it is obvious that the books were available throughout a good part of England. There is simply no sign of a clustering of such purchases around the Westminster-London area or of specific royal interest in "metropolitan" producers.[7]

Certainly, no single atelier of metropolitan illuminators could have filled the demand occasioned by the refurbishing of scores of royal chapels. Yet even Henry's most important chapels—

those at Windsor and Woodstock, for example—were stocked
with the requisite service books in the same offhand and rather
disinterested way. A chapel was fitted out for the king's daughter, Margaret, when she went north to marry Alexander III of
Scotland in 1251. Margaret's wedding was a glittering occasion,
and as the court moved slowly from Westminster to York, more
and more detailed orders were despatched to royal servants to
procure from artists and artisans the precious objects that were
to accompany the new queen to Scotland. Again, however, the
writs dealing with service books for her chapel were brief, terse,
and without amplification.[8] Books were needed; books were
bought; and that was that.

In his monumental volumes on thirteenth-century English wall
painting, E. W. Tristram noted an entry on the close rolls of
1252, addressed to Ralph Dungan, "keeper of the king's books."
A collection of books extensive enough to require a keeper
deserved to be called a library, and Tristram went on to extend
Dungan's title into "royal librarian." In the writ cited, the librarian was ordered to turn over certain paints he had in his possession to William, *pictor regis* and Westminster monk, then working at Windsor.[9] This is indeed an important writ if taken at face
value. It is significant evidence that Henry III was a bibliophile,
and it is impossible not to suggest that if he collected books, he
must have patronized their production. The linking of the royal
librarian to a supply of paint and to the royal painter is simply
too full of possibilities to be ignored in the quest for an atelier of
illuminators under royal sponsorship, although the paint in this
instance was apparently for mural decoration.

In the following year, too, one Roger Ros, tailor and buyer to
the king, was ordered in a letter close to give over to Ralph
Dungan a certain glossed psalter which he had in his possession.[10]
In this writ, which was apparently unnoticed by Tristram, the
royal librarian was linked to a specific book, and the fact that it
was a most common type of service book might be taken as
evidence that Henry's library was chosen with more attention to
the craft or artistry than to the nature of the books.

The royal librarian, however, requires a closer look. Dungan, fortunately, left many traces of long service as a royal clerk.[11] In 1252, he was at Windsor as custodian of the castle building works and of the royal children, who normally resided there when the king was on a progress around England. He is usually described in the rolls at this time as *"custodius puerorum regis,"* occasionally as *"custodius liberum"* or *"custodius liberorum,"* and once as *"custodius librorum."* The last, in Tristram's writ, is simply an unsuccessful attempt on the part of the enrolling clerk to spell *"liberorum"* and is evidence only of the calibre of clerical spelling in the thirteenth century. A clerk's mistake translated the keeping of the royal children into a librarianship that Dungan never held and a library that never existed. All of the very important implications of the writ collapse. The keeper of the royal children and of the construction works at Windsor gave over paint to a painter, and that is all that is left. Nor is the writ linking Dungan to the psalter of any special significance. He and Ros had been associated for some time as buyers for the king, at fairs and elsewhere, of all sorts of commodities—cloth, wax, spices, and the like. They bought and stored or passed on their purchases according to royal command. The psalter had no more special significance for Dungan, stripped of his library, than had the pepper, samite, or shoes he handled for the king in the same year.[12] The book was perhaps for a royal gift, more probably for a royal chapel.

If Henry's own records fail to show any real sign of interest in illumination and any evidence of the existence of a court School of illuminators under formal royal patronage, the quest must go on to Westminster Abbey. Palace and abbey were almost indivisible in the last quarter century of the reign, for Henry was patron of the abbey in the very fullest sense of the term. His interest enriched the abbey in every way he could devise, but it was an interest so strong that the dividing line between what pertained to the abbey and what to the king was often obscured. The king chose the design and color of hangings and banners for the principal feasts of the church; he transferred to his own works at St. Martin le Grand and at Windsor, building materials he had granted earlier to the abbey; he even borrowed and pawned a great treasure of precious ornaments from the shrine of St. Edward for funds to tide him over a severe economic crisis in the 1260s.[13] If there were illuminators working within the abbey itself, their relationship with Henry would certainly have been almost the same as if they had been under direct royal patronage in the palace precincts.

The existence of a productive scriptorium at Westminster Abbey in the thirteenth century has been posited on the basis of three factors: the attribution of the Westminster Psalter (British Museum, Royal 2A xxii) to the abbey, the selection of William, monk of Westminster, as *pictor regis*, and several passages in the Westminster *Customary*.

The first of these, the Westminster Psalter, can be related only remotely at best to the question of an abbey scriptorium after mid-century, but a Westminster origin for the Psalter would establish at least some precedent of illumination at the abbey, albeit half a century before the production of the manuscripts now attributed to the Court School. The Psalter is universally held to be from the late twelfth century.[14] That it belonged to the abbey is certain, for it has a Westminster calendar and it can be identified in abbey inventories of 1388 and 1540.[15] Where it was produced, however, is disputed. Saunders saw no clue to the manuscript's origin. James ascribed it to St. Albans; Hollaender accepted this attribution but wrote, nevertheless, of the influence of the "early Westminster school" on the Sarum illustrator. Millar, Ker, Tristram, and Boase gave the "provenance" of the Psalter as Westminster, implying only that it had been at the abbey, not necessarily that it was produced there. Wormald justified an "undoubted Westminster provenance" on the basis of the calendar, however, and his use of "provenance" clearly suggests that the Psalter was a Westminster production, for he sees the historiated initials at least as the work of a Westminster monk.[16]

Even if the Psalter might be assigned to Westminster Abbey, it would stand isolated as a work of that house. There are really no other illuminated manuscripts attributable to the abbey at that period and no links at all between it and the mid-century works now ascribed to the Court School. Acceptance of a Westminster origin for the Psalter, then, would establish at best a single precedent, not a tradition, of illumination within the abbey.

Bound with the Psalter, however, are several tinted drawings of a later date and unquestionably connected with the abbey, as they were added while the Psalter was in its possession. Again, a series of disputes has swirled around these drawings. They have been attributed to Matthew Paris, and this, in turn, has been denied. Their stylistic similarity to a mural head of Christ at Windsor has been noted, and as William, *pictor regis*, worked at Windsor for years, they have been tentatively attributed to him.[17] Wormald connects the drawings to the Westminster chapter house tiles and notes that the drawings are "indications of the vigorous activity of Westminster artists during the first part of the reign of Henry III." Henderson ascribes them to an artist of the Court School, "working for King Henry."[18]

These uncertain attributions serve at least to introduce William of Westminster, the one painter of the Court School period with undeniable ties to the Westminster chapter. Tristram sees William not only as the leader of Court School painters, but "as its main source of inspiration and the predominant influence in its formation and development." He suggests "there was probably an established school at Westminster in which he trained."[19]

The problem with William, of course, lies in the temptation he inspires to link a known and named artist to one of the few extant pieces of art from his time and place of work—a temptation which can seldom be resisted but which probably causes frequent damage to the truth. Nothing whatever can be told of William's Westminster Abbey career, if in fact he had one. After Henry had failed in an attempt to secure for him a prebend at Winchester Cathedral Priory, he very probably forced the Westminster chapter to take on the painter, who was already "Master" William. William was, at any rate, seldom at Westminster; he was most frequently in royal service at Windsor and elsewhere. He may have produced some or none of the works with which his name has been linked—the Windsor head, the extra leaves of the Westminster Psalter, the Painted Chamber, the Westminster St.

Faith, and the design of the chapter house tiles among them.[20] He stands, in fact, in isolation—a Westminster monk who was a muralist at least, but the details of whose life simply do nothing to support the idea of other artistic production within the abbey or of a "school" there.

The final bits of evidence cited frequently to connect Westminster Abbey to a Court School of illumination are contained in the abbey's *Customary*. These passages, on the surface at least, do lend support to the idea of a scriptorium of some sort in the abbey, and as it has been suggested, "unless we are to consider these as mere ideal precepts they do argue an interest in the production of books in the [thirteenth] century."[21]

Among the problems here are the precise dating of the *Customary* of St. Augustine, Canterbury. The Westminster *Customary* is widely held to have been completed in the last years of Henry's reign. Its relation to the Canterbury *Customary* is simply unclear; the connection is obviously very close, but whether one used the other as a model, or whether both filiated from another lost customary, is uncertain.[22]

The parts of the Westminster *Customary* of interest here are four:

    1. A passage describing the duties of the precentor, who was to oversee the making of ink and to provide vellum when necessary; to read, arrange, correct, and seal all official documents; and, with the succentor, to care for and repair the books of the abbey;

    2. A passage noting the limitations upon the movement of the precenter within the abbey and stating that although formerly he could not leave the cloister without permission except to make ink, since the *domus scriptoriae* was first made he was free to go, by whatever way, below the walls of the monastery without permission;

    3. A passage on writing within the monastery, an endeavor in which monks were to be employed only during proper hours and only for the use of the church and the perfection of their own souls;

    4. A similar passage which states that monks were not to work "*in scribendo vel illuminando*" unless they were certain they were benefitting the convent or themselves.[23]

Passages 1, 3, and 4 may be disposed of rather quickly. The first, of interest because the precentor was in charge of ink, vellum, and books, appears almost verbatim in the Canterbury *Customary*. The Westminster and Canterbury customaries also reproduce passages 3 and 4 in nearly identical form, and these passages at any rate derive directly and almost verbatim from the Statutes of a General Chapter of Benedictines at Bermondsey in 1249.[24] The Bermondsey statute, in fact, cautioned against writing *or illuminating*, and the omission of any reference to illuminating in one of the Westminster passages might argue against strong interest in that area at the abbey. These passages may, or may not, have specific relevance to Westminster Abbey. They seem remarkably close to "ideal precepts."

The second passage is not so easily dismissed as the others. It is obviously pertinent to Westminster Abbey and its specific physical layout, so it can be no ideal precept. It has caused flurries of speculation for decades about art activities in the abbey. The phrase, *domus scriptoriae*, appears nowhere else in the *Customary*, but these two words have been expanded into a monastic scriptorium in the fullest modern conception of the word, a true center of artistic production. The phrase has been the key factor in linking Westminster Abbey to a Court School of illumination. It has helped fill in the gap between the producer of the Westminster Psalter and Court School illuminators assumed to have centered there.[25]

The phrase needs more attention, however, in the context of the whole *Customary*. On the surface, at least, it means only the "writing place." Nor is there anything at all in the *Customary* that other members of the community shared the exemption. The precentor was the official most closely concerned with the abbey books and its official documents. He had charge of the cupboards in the carrel area of the north cloister where the books were kept. He made ink and provided parchment for writing. He prepared and sealed the abbey's legal documents. He performed for the chapter many of the functions of the chancery of the royal court, and it is significant that the royal writing office had been called, until very recently, the "scriptorium," a usage that can have had no other implication than the place where unadorned official and legal documents were produced.[26]

It seems likely, too, that the phrase *domus scriptoriae* had some relation to the dating of the *Customary* itself and to progress of Henry III's building works at the abbey church. The writing of the *Customary* appears to have been undertaken in 1266, at just about the time the abbey construction works had advanced to the quire, the five easternmost bays of which were completed during Henry's lifetime.[27] These bays were contiguous to the north walls of the cloister, where the study and writing carrels were located and where a good part of the precentor's attention was necessarily centered. There is disagreement as to the date of the rebuilt eastern end of the north cloister. Pevsner ascribes it to the 1240s, at the very beginning of the works at the church; others date it later.[28] More important than the date, however, is that the writing area was necessarily moved at some time for the demolition and reconstruction of part of the north walk. Even if the outside north cloister predates the work on the five bays of the church proper, as Pevsner suggests, it seems unlikely that this portion of the cloister could have been very useful for writing or study with an immense and noisy construction project going on immediately behind and above the cloister wall. Where the monks wrote and studied during this dislocation is simply not clear. They do not seem to have had access to the *domus scriptoriae*. Very likely, that *domus scriptoriae* was nothing more than a place of uncertain location designated to house the chancerial functions of the precentor when the north cloister was no longer usable. The phrase, at any rate, can support no wider definition than the "writing place" and to read more into it is simply untenable. The *Customary* as a whole gives a remarkably comprehensive portrait of life within the abbey just at the time a Court School of illuminators should have flourished. It offers no single bit of solid evidence, however, that such activities were a part of conventual life. If Westminster Abbey housed a Court School of illuminators, it kept it very well hidden indeed.

None of this is to deny that there was a definable Court *style* in illumination in the second half of the thirteenth century, or that it was related in its development, its inspiration, and its sophistication to the Court School of artists and builders who came to produce for Henry III. Nor is it to deny that the best contemporary illuminators might have been attracted by the warm patronal climate in the Westminster-London area and produced there the finest works of their day outside the formal patronage of king or any institution. It is to caution, however, that the exceedingly full records of Henry III and the very full records of Westminster Abbey are remarkably bare of any hints of specific interest in illumination or illuminators. If the Court School of illuminators was not in fact under royal patronage or within the royal abbey, it very likely had a mobility that could carry its members and its styles into the provinces with ease and speed. Before centripetalism sweeps everything excellent into the capital, more study is needed of the mobility of men, ideas, and styles in the thirteenth century.

Medieval Academe:
The Medical Masters at Montpellier

HOWELL H. GWIN, JR.

By 1258 the importance of Western Europe's first great medical school at Salerno was fast passing away in the political turmoil that was destroying southern Italy. But at Montpellier, in southern France, Jewish scholars expelled from Almohad Spain and an influx of masters and students from Salerno had already made that city a flourishing center of medical teaching and practice.

In 1220 a papal legate, Conrad of Urach, cardinal bishop of Porto and St. Rufine, granted the *universitas medicinae* of Montpellier a charter and body of statutes for its governance. This document, which placed the corporation of masters of medicine under the authority of the local diocesan the bishop of Maguelone, was confirmed by the Holy See and reinforced on several occasions with additional statutes between 1220 and 1340. At about the same time that the masters of medicine received their charter, the masters of civil and canon law organized themselves as a faculty, and later a faculty of liberal arts gained recognition at Montpellier. In 1289 Pope Nicholas IV recognized the schools at Montpellier as a *studium generale, a* designation enjoyed by only two contemporary universities, Paris and Bologna. Henceforth the faculties at Montpellier were entitled to grant to their graduates the coveted *licentiate docendi ubique,* the license to teach anywhere in the Christian world.[1]

In 1340 the Faculty of Medicine received a new body of statutes that was the framework of university governance for nearly two centuries. The statutes of 1340 apparently superseded all previous ordinances, but they were essentially a codification of earlier statutes. The new statutes established rules for every school activity: administration, teaching, student and faculty conduct, examinations, choice of lecture subjects and times, required courses, relations among masters and between masters and students, ceremonies, and other matters. Even the gifts students were expected to give their masters upon graduation were described in detail. Most important, the statutes of 1340 reiterated earlier statutes that had deprived the bishop of Maguelone of much of his authority over the medical school and faculty and given the masters a greater role in the administration of the university. After 1340 no change could be made in the school's statutes without the assent of the masters. At the same time the masters could not alter statutes that affected the students without student consent.[2] The fact that the statutes of 1340 remained viable for nearly two hundred years is a tribute to those who framed them. Certainly the rules were changed from time to time, but the modifications were made by those whom they most affected—the masters and the students themselves.

As with any institution, however—especially an institution of higher learning—rules and regulation could provide only the framework for the conduct of the true business of the corporate body, which was, in this case, the teaching and learning of medicine. It has been said that the medieval university was "built of men," and it was the masters themselves who gave Montpellier its reputation as *fons artis physicae*. Who, then, were these masters, and how did they conduct their business?

In order to be a master in the faculty of medicine, a man was supposed to possess three qualifications: legitimate birth, clerical status, and the approval of the bishop of Maguelone or, later, of the faculty of medicine itself. The first qualification, that of legitimacy, appears in the supplemental statutes adopted by the masters in 1313, but had probably been in force earlier. However, exceptions may have been made because the statutes of 1340 provided that any illegitimate men then on the faculty of medicine should be immediately removed from it. The Apostolic See could, however, grant exceptions to this rule, as Pope John XXII did in 1330 when he authorized the admission of Pons de Lunel, despite his illegitimate birth, as master because Pons had worked long and hard at his studies. In 1341, Anthonio de

Abbatibus was granted a similar dispensation, provided that he accept no office that involved the cure of souls.[3]

Second, masters and students had to be clerics as did all men who were even incidentally involved with the affairs of the Church. However, most medieval students, especially in medicine, never intended to become priests. They took minor orders to be eligible for a university education and in the hope of appointment to an ecclesiastical benefice that would give them the financial support necessary to pursue their studies. The statutes of 1220 required students and masters to wear the tonsure and the proper habit of their religious order. However, celibacy was not expected of those in minor orders. In 1320 the chancellor of the school of medicine was married, as were other masters, including Bernardo Alberti, Petro de Dacia, Roberto Tassilli, Petro de Romerario, and a future vice-chancellor, Bernardus Forestis.[4] Even John de Tornamira, personal physician to Popes Gregory XI and Clement VII, was married and had a daughter.[5]

As far as the admission of new masters was concerned, after the issuance of the supplementary statutes of Pope Clement V in 1309, the bishop's approval became a mere formality. Masters thereafter were admitted by the masters themselves, although the popes occasionally intervened and ordered admission of applicants as John XXII did in 1330 and 1334.[6]

As was common in other universities, Montpellier drew most of its regular teaching staff from among its own graduates. In 1340 prospective licentiates had to swear to teach for two years in the faculty of medicine after receiving the master's degree: only the bishop Maguelone could grant permission to depart before the term was finished.[7] Graduates of other schools also taught at Montpellier, but they were not always welcome. Gilles de Corbeil, who had studied at Salerno, practiced and taught at Montpellier before moving to Paris where he became the personal physician of Philip II Augustus in the early thirteenth century.[8] In 1307, the bishop's vicar, Raimundo de Agone, issued a letter in favor of Petrus Calbertus, stating that Petrus had been examined and was to be granted permission to teach and practice in Montpellier. Evidently the masters of the faculty of medicine objected either to Petrus's qualifications or to the bishop's interference because the mandate was renewed in 1310 and again in 1312.[9] Pons de Lunel, who had received his master's degree from Avignon in 1315, asked permission to teach and practice in Montpellier, but the faculty immediately went to court to prevent this, and the legal proceedings lasted until 1330. In that year, Pope John XXII settled the matter by ordering the masters of Montpellier not to disturb Pons in his teaching and practice.[10]

Although every master of medicine who lived in Montpellier was considered to be part of the *universitas* and a member of the faculty of medicine, not all of them had the same standing. The statutes distinguish between the reading masters, *magistri legentes*, and the nonreading masters, *magistri non legentes*, but the line is not clearly drawn between them. Since the faculty of medicine was essentially a gild for those engaged in either teaching or practicing medicine, or both, the nonteaching practitioners would obviously have to be members so that they might be regulated—a fundamental purpose of the medieval gilds. It is possible that the nonreading masters might be considered adjunct, or part-time instructors, who seldom taught or who periodically taught unusual courses in their particular areas of expertise. Considering the rigid structure of the medieval medical curriculum, however, this seems improbable. Dr. Dorothy Mackay Quynn has suggested that the fundamental role of the nonreading master might be comparable to that of the German *Privat Dozent*, an instructor who taught tutorially after receiving his degree.

The statutes define the reading masters as those who engaged regularly in lecturing from the Feast of St. Luke (October 10) or the Feast of All Saints (November 1) until Easter.[11] Only reading masters were allowed to participate in the examinations of those applying for the degree of master.[12] Reading masters were assigned two bachelors to assist them in their work and were entitled to a fee of twenty *sous* from each bachelor who chose to study with them. If a reading master violated the faculty statutes, he could be punished by revocation of his reading privileges for a year, thus leaving him with only whatever income he derived from his private practice.[13]

If a nonreading master wished to begin teaching, he had to announce his intention at the first faculty convocation of the year. Then, if the other masters did not object, he was allowed to choose his course in accordance with his seniority. However, he received only one bachelor to assist him. Apparently a nonreading master could actually teach without securing formal permission of the assembled faculty, but, if he did so, he was entitled to only half the fees normally received from students. The other half was paid into the faculty treasury.[14]

The medical masters were, of course, concerned primarily with the teaching and practice of medicine. In teaching, their books, methods, schedules, and most other details of academic life were closely regulated first by the Church and later by the masters themselves. In 1309, Pope Clement V, after consultation with his personal physicians, Arnaud de Villanova and John de Alesto, both masters from Montpellier, issued a bull listing the books which were to be taught by the faculty of medicine.[15] Their advice to the pontiff was wise, for the selection of required books included the core of the medieval medical canon. Hippocrates' *Aphorismorum*, *Pronosticorum*, and *De Regimine Aucutorum* and Galen's *Ars Magna*, *Ars Parva*, and *Tegni* comprised the Greek authorities. Muslim medicine was represented by the authors Rhases, Constantinus, and Isaac, but no specific titles were listed. Evidently any book written by the latter authors would suffice. The pope specified in addition that at least two of the required works would have to be studied in conjunction with authoritative commentaries, such as Johannitus's introduction to Galen's *Ars Parva*, but one book could be read without a commentary.[16]

The statutes of 1340 included a list of books that formed the basis for the faculty's curriculum. As might be expected, this list was not exactly the same as the one issued by Clement. Moreover, where Clement had merely stated which books should be studied, the new statutes organized the books into nine separate courses, each consisting of two or more books. Instead of simply specifying that Avicenna's *Canon* would be taught, the new rules indicated which parts of the book were to be included in the lectures. If there were more masters who wished to read than there were books available in the list, then there were alternate selections from the works of the approved authors, such as Isaac's *De Febris* and his *Dietis universalibus.*[17]

Since the books to be read were specified, it would be reasonable to assume that forbidden books were also listed. Such was indeed the case. The masters of Montpellier were permitted to lecture on only one book of natural science, Aristotle's *De Animalibus*. In addition, no master might read from any book of logic or grammar, because students were presumed to have finished their undergraduate training in the arts.[18]

The statutes also set forth a definite procedure by which the individual masters could choose the books upon which they would lecture. This scheme was apparently necessitated by quarrels among the masters over who should teach what books. Each master chose his books at the first official congregation of the year which was called by the chancellor in the week before the Feast of St. Michael in September. The oldest master in years of service was permitted to choose first. In the interest of fairness, however, the youngest master then selected his book. This process proceeded with the choices alternating between the next oldest and next youngest member of the faculty until all the masters had made their selections. Once a master had chosen his book, and his choice was written in the *Liber Lectionum et Clavium*, he was not permitted to alter his selection. Masters were forbidden to choose a book which another master had already selected, and no master was allowed to repeat his lecture on any one book within five years. Thus students were assured the opportunity to hear lectures on as many different books as possible during their years of study and were also able to hear different masters lecture on the same book if they so desired.[19]

The masters' lectures were also regulated by the university statutes. The earliest rules drafted by Cardinal Conrad had stated that the senior master was to regulate the time, number, and length of the masters' lectures. Once the format was established, no master could dismiss his students before the end of the period unless he became ill or was forced to end his lecture early because of compelling family necessity.[20]

As the faculty of medicine increased in size, more detailed regulation of lectures became necessary. The statutes of 1340 established the length of each class period and the time of day each class should be held. The masters were permitted to choose their lecture hours, but the selection procedure favored the senior masters. During the first five years of his teaching career, a master was allowed to lecture only during the first hour. After five years' experience, a master might choose to lecture during either the first or the second hour. After a master selected his time, he was not allowed to vary from it during the entire year.[21]

If a master was called to visit an important patient in a distant city, he was permitted to be absent from his lectures, provided he had no lecture responsibilities or other unperformed duties relating to the school. If his work was not completed, he was expected to resign from the reading masters and if he did not resign, he could be expelled, as was Nicholas Caresmel in 1455. In addition, when a master was absent on school business, he could be excused for any length of time, and another master would be asked to take over his classes.[22]

The statutes also provided sick leave for faculty. If a master became ill, he might have another master lecture in his place until he recovered. If he returned to work within one week, he was permitted to resume his lectures. If he did not return within this time, his class was given to another master, and he was removed from the list of reading masters. Any master who claimed illness and absented himself for more than a few days had to submit to examination by another master to determine whether or not he was truly sick. If the illness was feigned, then his name was removed from the list of reading masters.[23]

The statutes themselves give little information concerning the actual methods of teaching, but instruction undoubtedly followed the procedures of other medieval universities. The master sat or stood before his pupils with a large volume upon a lectern in front of him. The students sat upon the floor and took notes if they were fortunate enough to have money for ink and parchment. The lecture began with the peal of the faculty bell, but it was not a lecture in the modern sense of the word: the master literally read the book to his students. As he read, he might illustrate certain points from the book by recalling experiences from his own practice. For example, if he was reading Johanni- tus's *De Pulsibus*, he might describe the difficulties he had expe- rienced in taking the pulse of an extremely obese person. Then he might relate a method he had discovered which made the task easier.

Unfortunately, verbatim records of medieval medical classes do not exist. However, Bernardus de Gordino, a master in medicine at Montpellier, wrote a book on the professional con- duct of physicians, and used much of the same information in his classes that he later included in his book. To illustrate how a medieval lecture in medicine might have sounded, a few of his comments from his *De Practica* follow:

> If you do not know what the urine you are examining denotes, you should say, 'there is a liver obstruction here.' If the patient should say, 'No, Master, my head hurts,' you should hasten to say, 'That results from the liver obstruction' . . . Use the word *obstruction* often, for none know its meaning.
>
> It may happen that even after observing a patient you do not recognize his illness. In such a case, speak to him of accidents of which he has previously told you, and he will have confidence in you. When you leave such a patient, do not omit to say that his condition is very serious. If he recovers, your glory will be all the greater, while if he dies, his friends will not forget to say that you had despaired of him. When you visit a patient in a far-distant city, do not accept his offer of food and lodging; get them at the inn. If you dine and rest with him, he will always deduct the cost of his hospitality from your fee.[24]

In addition to the ordinary lectures which were delivered by the masters, there were also the cursory lectures. Cursory, or extraordinary, lectures were given in the afternoons and usually served as review sessions. They might also be devoted to the less important books in the curriculum. In any event, they were conducted exclusively by bachelors, who were required to read cursorily for two years before being eligible for promotion to the rank of master. Such a provision gave the bachelor practical teaching experience, an opportunity to earn extra money, and allowed the masters to spend their time on the more important ordinary lectures.[25]

As in all medieval universities, the disputation was used as a teaching device. A disputation was "the presentation, explanation, and proof of some statement of theory and the answering of objections against it which were put by an opponent."[26] Since medieval medicine was a logical and theoretical skill rather than a practical one, a man was judged upon his familiarity with the important authorities and his prowess in verbal battles. Consequently every examination during a student's career included at least one disputation, and to perform well, skill and experience were necessary.

At Montpellier disputations, like formal lectures, were closely regulated. The statutes decreed that the hour of vespers be set aside for the masters and bachelors to dispute so that the bachelors might receive practice in this important activity. No lectures, neither ordinary nor cursory, were permitted during this time. On Wednesdays, the "day of Hippocrates," and university holidays, disputations could take place at any time. If several masters wished to dispute at the same time, preference was given to the senior among them. If, however, a bachelor who was to be promoted in the near future wished to dispute, then he took precedence over everyone else. Each disputation was limited to one hour, but if no one else wished to dispute, the disputant was allowed an extra hour.[27]

Disputations could become more physical than mental exercises. In the early thirteenth century, Gilles de Corbeil visited Montpellier after having attended the medical school at Salerno. Perhaps wishing to uphold the reputation of his school, he engaged in a disputation with several masters of Montpellier that degenerated into a brawl. In the middle of the debate, according to Gilles, the masters set upon him and beat him severely "as if he had been a churl or a fool."[28] Presumably few disputations reached such a pitch of academic enthusiasm.

An unusual feature of medical instruction at Montpellier was that every student was required to observe an anatomical dissection before receiving his master's degree, because, according to the statute, "experience is the best teacher in all things."[29] These dissections were to be held every two years at least, and the chancellor and one nonreading master were to conduct them. Bodies for the demonstrations were obtained from the political authorities. In 1376, Louis of Anjou ordered his lieutenants in Languedoc to give the body of an executed criminal to the medical faculty at Montpellier.[30] Thereafter the masters received something approaching regular deliveries of bodies from the authorities,[31] although occasionally the faculty had to remind them to send the promised cadavers.[32]

Although the statutes of the faculty of medicine give no specific information concerning the rules for conducting dissections, the procedure probably followed the one used at Bologna in 1405. A limited number of students were invited to each dissection, so that everyone in attendance could see the process. Twenty students could attend the dissection of a male, but thirty could view one of a female, since female bodies were more scarce. No student was admitted to a dissection until he had studied medicine for two years so that all who attended would have sufficient knowledge to benefit fully from the demonstration. The students who observed the dissection were responsible for paying the expenses of procuring, preparing, and burying the subject up to the amount of sixteen *livres* for a male specimen and twenty for a female. The master who performed the dissection was paid one hundred *sous*.[33]

The actual methods used in medieval dissections were described by Gui de Chauliac in his famous work on surgery, *La Grande Chirurgie*. According to Chauliac, the procedure usually consisted of four parts or sessions. In the first part the dissecting master and his students examined the abdominal organs such as the stomach and intestines. The second lesson consisted of the thoracic organs, including the heart and lungs, while the brain was examined in the third. Following the third lesson, the students were responsible for removing of the remaining flesh by boiling or exposing the cadaver to the sun. This procedure made the bones, ligaments, and joints more accessible for the fourth and final session on the skeletal structure. The order in which the dissection proceeded was dictated by the normal progress of putrification. The digestive organs decayed first, followed by those in the chest; since the bones did not degenerate, they were reserved for the final lesson. After completion of the demonstration, the students were responsible for burying the remains "in a Christian manner."[34]

In addition to his teaching and private practice, a master of medicine at Montpellier had to participate in the governance of the faculty and school. After 1307 one of the masters was elected by his colleagues to serve as chancellor, or head of the faculty. The chancellor-elect still had to receive the formal approval of the bishop of Maguelone, and before he could assume his office he had to swear to provide justice to all members of the faculty; to promise that he would not accept money or other gifts and would not be moved by love or by hate in making decisions; and to pledge that he would keep the statutes of the university intact for his successors.[35]

The chancellor was expected to consult regularly with the masters and to regulate the affairs of the school with their advice. According to the statutes of 1340, the chancellor was to assemble the faculty whenever internal or external problems troubled the school. In addition to extraordinary assemblies, the chancellor was expected to summon the masters to two regular convocations each year. The first regular meeting was held in September during the week preceding the Feast of St. Michael and the second during the week after Easter. It was in these meeting that the real business of the faculty took place, and all masters were required to attend unless they had a valid excuse for absenting themselves. The first regular assembly in September was the most important one, for it was at this convocation that the masters chose their courses; the statutes of the faculty were read; keys to the archives were distributed; and lesser officials were chosen.[36]

Second in importance to the chancellor was the dean. In the earliest statutes, the senior master was given precedence in all processions and seating, and had authority to set the times of vacation, establish the length of lectures, and assign lecture hours for the other masters. By 1340, the faculty decided that the senior member of the faculty who was still actively reading would be called *decanatus*, or "dean." Since lectures were now regulated by statute, the dean seems to have had few duties beyond enforcing observance of the statutes pertaining to teaching and determining vacation periods. In 1364 the responsibilities of the office were not sufficiently burdensome to prevent masters from requiring their dean to lecture. They recognized, however, that old age brings infirmity, and the masters provided that another master could read in the dean's place if he was too sick to fulfill his duty.[37]

The statutes of 1340 also mention financial officials for the first time. The faculty's growth had evidently made it impossible for the masters and chancellor to handle such matters as the collection of fees and the purchase of supplies. Consequently the statutes provided for the annual selection of two proctors who were chosen from among the masters by a procedure similar to that used in selecting courses. The first year the oldest and the youngest masters in years of service filled the office. The following year the next oldest and youngest served as proctors, and the process continued until all had served when, presumably, the procedure began all over again. It was the proctors' sworn duty to keep safe the goods of the faculty and to render a strict accounting at the end of their term of office for what had been entrusted to them. Faculty funds were kept in a chest, or *archa*, that was placed in the home of the elder proctor. The chest was locked with three keys, each of which was entrusted to a different master. Although the statutes do not identify the holders of the keys, it seems most likely that they were held by the chancellor and the two proctors. Since it took the presence of three persons to open the chest, it was customary for the proctors to keep fifty or sixty *sous* in their purses to cover the immediate expenses of the school.[38]

Since the masters of Montpellier belonged to a *universitas*, or gild, they were bound by some of the same regulations, and observed some of the same customs, as members of the craft guilds. One of the earliest rules of the faculty of medicine required the members to assist any fellow master or student who was injured by a person not connected with the school. As in other gilds, the masters were expected to attend mass together at least once a week in a church chosen by vote of faculty. Masters who were not present were fined six *denarii*, which was collected by the proctors and used for the good of the faculty. The masters were also expected to attend the funerals of all deceased faculty members. However, by 1335, this rule was relaxed to require attendance only at an annual requiem mass for the souls of all departed colleagues celebrated on the Feast of All Saints.[39]

In addition to teaching, most masters at Montpellier engaged in private medical practice, which, like their academic activities, was regulated by the faculty statutes. According to the statutes, no physician could practice in the region of Montpellier until he had been examined and approved by the faculty of medicine. However, if a nonaccredited practitioner was persistent, only the civil authorities could restrain him, and their cooperation was not always easily obtained. In 1281, when the faculty wished to prevent John de Chipro from practicing until he submitted to an examination, its officials had to write no less than four letters to the authorities, and even then the outcome of the dispute with Chipro remained in doubt. Another statute, intended to prevent unfair competition among the practicing masters, specified that no master should pay an innkeeper more than a five *sous* referral for sending him a patient.[40] The statutes also attempted to delineate the proper sphere of physicians of the body from that of physicians of the spirit, by requiring masters to summon a priest before attending a woman in the last stages of labor, or treating a patient with a severe fever, for "in such matters . . . the soul's health is to be treated first."[41]

Besides regulating medical practice, the statutes and the faculty of medicine also sought to control the activities of apothecaries in the city. Each year the faculty elected two masters to visit the apothecary shops to ascertain that the proprietors were properly licensed by the bishop of Maguelone and to admonish them not to sell laxatives except by prescription from one of the masters of medicine.[42]

The private practice of the masters often took them far from Montpellier. As early as the thirteenth century the school had acquired sufficient renown to cause great men throughout Europe to seek consultants and personal physicians from among the masters of its faculty. In 1253 John of St. Giles was called to London to treat the illustrious Robert Grosseteste, bishop of Lincoln.[43] In the fourteenth century the Avignonese popes chose their personal physicans from the medical faculty at Montpellier, and dispatched them to treat distinguished friends of the papacy, including the count of Armagnac and the wife of the duke of Normandy.[44] Because the masters of Montpellier were considered to be especially expert in the diagnosis of leprosy, one of the great scourges of the Middle Ages, the faculty played an important role in public health. In 1372, for example, the examining board for suspected lepers in the city of Nîmes consisted of two masters and a bachelor from the school at Montpellier.[45]

Such was the life of a medieval master in medicine; it was not, after all, very much different from that of a modern professor. His world was one of books, students, lectures, and examinations. He had to attend faculty meetings, fulfill administrative duties, and often travel on behalf of the school. He devoted time to research and writing and to his medical practice, much as modern professors engage in consulting work. If the medieval university was truly "built of men," the faculty of medicine at Montpellier formed a strong and efficient edifice for the transmission of knowledge. Of them might it truly be said that "gladly would they learn, and gladly teach."

Women's History

The Indomitable Belle:
Eleanor of Provence,
Queen of England

MARTHA BILES

Eleanor of Provence was the second of four daughters born to Raymond-Berenger, count of Provence, and his wife Beatrice, daughter of Count Thomas of Savoy. Eleanor grew up in a gracious and cultivated court where she acquired a dignity and cultural sensitivity uncommon in that age even for a woman of rank. Ordinarily when a younger daughter of a comital family came of marriageable age she could expect, at best, suitors from the lesser baronial houses. However, the counties of Provence and Savoy were not without importance in the politics of thirteenth-century Europe, and perhaps more significantly, the daughters of Raymond-Berenger had a reputation for beauty. The count's eldest daughter, Margaret, was already married to King Louis IX of France, and this alliance certainly improved Eleanor's chances for a marriage of consequence.

Perhaps Europe's most eligible bachelor was King Henry III of England, whose ten-year quest for a bride had assumed the proportions of an epic. Henry began to negotiate for Eleanor's hand in 1235. Count Raymond was so pleased at the prospect of numbering a second queen among his progeny that the English envoys were able to exact from him the promise to provide a dower for Eleanor of 20,000 marks, a sum equal to that which he had settled on Margaret. The count, of course, did not know that Henry was so enraptured by the descriptions of Eleanor that he had privately instructed his envoys to contract the marriage with or without a money settlement. Indeed, the emissaries had been instructed to bring the girl to England as quickly as possible, even if Raymond failed to agree to other terms in the articles of marriage.[1]

The preparations made in London for receiving the new queen

were unprecedented in the history of the city. Stories of the loveliness of "La Belle de Provence" preceded her, and the citizens, whose expectations of their new queen had been heightened by years of anticipation, spared nothing for her reception. The young girl, not yet thirteen years of age, landed at Dover in January 1236 and was escorted immediately to Canterbury. There she met Henry, who "rushed into the arms of the messengers, and, having seen the lady and received possession of her, . . . married her at Canterbury."[2] The ceremony took place on January 14 and was followed six days later by her coronation at Westminster.

The love that Henry and Eleanor inspired in each other endured through thirty-six years of marriage. She bore Henry nine children, only four of whom, Edward, Margaret, Beatrice, and Edmund, survived to adulthood. The family environment that Henry and Eleanor provided for their children was rare in the thirteenth century. In an age when indifference and even cruelty were commonplace, they were affectionate and compassionate parents. In an age when marital fidelity was much praised, but seldom observed, their devotion to each other was exemplary. And in an era when cruelty and insensitivity abounded, they taught their children to appreciate beauty. The attention that Henry and Eleanor lavished on the children was returned, for they always remained loyal to their parents and to each other, and their own marriages were uncommonly happy.

Whatever the people who had welcomed Eleanor to England with such joy and high expectations came to think of her in the later turbulent years, she proved herself a loving, tender wife and mother, a trusted counselor, and, when necessary, a relentless enemy who could fight with animal ferocity when the welfare of her family was threatened. It was her intelligence and strength of character together with the influence she exerted through her husband, children, and other relatives that enabled Eleanor to affect events in England and even beyond the borders of the realm.

Queen Eleanor got her first opportunity to play a significant role in the governance of England in 1253 when Henry decided to visit his Gascon lands. Simon de Montfort, earl of Leicester and the king's brother-in-law, had been Henry's lieutenant in Gascony, but he had so wretchedly managed his office there that he had to buttress his authority with bands of mercenaries. Although Earl Simon retired to France in the spring of 1253, his retreat failed to undo the mischief he had set in motion. Henry's Gascon subjects were threatening to renounce their allegiance and to align themselves with Alphonse of Castile. The situation was so serious that King Henry believed the duchy could be saved only if he went there in person.

Prior to his departure King Henry appointed Eleanor regent of England, Wales, and Ireland, with authority to govern these lands with the counsel of his brother Richard of Cornwall, until his return from Gascony. He also made his will and saw to the comfort of his queen, who was expecting another child. On June 22, 1253, Henry announced that he was entrusting the great seal of England to Eleanor and warned that if, during his absence, anything detrimental to the crown was sealed with any other seal, the act would be null and void.[3] He dictated his last will at Southwick on July 1, and nothing illustrates better than this document his affection for and trust in his queen. To Eleanor Henry committed the guardianship of his eldest son and heir, Edward, and his other children. It was also his wish that she should rule as regent over England, his lands in Wales, Ireland, and Gascony until his heir came of age.[4] The following day Henry wrote to his son-in-law, Alexander III of Scotland, asking that he allow his queen, Margaret, to come to England and stay with her mother during the remainder of Eleanor's pregnancy, as she was in need of "some small grain of consolation."[5] Although Alexander respectfully denied the request, Henry was at least able to provide for his wife's material needs, ordering that venison be provided for her from the royal park at Windsor and that good wine be supplied her when she resided in London.[6]

Henry's departure was delayed by unfavorable winds and by baronial opposition to the expedition. Richard de Clare, earl of Gloucester and Hertford, and many other prominent men were slow to the answer the royal summons.[7] At last, however, the contrary winds, which had blown across the Channel from France, and the grumbling of the barons subsided sufficiently to allow a crossing, and, on August 6, the king and his party sailed from Portsmouth.

During her reign as regent, Eleanor left many routine tasks to Master William de Kilkenny, archdeacon of Coventry, who held the seal of the exchequer, but she personally performed the more important tasks of governing, including that of sitting as judge in the curia regis. The birth of a daughter, Katherine, on November 25, 1253, interrupted Eleanor's duties, but she seems to have resumed them immediately after her purification.[8]

Eleanor's main concern as regent was to raise more men and money for the king's Gascon campaign. Shortly after his arrival in Gascony Henry ordered all tenants-in-chief who had ignored his call for military support to appear before the queen and royal council to explain their actions. Richard of Cornwall joined Eleanor in urging her son-in-law, Alexander III of Scotland, to aid Henry. This appeal, however, failed to persuade Alexander and his stubborn Scottish lords to support England's cause.[9]

The honeymoon between Eleanor and the turbulent Londoners had been over for a long time. She was now the hated foreign queen, and her actions as regent aggravated the hostility of the city. Eleanor not only rigidly enforced the payment of a tax on every boat loading or unloading at Queenhithe on the Thames, but also squeezed from the citizens everything possibly due her in queen's gold, an honorarium payable to her when anyone entered into a voluntary fine or obligation with the crown that was figured at one-tenth the value of the fine, but was owed in addition to the obligation. Richard Picard and John de Northampton, sheriffs of London, refused to cooperate with the regents and were arrested and held in the Marshalsea Prison. The Lord Mayor, Richard Bardell, joined the sheriffs when he refused to produce the aid imposed on the city for the Gascon expedition.[10]

In December 1253 King Henry informed Eleanor and Richard that he would have to have reinforcements. He instructed the regents to require all free tenants with annual incomes of £20 or more to be knighted and to prepare themselves for service in Gascony. On December 27 the regents summoned the lay and ecclesiastical magnates to a parliament that was to convene in one month. Henry sent Roger Bigod, the earl marshal, and John de Balliol home to inform the assembled notables of his urgent needs. Unfortunately the emissaries were delayed by twelve days of unfavorable winds, and by the time they arrived in England the parliament had already met and adjourned. The only promise Eleanor had been able to exact from the magnates was a pledge to grant the king financial aid in the event Alphonse of Castile invaded Gascony.[11]

Meanwhile, Eleanor and Richard, on February 11, 1254, summoned another parliament to convene two weeks after Easter. Only the great lay and ecclesiastical lords who traditionally attended the king's parliaments had come to the first meeting in January, but the new summons included, in addition to the magnates, representatives from the lesser nobility. The summons, which was sent to the sheriffs, read as follows:

> Earls, barons and nobles will come to London Easter Day for three weeks with horses and arms, ready to go to Portsmouth to cross to Gascony against the King of Castile about to enter with force into Gascony. . . . We order you that you will constrain to the same all those of your jurisdiction who hold twenty librates of land and in our ward; in addition make appear before us at council at Westminster within a fortnight of Easter, four legal and discreet knights of the aforesaid shires whom the shires shall elect for the purpose to provide aid.[12]

Because of the inclusion of a representative element this summons was a landmark in parliamentary history. The sheriffs received with the parliamentary summons mandates directing them to appear before the exchequer on the date set for the parliament, prepared to pay all their debts to the king. Failure to appear, they were warned, would result in their arrest and the forced levy of their obligations from their lands and other holdings.[13]

The Easter parliament, attended by representatives of the clergy from each diocese and by elected knights from the shires, was even less willing than the previous assemblage to grant

Henry the financial aid he requested. No doubt Simon de Mont-fort's return from France and his assertion that no danger existed in Gascony influenced the decision of the assembly. The con-certed response of those present was that the king had troubled and impoverished them so that they could hardly breathe.[14] No aid was forthcoming.

Consequently, the conditions of royal finances both at home and in Gascony continued to deteriorate. Eleanor was reduced to raising money by any means possible including borrowing from Richard of Cornwall, Italian merchants, and others. Henry's needs were so desperate that he asked that the royal treasure be sent to him so he could pawn it to obtain money to pay his soldiers and other mounting debts.[15]

Nevertheless, all was not black for the royal couple. Since Alphonse of Castile was behind most of the trouble in Gascony, Henry decided that he could solve his problems through that most important device—a marriage alliance. A marriage between Henry's heir, Edward, and Alphonse's half sister, Eleanor of Castile, would secure the borders of Gascony and, at the same time, add to the duchy several important fiefs that the prospective bride had inherited from her mother. Henry was delighted when, after lengthy negotiation, the formal marriage agreement was concluded in April 1254.[16] Henry then sent for Queen Eleanor and Edward. He chose the portsmen of Yar-mouth and Dunwich to escort his family to Gascony, and took the precaution of informing the unruly barons of the Cinque Ports that if they harmed the queen or interfered with her pas-sage, he would "betake himself to the bodies of them, their wives and children, their lands and tenements in the realm so that they shall forever feel themselves aggrieved."[17]

On May 29 Eleanor resigned the regency fully to her brother-in-law Richard and set sail for the continent in the company of her uncle, Boniface of Savoy, archbishop of Canterbury; her sons, Edward and Edmund; her sister, Sanchia; and a courtly retinue of knights and ladies. Within a few days she was reunited with her husband, and the royal family then traveled together to Castile. When they arrived Alphonse knighted Edward, and the marriage of the prince and Eleanor of Castile was celebrated at the monastery of Las Huelgas.[18]

Henry had accomplished the main objectives of his Gascon venture. Most of the Gascon insurgents had been pacified, the southern border of the duchy had been made secure, and he had obtained an influential kinsman and ally in Alphonse of Castile. Henry felt sufficiently relieved to spend several weeks visiting cities that had heretofore been only names to him. On November 9, 1254, the royal family and its entourage moved north from Cognac to Fontevrault Abbey where Henry and Eleanor visited the tomb of his mother, Isabella. King Louis IX met the English royal family at Chartres and personally escorted Henry and his queen on to Paris. Louis offered his English relatives the use of his own palace, the Louvre, or any other residence in the city they might prefer. But Henry, who was normally an aesthete, was apparently in an ascetic mood, for he chose as his residence the Old Temple, a somber and severe stronghold.[19]

In Paris Eleanor enjoyed, for the first time since her marriage, a reunion with her mother, Beatrice of Provence; her three sisters; Margaret, queen of France; Sanchia, countess of Cornwall; and Beatrice, countess of Anjou; and her sisters' children. On the second evening following their arrival Henry entertained his French host at a feast that contemporary chroniclers vowed had never been equalled, even in the courts of Arthur and Charlemagne.[20] The feast temporarily interrupted family unity, for while the queenly sisters, Eleanor and Margaret, were seated on thrones for the meal, royal etiquette relegated the countesses to stools.[21]

In this age, family affairs and affairs of state were inseparable. For eight days Henry and Louis engaged in cordial discussions. Before the talks ended a personal friendship had developed that was invaluable during the troubled years that were facing Eleanor and her husband. Queen Margaret, like Louis, grew fond of Henry, and her natural affection for Eleanor never wavered. After this pleasant family gathering Margaret freely corresponded with her brother-in-law, and, in the years following Henry's death, continued to exchange letters with his son, Edward I.[22]

The English barons, however, failed to see the long-range benefits of this family reunion and became increasingly critical of Henry's long absence from England. Many of these disgruntled magnates blamed Eleanor for what they saw as dalliance on Henry's part. Although the barons had enthusiastically received her in 1236, their euphoria, like that of the Londoners, had not lasted. By 1255 their feelings for the queen had hardened into bitter resentment. She was, they believed, partly responsible for the horde of foreigners who had descended on England like a plague of locusts. Eleanor's Provençal and Savoyard relatives, like King Henry's half brothers, the Lusignans, had come to England to seek their fortunes and had received from the crown offices and lands that the English nobles and ecclesiastics thought should have been theirs. The chronicler Matthew Paris reflected the prevailing mood of the country when he observed that the barons were asking why the queen's uncle, William of Savoy, bishop-elect of Valence, did not "betake himself to the kingdom of France . . . to manage the affairs of the French kingdom, like he does here, by reason of his niece the queen of that country?"[23] Indeed, so many of Henry's foreign relatives had found favor at court that the barons believed the king preferred the company and counsel of the aliens to his "natural" counselors, who were, of course, they themselves.

Eleanor and Henry returned to England at the end of December 1255. They were at home in time to bring in the new year—a new year that began a decade of trouble and tragedy for the king and queen. There would be concern for the welfare of their daughter Margaret, who found life in Scotland both uncomfortable and dangerous, and for the health of baby Katherine. Their ambitious dream to see their son Edmund crowned king of Sicily would vanish as all fantasies do. But fate would be cruelest to them during the Barons' War (1264-1265) when Henry and Eleanor would have to face the humiliation of defeat, the anguish of separation, and the fear of death. All these trials lay in the future, but even at the beginning of 1255 Eleanor and Henry were being hounded by their creditors. Many of the debts they had incurred before the Gascon campaign resulted from their own extravagant spending, but to these obligations were added the staggering expenses of the Gascon enterprise which the lay and ecclesiastical nobles had steadfastly refused to help defray. Henry and his queen had to face the unhappy fact that the incomes of their wardrobes were not sufficient to meet current expenses to say nothing of reducing their debts.[24]

In 1258 Henry and Eleanor's financial problems paled into insignificance when the hostility of the barons, who always had their individual grievances and grudges, began to congeal into a common antipathy for royal policy. Nature herself seemed to desert Henry and his queen as uncommonly heavy rains followed severe frosts and caused crop failures throughout England, arousing a general unrest in the countryside. Parliaments were held in April and again in June, giving the barons the opportunity to vent their wrath against the crown. Henry agreed to the barons' demands for reform presented to him in a document known as the Provisions of Oxford.[25] However, Henry's half brothers, the Lusignans, denounced the Provisions that would have deprived them of much of their influence. When it became obvious that their opposition would not deter the barons, they fled to the palace of Aymer de Lusignan, bishop-elect of Winchester and youngest of the Lusignan brothers. The barons pursued them, seized the palace, and forced the brothers to leave England.[26] Eleanor had never been a favorite of the Lusignans, and now they blamed all their troubles on her. Louis IX, who was aware of their feelings toward his sister-in-law, refused the Lusignans safe conduct through France, and they remained restricted to the port of Boulogne after their flight from England.[27]

Meanwhile, the work of reform in England went forward, and by the end of 1259 the situation was stable enough for King Henry and Eleanor to again travel to France. This visit, unlike their earlier sojourn, was an affair of state. After several years of negotiation a treaty of peace between England and France, in which Henry formally acknowledged the loss of Normandy and other Angevin possessions on the continent nearly a half century earlier, was close to realization. The final details were worked out by the two kings and their advisors in late November and early December of 1259, and on December 4 of that year the Treaty of Paris was sealed and published.[28] Again the English royal family's stay in Paris was a pleasant one, and Eleanor and Henry lingered there for more than a month savoring their temporary liberation from the tumult of English politics. Undoubtedly, the highlight of the visit for the royal couple was the marriage of their daughter Beatrice to John, duke of Brittany.

After their return to England Henry and Eleanor resided mainly at the strongholds of Windsor and the Tower of London. They spent Christmas of the year 1260 with their daughter Margaret, queen of Scotland, but before February Henry moved quietly to the Tower. The uneasy relationship between the royalists and the baronial opposition was breaking down, and the barons were bickering among themselves. Henry proposed referring the differences between himself and the barons to the arbitration of Louis IX, or, if he should decline, to Queen Margaret and Peter, chamberlain of France.[29] Margaret indicated that she was willing to accept the responsibility, but it was not necessary for her to do so because in April 1261 Henry received papal absolution from his oath to observe the Provisions of Oxford.[30]

Henry dismissed the council the barons had imposed on him and shook off the other restraints of the Provisions of Oxford. The baronial opposition was a house divided and could offer no effective resistance to the king's bold moves. Simon de Montfort, the most spirited and effective leader of Henry's baronial opponents, left England in disgust and returned to France. The De Montforts were one of the great families of France, and Henry feared that Simon would use all the influence his relatives possessed to turn King Louis against him. Henry, therefore, decided to go to France himself to counter any of the earl's machinations. He and Eleanor again crossed the Channel in July 1261, and on arriving in Paris, found to their relief that Simon had not been able to drive a wedge of mistrust between the royal families. Their reception in Paris was warm, and King Louis and Margaret evinced genuine concern for the welfare of their kinsmen, promising to aid them in their troubles with Simon.[31] Louis and his queen sincerely hoped that Henry could peacefully settle his differences with his barons without having to surrender any of what they believed to be his regalian rights. Their hope, unfortunately, was in vain.

Henry had thrown the gauntlet in the face of his enemies. He would never agree of his own free will to a baronial reform plan that would limit his prerogatives, and his baronial opponents would not accept the status quo. There was no room for compromise, and one side or the other would have to yield. Simon de Montfort returned to England shortly after Henry and his queen, and began to rally the dissident barons. Insurrections broke out on the Welsh border and in the south of England. When Henry's attempts to raise an army at Worcester failed, he took his family to the safety of the Tower of London. For reasons which are difficult to fathom, the king's enemies blamed Queen Eleanor for the tragic state of affairs in England. William de Rishanger, a chronicler who sympathized with the baronial cause, observed plaintively that Henry had been a good king as long as he had remained a friend of Christ and a single man.[32] Other enemies of the king and Eleanor, however, were not content to express their feelings toward the queen in mere words. The rebellious barons seized her lands and castles, and, when Eleanor boarded a barge at the Tower in an attempt to join her son Edward, who was holding out against the barons at Windsor Castle, she was attacked by a mob on London bridge. Angry citizens assailed her with the foulest epithets. Some screamed "drown the witch," and many hurled at her barge mud, rotten eggs, and stones large enough to sink it. Eleanor finally managed to escape the mob and sought sanctuary from the bishop of London. The following day the queen returned unhurt to the Tower of London.[33] Nevertheless, the time was to come when the Londoners would pay dearly for their vicious insults.

Henry meanwhile, having discovered that he could not rally sufficient support to resist the demands of the barons, capitulated on July 16, 1263, and effectively surrendered the government of England into the hands of Simon de Montfort and his baronial partisans. In a parliament of lay and ecclesiastical magnates held at St. Paul's in London on September 9, Henry formally accepted the terms of the peace which again imposed on him the limitations of the hated Provisions.[34]

Fortunately for Henry and Eleanor, Louis IX had been kept informed about events in England by the queen's uncle, Boniface of Savoy, archbishop of Canterbury, and Henry's most trusted clerk, John Mansel, who had both discreetly decided to remain on the other side of the Channel. Louis, exercising his right as Henry's feudal lord, commanded the English king to appear before him at Boulogne. This action caught Simon de Montfort and his colleagues on the horns of a dilemma. The earl of Leicester feared the results of a meeting between the two kings, and yet he and his supporters could ill-afford to incur Louis's wrath. Convinced of the righteousness of their cause, Simon and the baronial insurgents would not believe that Louis, whose reputation for fairness was the marvel of Christendom, would take Henry's side in the dispute. Thus, the barons allowed the royal family to leave England, but only after each member pledged to return promptly at the conclusion of the talks. Henry and Eleanor; their sons, Edward and Edmund; and Richard of Cornwall's son, Henry of Almain, made the crossing in the disagreeable company of Earl Simon, who was determined to lay the baronial case before King Louis.

King Louis and Margaret; Louis's brother, Charles of Anjou; and Eleanor's uncles, Peter of Savoy and Boniface, archbishop of Canterbury, greeted the royal party upon its arrival at Boulogne. Much to his dismay, Simon found himself a stranger at a gathering of the clan. Eleanor's uncles and other royalist exiles at Boulogne urged Louis to denounce Henry's baronial opponents. Simon and the baronial proctors haughtily replied that they were not bound to answer for their actions in the court of the king of France. Thus the meeting came to an abrupt end. Henry and Edward returned home on October 7, 1263, but Eleanor and Edmund stayed in France with Margaret and remained there for more than a year.[35]

Eleanor and her French relatives immediately began to do everything they could to succor Henry. Louis and Margaret wrote to Pope Urban IV, informing him of the English king's predicament. On November 22 Urban appointed Guy, cardinal bishop of Sabina, his legate in England, and commanded the English clergy to obey him. The pope instructed his legate to absolve the oaths exacted from the royal family, especially the pledge that bound Eleanor and her son Edmund to return to England. Urban then sent letters to King Henry, Queen Eleanor, the Lord Edward, and to Simon de Montfort, "the chief disturber of the realm," informing them that the legate's mission was to restore the king and royal family to their former state and to bring peace to the land. Of course the barons refused the legate permission to cross the Channel.[36]

Meanwhile a tense political stalemate had developed in England. Neither Henry nor his baronial opponents were yet prepared to risk war, and there was still an important faction of moderates headed by the king's brother, Richard of Cornwall, that was urging Henry and Earl Simon to compromise. In December 1263 both the king and the baronial reformers accepted King Louis's offer to mediate the dispute after Henry pledged that he would never abandon his oath to govern in accordance with the Provisions of Oxford. In January 1264 Henry and representatives of the baronial party met Louis at Amiens. After only a few days of discussion Louis gave his judgment in the Mise of Amiens. He found for King Henry on every point. Since the pope had annulled the Provisions, they were, Louis pronounced, of no effect. After Amiens Earl Simon and his adherents were left only with the choice of either complete capitulation or war, and they chose war.[37]

King Louis's decision at first confused the barons, but when they understood the full implications of the pronouncement, they were disappointed and angry. Not surprisingly some of Henry's embittered opponents held Queen Eleanor responsible for Louis's betrayal of their cause. One chronicler no doubt expressed the feelings of many when he wrote that:

> by the fraud of a woman, that is the queen of England, the king of France was seduced and deceived. For it is written, no fraud is beyond the fraud of a woman, for a woman deceived the first father,

King Solomon, David the prophet, and others. The heart of this king
was changed from good to bad, from bad to worse, and from worse
to worst.[38]

While King Henry and his enemies prepared for war, Eleanor
rallied the small but distinguished group of émigrés who were
hovering near the coasts in Boulogne, Montreuil-sur-mer, and
other places. The queen now directed her whole energy into
planning and organizing an invasion force that would aid Henry
in destroying his enemies. While King Louis did not overtly
support Eleanor's efforts, he did nothing to obstruct her. The
French queen, on the other hand, worked tirelessly to obtain
ships and men for her sister. On May 15, 1264, Simon de
Montfort's army inflicted a crushing defeat on the royalist forces
at Lewes, capturing Henry and his son Edward. However,
several important royalists, including John de Warenne, earl of
Surrey; William de Valence, earl of Pembroke; Guy de Lusignan;
and Hugh Bigod, the former justiciar, escaped from the disaster
at Lewes and joined the queen.[39]

The royalist collapse in England gave greater urgency to
Eleanor's efforts to lead a relieving army across the Channel.
Money to finance the invasion was the first obstacle she had to
surmount, and in this endeavor Louis was most helpful. On June
1, 1264, Louis paid Eleanor and Peter of Savoy 58,000 livres of
Tours of the 134,000 livres promised Henry in the Treaty of
Paris. The treaty specified that the money was to be used to
support five hundred knights in the service of the Church, but to
Eleanor, no cause was more sacred than that of her husband and
her son.[40]

After the defeat at Lewes Earl Simon and the rebel barons had
forced King Henry and the Lord Edward to append their seals to
a peace agreement known as the Mise of Lewes. A copy of the
document was sent to King Louis in the hope that he would
consider Henry's submission to the barons irrevocable and dis-
suade Eleanor and the other royalist exiles from further efforts to
invade England. They obviously failed to take into account the
character of the queen, who believed herself far from beaten.

In the fall of 1264 Eleanor was poised on the Flemish coast

with a large army of German, Gascon, Breton, French, and Spanish mercenaries. Across the Channel, at Barnham Down near Canterbury, Simon de Montfort waited with a force to repel the invasion. Providence, however, dictated that both armies would wait in vain. For weeks unfavorable winds blew into the face of Eleanor's fleet, and her war chest shrank with each day's delay. She desperately sought additional money from Louis and went so far as to pledge Henry's rights in Aquitaine. But what she got was not enough. When the mercenaries realized that they would have to accept promises for pay, they soon drifted away, and by October Eleanor found herself the leader of a phantom army.[41]

Neither the loss of her army nor a letter from Henry demanding that the king of France not permit the sale or alienation of his lands and prerogatives in Aquitaine as proposed by "certain persons," deterred the redoubtable Eleanor.[42] The letter was so obviously the work of Simon de Montfort and his cohorts that she could dismiss it as the travesty that it was and continue to raise money from any possible source. She also urged Pope Clement IV to send a papal legate to England. Clement, formerly Guy, cardinal bishop of Sabina and papal legate to England before his elevation to the papacy, was well acquainted with the situation in Henry's realm and was no friend of Simon de Montfort and the baronial rebels. The pope chose as his emissary Ottobuono Fieschi, the future Pope Ardian IV, and armed him with power to deal with the rebels and to preach a crusade against them if necessary. The legate was not, however, to make peace with the insurgents until Simon de Montfort, "that pestilent man, with all his progeny, be plucked out of the realm of England."[43]

Meanwhile in England Earl Simon's domineering personality, the arrogance of his sons, and complacency of his supporters were rapidly undermining the baronial cause. Young Gilbert de Clare, earl of Gloucester and Hertford, whose power and influence none but the king's brother, Richard of Cornwall, could rival, quarreled with Simon and withdrew to his stronghold in the March of Wales to brood. At the same time William de Valence, the king's half brother, and other royalist exiles crossed from France and landed in William's great earldom of Pembroke. But the most ominous news that Earl Simon heard was that the Lord Edward had, with the aid of Gilbert de Clare, escaped from custody. Roger Mortimer and the other turbulent lords of the Welsh March quickly joined Edward. Simon led his forces west to deal with the threat, and the decisive battle was fought at Evesham on August 4, 1265. There Edward's army annihilated the rebel host. Simon, his son, Henry de Montfort, and many other baronial partisans were killed. King Henry, although wounded by his own rescuers in the mayhem of battle, was at last free, and could once more rule England without the shadow of Earl Simon falling across every royal writ and letter.[44]

On October 28, Eleanor and Edmund arrived at Dover and were reunited with Henry at Canterbury. From there the royal party moved to London and entered the city in triumph. The day of reckoning had arrived for the citizens, who were informed that they must surrender themselves, their property, and the keys of the city to the king's mercy. They were further required to remove the gates and road chains which symbolized their independence. The bridge from which Eleanor had been insulted was given to her, along with its tolls.[45]

Henry did not wish to punish the rebels by shedding blood. His policy instead was to confiscate their lands and distribute them among his faithful followers. Leicester's earldom he gave to Edmund. Simon's widow Eleanor, countess of Leicester, had held out at Dover Castle for a time, but escaped to France the day before the queen returned to England. The queen must have sympathized with her sister-in-law's loyalty to Simon. It was the same quality of character that had driven her to fight for her husband. At any rate, Henry first refused to consider his sister's return to England; later, he not only offered her safety and justice there, but also granted her an annual pension of £500. It was generally recognized that Louis IX and Eleanor were responsible for Henry's change of heart.[46]

Relative peace at last settled over England. Never again would Eleanor be called upon to assume so important a role in the affairs of state. Nevertheless, the crisis of the baronial revolt had proved that Eleanor, whose moral character and devotion to her faith and family were above reproach, was also a woman of courage and determination. Eleanor and Henry shared seven more years during which time the king's health grew steadily worse. On November 16, 1272, realizing that death was imminent, he summoned Gilbert de Clare to come to him and requested the earl to swear to preserve the kingdom until Edward's return from the Holy Land. Later the same day Henry III died, and the following morning the chancellor, John de Kirkeby, surrendered the great seal to the council of regency.[47]

No son could have been more solicitous of his mother than Edward was of Eleanor during the years remaining to her. After his coronation he increased her lands and augmented her income in a variety of ways.[48] While Edward was preparing for her future, Eleanor was apparently giving thought to it herself. In January 1275, Edward gave her permission to make her will, and the following year she entered the convent of Amesbury in Wiltshire.[49] It was not at all strange that she would choose to spend the latter years of her life in a religious house, for she and Henry had always shown an active interest in convents and monasteries. Moreover, medieval convention almost demanded that dowager queens and other noble widows enter convents at some point near the end of their lives. Although Eleanor became a resident at Amesbury in 1276, she did not wear the habit of her order until July 7, 1286.[50] During the intervening years she did not cease to fight energetically for her rights in regard to property and income; nor did she remain cloistered, but instead moved about visiting her castles and taking an active part in secular affairs.

In 1290, the queen mother was associated with Edward in an action which did no honor to either of them. As king, Edward had assumed a more severe attitude toward the Jews of England than had his father. Where Henry had hoped to convert his Jews to Christianity, Edward seemed bent on expelling them from his kingdom. Eleanor had already decreed that no Jew could live, or even stay, in any towns which she held in dower.[51] Some felt that in 1290 when Edward expelled the Jews from England, it was with the counsel of the queen mother.[52]

Edward continued to consult his mother, especially on family matters, during the remaining years of her life. In 1289, in the midst of the crisis over the Scottish succession, Edward spent two weeks at Amesbury with the dowager queen. When he left for Clarendon to meet with envoys from Norway and Scotland, he had decided that Eleanor's great-granddaughter, Margaret, "the Maid of Norway," who was the only heir of the late Scottish King Alexander III, should be brought from her Scandinavian home and married to his eldest son, the future Edward II. In April of the following year Edward and other members of the royal family gathered at Amesbury to discuss with the queen mother the betrothals of her granddaughters, Margaret and Joan of Acre, and to plan the succession to the throne. The king was preparing to lead a crusading army to drive the Mamelukes from the Holy Land, and he wanted to see all family matters settled before his departure. That same year Joan of Acre was married to Edward's mightiest subject, Gilbert de Clare, earl of Gloucester and Hertford, and Margaret was married to John, duke of Brabant.[53]

Edward could turn to his mother for consolation as well as advice. In the fall of 1290 while hunting in the north, the king received news that the Maid of Norway had died during the voyage to Scotland, raising the spectre of a war of succession in Scotland. Then came the disturbing news that his beloved queen, Eleanor, was desperately ill at Harby near Lincoln. Edward rushed to her and was at her side when she died on November 28, 1290. The same day the grief-stricken king wrote to the bishops, beseeching masses and prayers for the soul of his queen. Edward decided that Eleanor's body should be taken to Westminster for burial, and he personally followed the cortege back to London. At each place where Eleanor's bier rested for the night, Edward marked out a spot where a cross should be erected in her memory. Eleanor was buried in the abbey on December 17, and after the funeral Edward went into seclusion at the monastery of Ashridge where he remained until the end of January. He then went to Amesbury and his sixty-seven-year-old mother, whose health was failing. Eleanor died on June 25, 1291, while her son was away in the north deeply immersed in the Scottish problem. Her body was preserved, but lay unburied until Edward's return. A multitude of English and French nobles and churchmen gathered at Amesbury for her burial on September 8, 1291. As she had requested, her heart was then taken to London for interment in the church of the Franciscans.[54]

Although there were many French and English notables among the mourners, there were few of her old friends. Her Savoyard uncles, Peter, Boniface, and Thomas, had preceded her in death. She had survived her husband; her three daughters; two of her sisters; and her brothers-in-law, Louis IX and Richard of Cornwall. Those who were at Amesbury saw Edward pay his mother the respect she had earned and which England had so often withheld.[55]

Josefa Amar y Borbón:
A Forgotten Figure
of the Spanish Enlightenment

CARMEN CHAVES McCLENDON

Spain, a proud, religious, and bigoted nation where the Inquisition and the Index of Forbidden Books were still considered necessary in the eighteenth century, remained largely impervious to the scientific and intellectual ferment of the Enlightenment. Yet, ideas and books have never respected political frontiers, and despite offical efforts to enforce intellectual conformity, the thoughts of the philosophers drifted across the Pyrenees. Seized and nurtured by a samll group of educated Spaniards, Spain's enlightened elite, these new ideas played a small and relatively unknown part in Spain's history. The enlightened elite, composed of women as well as men, espoused scientific and economic progress, educational reforms, and social justice, but they remained devoted to the basic tenets of the Catholic faith. They sought not to destroy the existing social and political order, but rather to modify and reform it. It was to this group that Josefa Amar y Borbón belonged.[1]

Josefa was born in the city of Saragossa on April 15, 1752.[2] She was still a child when her father, Dr. José Amar, was appointed chamber physician to King Ferdinand VI and the family moved to Madrid. As the king's personal physician, Dr. Amar was expected to reside at court with his family. It was there that Josefa received her remarkable education. One of the king's librarians, Don Rafael Casalbon, taught her French and Latin and encouraged her interest in books, including works of the French Enlightenment that had been obtained for the royal library. Antonio de Verdugo tutored her in Greek and philosophy and taught her to appreciate research and the scientific method. Josefa was a precocious child who found pleasure in reading and study. Before she was fifteen, she had achieved proficiency in Greek, Latin, Italian, and French. When Josefa was eighteen she began translating classical works into Spanish for which she eventually achieved modest fame.

During the half century before Josefa's birth, Spain had experienced wrenching changes. In 1700 Charles II, the last of the Spanish Hapsburgs, died, and Europe rushed headlong into the War of the Spanish Succession. Charles had named as his successor Philip of Anjou, a grandson of Louis XIV of France, but the possibility of an eventual union of the kingdoms of Spain and France made the settlement unacceptable to the rest of Europe. Philip ascended the Spanish throne as Philip V, but the enemies of Louis XIV only accepted a Bourbon in Madrid after thirteen years of bloody fighting. Philip's main concern had been to make the new dynasty secure, but he had also attempted to duplicate in Spain the great intellectual edifices of his native France. In 1712 he established Spain's National Library. The following year the Royal Academy of Letters was founded to preserve the purity of the Spanish language, and the Academy of History was created in 1735. All of these events would influence and affect Josefa's life.

If Spain had an enlightened monarch it was Charles III (1759-1788), who succeeded Ferdinand VI. He restrained the Inquisition and expelled the Jesuits from the country. He legislated wisely, surrounded himself with advisors from the middle class, built roads and canals to improve communication, and patronized art, music, and literature. Change, however, did not come without opposition. Conservatives took up their pens to denounce everyone and everything they believed threatened traditional Spanish values, and they were answered by the liberal elite, who defended change with all the passion of its critics. For a generation Spaniards waged a war of words with the same zeal that their ancestors had fought the infidel and carved out an empire in the New World, and it was in this struggle that Josefa Amar y Borbón played her small part.[3]

Josefa married Joaquin Fuertes Piquer in 1770 and returned to Saragossa where her husband became a judge in the *Audiencia* of Aragon. She continued her intellectual pursuits, and in 1782 she was elected to membership in the local Economic Society. In

1787 she was chosen to join the *Junta de damas* of the Economic Society in Madrid.[4]

The economic societies, which had become one of the most important forums for the discussion and dissemination of enlightened thought, had had their beginning during the reign of Ferdinand VI (1747-1759) when intellectuals in the Basque region formed the first Economic Society of Friends of the Country. The economic and scientific ideas propounded in the Society quickly aroused the interest and enthusiasm of educated Spaniards everywhere, and by 1789 at least fifty-six economic societies had been organized throughout Spain. The members of these societies, however, were from the intellectual elite, and their discussions and suggestions had little impact on the masses. As one contemporary pundit explained, the Friends of the Country were rich people "who wanted to improve the agricultural and commercial efficiency of the country . . . by trying to encourage progress in manual work in which they themselves were not engaged."[5]

Josefa traveled often to Madrid after her election to the *Junta de damas*, and it is reasonable to assume that there she met the leaders of the Spanish Enlightenment, for from 1770 to 1790 Madrid was the center of enlightened thought in Spain. There, despite efforts of conservatives to condemn the new thought as "Jansenist" and heretical, the ideas of enlightenment were nurtured and molded into form compatible with the Spanish character. Madrid's leadership was due in no small part to the emergence of such enlightened personalities as Gaspar Melchor de Jovellanos[6] and the Countess of Montijo, whose popular *tertulias* were frequented by the intellecutal elite. Madrid could also claim as its own such literary figures as Melendes Valdés and Cadalso.

It was during this period that Josefa, almost certainly inspired by her experiences in Madrid, began to write. In the 1780s she published numerous essays and treatises whose subjects fall into three broad categories: science and medicine, letters and the humanities, and attacks on superstition.[7] For her publications and philosophical position, she continued to receive recognition in educated circles. In 1790 she was elected an honorary member of the Medical Society of Barcelona—obviously a rare and coveted achievement for a woman of her time and place. In that same year, 1790, she made her principal contribution to the Spanish Enlightenment, a treatise on the education of women, *Discurso sobre la educación física y moral de las mugeres.*[8] It provided women with practical medical information, child-rearing advice, and a guide to studies for females. A product of her class, Josefa wrote not for all women, but for those who "were not satisfied with the mechanical duties of the household,"[9] and women who expected to "marry gentlemen and would need to learn how to communicate intelligently with them and their friends."[10] Some women, she observed, must be satisfied with the daily household routine "in order to preserve a balance in society."[11] Josefa's elitism does not alter the fact that she was the first Spanish woman to write on physical education strictly for women. The *Discurso* is also important because Josefa acquainted her Spanish readers with many important works on pedagogy in an extensive annotated bibliography.

Even though the Spanish Church had added Jean Jacques Rousseau's works to its Index of Forbidden Books and had publicly burned his *Émile* in 1765, Josefa was familiar with his ideas on education. However, her own thoughts on education were probably influenced more by M. de Leveson's *Émile Chretien, ou de l'education*, which she described as the "counterpart and complement of Rousseau's *Emile*"[12] than they were by the *Émile* itself. In her discussion of "moral" education she contends that children learn best in an environment that encourages their curiosity and allows them to develop "naturally."[13] Children were naturally curious, and this curiosity caused them to ask many questions about their surroundings. These questions, Josefa admonished her readers, should never be answered in anger or disgust because this attitude would "instill fear and deprive children of the freedom to explore and satisfy their curiosity."[14] Example was also very important in Josefa's system of education. It was her conviction that instruction that imparted only dry and rigid precepts was a bore. She suggested that the

"advantages of orderly conduct are learned only through example."[15] And, only through examples from nature would children
understand complex lessons, such as those pertaining to religious
belief. To her readers she suggested that:

the knowledge of god and of religion should always be accompanied
with examples, so that they may make a lasting impression in the child's
memory . . . .[16] For example, the intensity and beauty of the sky,
the multitude of stars, the brightness of the sun and the moon,
the greatness of the oceans and lands, the innumerable species of
animals and fruits, the differences in the faces of mankind though
composed of the same parts, and other signs all lend credence to
the existence of God.[17]

She was naturally critical of those who insisted on teaching
children religious doctrine by requiring rote memorization
without the benefit of examples to reinforce moral lessons.

Josefa believed strongly in a broad education for females.
Education moulded character, and, since women had such limited experiences outside the home, it was essential that they be
instructed through reading and personal study. All girls should
be taught to read and write, and encouraged to express themselves creatively. It was simplistic and naive to argue, as many
Spaniards did, that teaching women to read and write would
result in the moral decay of the country. Josefa insisted that
ignorance and illiteracy were no assurance of morality. She
believed that the major flaw of the "system" was that women
were not given as many educational opportunities as men and
yet, women were given the role of early childhood educators.

According to the *Discurso*, once reading and writing skills
were mastered young women could begin the most important
part of their education—the study of classical languages and then
Greek and Roman literature. But Josefa was encouraging more
than a moribund classical education. She believed that girls
should be familiar with the literature of their own country and
that they should learn French, English, and Italian so they could
read the great literary works of those nations. Moreover, they
should not neglect the study of history because its lessons pro-

vided many excellent topics for conversation and were a splendid source of moral example. The study of geography was also important because a knowledge of topography and people made history more relevant.

Despite her concern for the intellectual development of women, Josefa believed the traditional social and domestic accomplishments were important. Girls should also learn to dance and to appreciate art and music so that they could perform their proper role in society, and their domestic education should not be neglected. Josefa felt that if a woman's eduction was complete, she should be able not only to converse intelligently but also to do needlepoint, sew, knit, and have a sufficient grasp of the fundamentals of accounting to plan and manage her household budget.

For Josefa religious faith was an important aspect of moral education, and one that the mothers, for whom she was writing, should be prepared to discuss intelligently with their children. "True devotion," she suggested, "does not consist of attending church and reciting prayers . . . true virtue is doing that which is good and hating evil, restraining passions, dulling appetites, practicing charity, and, above all, being faithful to one's duties."[18] She was sensitive to the great debate between the defenders of public devotion and the proponents of personal piety. Each side had its polemicists who contended with each other in the Economic Societies and the literary journals. The issue was a favorite topic of conversation in the *tertulias*, and the idle rich, for whom daily attendance at church was just another social function, were ridiculed in the theatre. Josefa professed an unwillingness to take sides in the controversy, but her reticence did not prevent her from suggesting that "without the practice of the Commandments and the fulfilling of individual responsibilities, one cannot experience true virtue."[19]

Perhaps the most novel contribution of Josefa's treatise is her instructions on health for mothers and children. She compared the human body to a complex machine all parts of which were interdependent, so that if one part failed, the others would suffer.[20] Josefa offered advice on diet during pregnancy, on childbirth and nursing, on the care of nursing infants, on childhood diseases, and on physical exercise. She also discussed many health-related customs in Spain, such as the practice of binding babies' heads after birth to alter shape and of wearing corsets. She traced each custom back to its origin and attempted to explain the reason for its existence and persistence. Josefa realized that attachment to these customs and traditions was strong and not easily broken, so she did not condemn them, but she did point out that many of them were unreasonable.[21]

Even though Josefa discussed the scientific method of inquiry and explained its advantages to her readers, she was neither a practicing physician nor a medical researcher. Consequently she based her discussion of childhood diseases and their treatment on a careful study of the writings of acknowledged experts in the field of medicine. These she quoted at length in her own work, and thus preserved a wealth of interesting information about the medical practices of her day. Moreover, her own comments on contemporary medical procedures suggest the attitude of educated Spaniards of the eighteenth century to the new knowledge. For example, in her discussion of smallpox, she included the arguments for and against vaccination, which was a subject that was being passionately debated in Spain. Her own feelings were, that because of the risks of vaccination itself, she would advocate general vaccination of the populace only if there were a threat of an epidemic.[22]

Josefa was aware that her educational proposals were demanding and not suitable for every mother, but her own life and experience had proved to her that they were not unattainable. Women, she believed, could accomplish much if their lives were well ordered. "Let us form an orderly plan," she said. "Let us teach girls to distribute their hours wisely, and we will see that there is sufficient time for everything and that some occupations, far from detracting from others, will actually facilitate the understanding of all things."[23]

The *Discurso* did not bring Josefa Amar y Borbón literary fame, but it showed that enlightened ideas had penetrated Spanish society, and it was an important precursor of the literary effort to enhance the status of women.[24]

Bertha von Suttner
and Rosika Schwimmer:
Pacifists from the Dual Monarchy

REBECCA S. STOCKWELL

In contrast with the neutral position of contemporary Austria, the old Austro-Hungarian Empire was hardly associated with ideas of neutrality or pacifism.[1] Even the most favorable interpretation of Austria's part in the outbreak of war in 1914 assigns some of the blame to her, while the less charitable view holds her largely responsible for the disaster. If Austria-Hungary made a contribution to world peace in the late nineteenth and early twentieth centuries, then it was certainly not made at home. Yet, ironically, leaders of the peace movement in the multinational empire were able to exert an influence in the neutral United States. Two of these leaders, Bertha von Suttner (1843-1914) and Rosika Schwimmer (1877-1948), are the subject of this study.

Bertha von Suttner first heard of the International Arbitration and Peace Association in 1886. Learning of its existence and work crystallized her own growing concern for peace, and she decided to do what she could for the movement. Since she was already a writer with several published works, her contribution took the form of a novel, *Die Waffen Nieder! Eine Lebensgeschichte*, published in 1889. Although critics' reviews were mixed, the public loved the book, and by 1905 it was in its thirty-seventh edition. It had been translated into all the major European languages (in English as *Lay Down Your Arms*). The sensation caused by Suttner's novel had been compared to that of *Uncle Tom's Cabin*. The eminent Russian author, Leo Tolstoy, was one of those who hoped that her novel would bring an end to war just as Harriet Beecher Stowe's work had aroused the abolitionist sentiment that had doomed slavery.[2] Instead, the European powers continued to build their alliance systems and to arm for war.

Suttner's next act in the peace movement, initiating the formation of the Austrian Peace Society, contributed indirectly to the
establishment of the Nobel Peace Prize. The Peace Society was
organized in time to send delegates to the third world peace
congress that met in Rome in November 1891. It was as a
delegate to this congress that Suttner made her first major public
speech. The following year the congress met in Zurich, and there
Suttner saw Alfred Nobel and renewed her efforts to interest him
in the peace movement. They had first met in 1876 when Suttner,
then Countess Kinsky, had worked briefly in Paris as Nobel's
secretary. She had maintained an intermittent correspondence
with him, and she and her husband, Baron Artur von Suttner,
had seen him in Paris in 1887. The encounter in Zurich was to be
their last meeting, but they continued to exchange letters until
Nobel's death in 1896. During those years Suttner urged him to
consider seriously her cause. Although she could notice no progress, her private diplomacy was successful, and she is generally
credited with having persuaded Nobel to include the peace prize
in his testament.

News of Nobel's death reached Suttner on December 15,
1896. Waiting anxiously to learn whether his will included a
direct gift to the Peace Society, she seems not to have realized at
first the significance of his bequest to Stockholm University.[3] She
was bitterly disappointed, but not really surprised, that he had
not named her or the Peace Society in his will.[4] But Nobel's
endowment of a prize for contributors to peace at least gave the
movement a great deal of favorable publicity. Although Suttner
was probably also disappointed not to be one of the first recipients of the peace prize, in 1905 she became the first woman to
receive the peace laureate. The Nobel Prize added to the continued success of *Lay Down Your Arms* and assured Suttner's
international reputation as the foremost woman pacifist.

The world situation in those years was very discouraging for
Suttner and her co-workers. Since she had become actively
involved in the peace movement, there had been war between
China and Japan (1894-95); Italy and Ethiopia (1895-96); the
United States and Spain (1898); the British and Boers (1899-

1902); and the Russians and Japanese (1904-05). In the next few years the crises continued in North Africa and the Balkans. The European powers seemed determined to frustrate the efforts of peace advocates to commit them to binding arbitration and disarmament agreements.

The recalcitrance of the European nations made the pacifists look with greater hope and expectation toward the New World. Concern for American opinion was one of two recurring themes in Suttner's letters from 1890-1911.[5] She also mentioned frequently her quest for a patron who would make a really sizable financial contribution to peace—a gift that would compare favorably with the sums spent on scientific expeditions.[6] Nobel had made contributions from time to time, but only of small amounts, and those rather grudgingly.[7] Still he was more responsive than Andrew Carnegie, who did not even reply to her letter.[8]

When an agent offered to arrange a tour of the United States for Baroness Suttner to read from her works in 1902, the thought perhaps crossed her mind that an American millionaire might yet be found for her purposes. But her husband, Artur, already seriously ill, died that year, making a tour impossible.[9] She made her first trip to the United States in 1904 to attend the thirteenth world peace congress in Boston.[10] Edwin D. Mead, director of the Boston World Peace Foundation, later wrote that Suttner's presence was one of the most noteworthy aspects of the Boston congress.[11] He especially praised her "charming personality" and "clear and excellent English." Although Suttner stayed in America for three weeks and spoke in several large cities, no millionaire was forthcoming. The only monetary contribution she reaped was a $100 gift from Joseph Pulitzer, whom she met in New York.[12]

There were less tangible rewards, however. President Theodore Roosevelt received Bertha von Suttner on September 17, and they talked privately about her favorite subject.[13] She was impressed with Roosevelt, despite his "Roughriderdom," because he spoke of calling a new Hague Peace Conference and of negotiating arbitration treaties with "all nations." Although Czar Nicholas II actually called both the 1899 and 1907 Hague

Peace Conferences, Roosevelt's initiatives were responsible for the summons in 1907.

Suttner, who attended both conferences, was credited with some part in influencing the Czar to call for a world court. One reviewer wrote that *Lay Down Your Arms* had helped in "bringing about the Hague Tribunal,"[14] and another writer referred to Suttner as "the woman who moved the Czar."[15] Another said that "before her persuasive, gentle eloquence, the Czar of the Russias abandoned his long-cherished prejudice against taking a woman's advice."[16] Zionist leader Theodor Herzl was so confident of her influence with the czar that he asked her to write a cover letter to his request for an interview in 1903.[17] Herzl had already subsidized Suttner's trip to the 1899 Hague Conference in return for introductions to peace representatives who frequented her "salon."[18]

Baroness Suttner had had no special motive for her American visit in 1904, unless it was to find a wealthy benefactor for her cause. She simply talked and listened, and apparently her impression of the country and its people was as favorable as the one she herself made. She left "richer in magnificent impressions, with her mental horizon enlarged." She had "looked through a new window . . . into the universe."[19] She spoke of America as "the hope of mankind" and said that she "could carry on her campaign conscious of a great America supporting her of which she was before unconscious."[20] The United States was "the land to which she had begun to look for light and strength."[21]

Eight years after the first brief visit to the New World, Bertha Suttner returned for a six-month lecture tour, July through December 1912. The intervening years had seen many threats to peace: the first Moroccan crisis (1905); Austria's annexation of Bosnia-Herzegovina (1908); the Turko-Italian War; second Moroccan crisis; and Chinese revolution (1911). And the first Balkan war would begin during her tour. However, the same period offered some encouragement to pacifists. Norway and Sweden had separated peacefully in 1905. In 1905 she had received the Nobel Peace Prize, and the second Hague Peace Conference had been held in 1907. Probably referring to the

Hague meeting, Suttner said that "Roosevelt had kept some of the promises he made her in 1904."[22]

One event which surprised and gratified Suttner was the establishment of the Carnegie Peace Endowment in 1910.[23] She had tried for years to interest Carnegie in the peace movement with no apparent success and she claimed to have "absolutely no influence" on him.[24] Thus she was not surprised to be excluded from the governing committee of the endowment. As late as November 1911 she still found no encouragement from Carnegie himself.[25] However, her lecture tour was partially financed by the Carnegie Foundation,[26] and she had addressed the first general meeting of the European section of the Carnegie Foundation in Paris, May 29, 1912, before leaving for New York.[27] After the American tour Suttner received a letter from Carnegie granting her a monthly pension beginning in January 1913.[28]

Mrs. Andrea Hofer-Proudfoot, who had arranged Suttner's tour, was apparently responsible for Canegie's change of heart.[29] Although Mrs. Hofer-Proudfoot had lived in Vienna for several years,[30] she actually belonged to the American branch of the family descended from the Tyrolese hero Andreas Hofer, who had won fame for his resistance to Napoleon.[31] Hofer-Proudfoot was also a friend of the Boston publisher and pacifist, Edwin Ginn, who published the English-language edition of Suttner's memoirs in 1910. During the strenuous lecture tour, the Ginn home in Boston provided a refuge for Suttner for some three weeks.[32]

The tour must have been strenuous since Suttner, who was then sixty-nine years old, gave at least one hundred fifty lectures.[33] The highlight of her odyssey was a speech to the General Federation of Women's Clubs in San Francisco on July 4, 1912. However, on July 2 she had an opportunity to speak briefly to the delegates about her new plan to start a daily paper "devoted to peace and to truth."[34] Suttner continued to seek financial backing for her newspaper during the remainder of her visit. Although her proposal for a pacifist newspaper "was warmly applauded. . . and received unanimous endorsement"[35] in San Francisco, she needed more than moral support for the venture. After she returned to Boston in October,[36] Suttner made a quick trip to New York to present J. P. Morgan a letter from the prince of Monaco,[37] and she, of course, took the opportunity to plead for support for her pacifist newspaper. Although Morgan received her cordially in his library, he was not interested in the project. His indifference led Suttner to conclude that beyond Ginn and Carnegie the American "Millionenwelt" remained closed to pacifism.[38]

Suttner's July 4th address in San Francisco was not only a general appeal for the prevention of wars, but also included warnings especially tailored for her American audience. Besides the obvious danger that the United States would be drawn into any European conflict, she pointed out another subtler threat which she called the "immigration evil." America would be protecting its own interests by helping to end all wars, because with every conflict there would be a "rush of aliens" to its shores who would bring unimaginable trouble to the nation.[39] She so impressed the one-million-member American Federation of Women's Clubs that they inscribed the word "pacifism" on their flag.[40]

Sometime during her tour in the autumn of 1912 Suttner met informally with President William Howard Taft at Beverly, Massachusetts.[41] By this time she had become skeptical of Theodore Roosevelt, whom she now described as one of the small minority of Americans with "eine angeborene Vorliebe für das Kriegerische."[42] Taft, on the other hand, had already become to Bertha von Suttner the "greatest apostle of peace."[43] Taft was in sympathy with the peace movement and would shortly found the American Peace League.

There is no way to accurately measure Bertha von Suttner's influence on American public opinion, but pacifism was certainly popular in the United States on the eve of the outbreak of the First World War. Although disappointed in many of America's political and financial leaders, she had found most students and teachers to be sympathetic with the peace movement.[44] All of Suttner's audiences had received her warmly and had listened to her with interest. The American reaction to her message was so favorable that the European press described her tour as a "Triumphzug."[45] And, one American journalist voiced the apparent feelings of many when he said she was "in many respects the foremost worker in Europe for worldwide peace . . . an authority on international relations, and a brilliant writer."[46] Suttner herself considered her American tour to have been a great moral success.[47]

Many Americans had also read *Lay Down Your Arms*, the English edition of Suttner's book that had been available since 1892. After she received the Nobel Peace Prize there was renewed interest in the book, and a new edition, entitled *Ground Arms*, appeared in 1906. Both editions were widely reviewed and most of the reviews were quite favorable. Fanny Hertz described *Lay Down Your Arms* as "the most forcible protest ever uttered against the stupendous evils, the egregious madness, of war."[48] *The Outlook* said of the second edition that it was a "powerful human document" whose argument "in favor of the settlement of disputes between nations by an international court . . . [was] stronger than the story."[49] As late as 1911 *Lay Down Your Arms* and its author were still receiving acclaim. *Review of Reviews* referred to the work as "the Uncle Tom's Cabin of the peace movement," and said of Bertha von Suttner: "It has not been permitted to many women to exert so widespread, intelligent and effective an influence toward general peace between nations."[50]

Despite Bertha von Suttner's eloquence and tireless efforts Europe moved ever closer to the Armageddon she feared. She seemed to sense the imminence of an international incident that would ignite a conflict which would spread rapidly and involve all the European powers. Ironically she died only one month before the assassination of Archduke Franz Ferdinand. Mrs. Mary Ellen Slayden spoke for many of Suttner's friends when, at the outbreak of the Great War, she expressed gratitude that the baroness was not there to witness the "hideous culmination of all her fears."[51]

After the death of the baroness a young admirer of Suttner's work, Rosika Schwimmer, quickly moved to the fore of the peace movement.[52] Rosika, unlike Suttner, had begun working for peace at a young age. Her uncle Leopold Katscher had organized the Hungarian Peace Society and had helped Bertha von Suttner publish her antiwar novel. He had continued to correspond with Suttner, and it was through this relationship that Rosika became acquainted with the baroness and her efforts in behalf of world peace. Before the outbreak of the First World War Rosika had become a respected journalist and was active in the struggle of woman's suffrage. When the Hague Peace Palace was dedicated in 1913, Schwimmer was one of only two women journalists admitted to the press gallery.[53]

Rosika Schwimmer was in London working as press secretary for the International Woman Suffrage Alliance in 1914 when the German army rolled across the Belgian frontier. She immediately appealed to the United States and other neutral countries to offer contiuous mediation to the belligerents and cabled women's organizations on five continents urging them to request President Woodrow Wilson to call a conference of neutral nations.[54] She then left England, where she was an enemy alien, and arrived in the United States on September 3, bringing with her endorsements for her plan of mediation from prominent people and organizations all over the world.[55]

On September 16, Rosika Schwimmer and Carrie Chapman Catt met with Secretary of State William Jennings Bryan, who had dedicated himself to attaining peaceful settlements of international disputes. Two days later President Wilson agreed to see Mrs. Schwimmer, who urged him to call immediately for a neutral conference and continuous mediation. The president was not opposed to the plan and had already told the belligerents to "let me know when you are ready," but Schwimmer argued that a more forceful invitation was required. She suggested instead that Wilson summon the neutral countries to meet in Norway. Norway seemed to her the best site because it would probably be the last neutral state to be drawn into the war and because Norway, which had peacefully separated from Sweden in 1905, exemplified, by its independent existence, what could be accomplished by negotiation.[56] Wilson's response was polite but noncommittal. The press largely ignored the interview, except to comment that Wilson would not be pressured by such proposals.[57]

Schwimmer then began a speaking tour through twenty-two states during which she persuaded thousands of men and women to support her plan for continuous mediation. Many in her audiences soon let President Wilson know their views on the situation in Europe.[58] Schimmer's arguments were forceful, but diplomatic. She warned that if the war were not ended soon the United States would be drawn into it. But President Wilson, she said, "was a great force for peace," and the United States could "bring this fearful slaughter to an end." Since America had taken in immigrants from all the warring nations, it had "the best right to interfere."[59]

Rosika Schwimmer was convinced that any aid to the belligerents would only prolong the war. Unfortunately this belief prompted her to criticize the activities of the American Red Cross. These remarks rang as false notes in the ears of her American audience, but her other efforts produced more positive results. Her influence on Jane Addams led to the establishment of the Woman's Peace Party in January 1915.[60] Jane Addams became president of the new party, and Rosika Schwimmer served as its international secretary. Addams also headed the Emergency Federation of Peace Forces that was an amalgamation of several peace groups that supported Schwimmer's plan for continuous neutral mediation.[61]

Rosika Schwimmer and Jane Addams both attended the International Congress of Women that met at the Hague from April 28 to May 1, 1915. The Congress organized a Women's International League for Peace and Freedom under the presidency of Jane Addams with Dr. Aletta Jacobs of the Netherlands and Rosika Schwimmer as vice presidents. The Congress also unanimously adopted Schwimmer's resolution calling for a neutral conference for continuous mediation and her suggestion that members of the Congress personally deliver copies of the resolution to the various nations.[62] Jane Addams headed the delegation to the belligerent countries while Rosika Schwimmer led the mission to the neutrals.

Germany, Britain, France, Belgium, and Russia responded favorably to the delegates' proposal for a neutral conference. The foreign minister of Austria-Hungary, Count Stefan Burian, also thought a conference should be called immediately, but not by the United States. "America," he said, "did not know enough about European interests."[63] Regarding President Wilson's earlier offer of mediation, he confirmed Schwimmer's assessment that the wording of the offer had obliged both sides to refuse it. Instead of the United States serving as an arbiter between the belligerents, Burian favored a conference of neutral nations that would present to the belligerents proposals for a resolution of the conflict and, if necessary, would offer new proposals and modifications until they arrived at something both sides could accept.

When Jane Addams returned in July from her visits to the warring nations, she met with President Wilson to tell him of their favorable response to the mediation plans.[64] By September Rosika Schwimmer and her delegation had also returned to the United States, and, when it became apparent that they had not persuaded Wilson to call a neutral conference, they issued a manifesto declaring that all the neutral and belligerent states were ready for mediation and were waiting for the United States to take the lead. Afterwards Schwimmer and the other European delegates began a nationwide speaking tour.[65] Rosika and Crystal MacMillan, an English delegate, spent several days in late September convincing the wavering Jane Addams to remain firmly behind the neutral conference plan rather than to support Wilson's wait and see policy.[66] Schwimmer then traveled to Chicago with MacMillan and Aletta Jacobs, and in October she appeared on the program of the International Peace Congress in San Francisco. The following month she spoke in Lexington, Kentucky. As a result of this address the Kentucky suffragists sent a resolution to Wilson urging him to call a neutral conference.[67]

A few days later Schwimmer was speaking in Detroit to receptive audiences. Someone there suggested to her that "Henry Ford was a man, who, if he were but approached, would at once grasp the vision of these women."[68] Here at last was a chance to realize

Bertha von Suttner's dream of enlisting a New World millionaire to help the Old World come to its senses before it was truly too late! Rosika was able to meet Mr. Ford on November 20, 1915. She already had an appointment arranged with President Wilson for November 26, and was scheduled to sail for Europe the following day. However, the meeting with Ford completely altered her plans.

In March 1915, or perhaps even as early as December of the previous year, Rosika Schwimmer had suggested sending a "peace ship" to Europe.[69] According to newspaper accounts at the time, the idea was to transport American women pacifists to Europe where they would attempt to persuade the belligerents to lay down their arms. The women themselves would raise money to charter a ship that would take at least a thousand of them to see "the kings of Europe."[70] However, newspaper speculation about the mission of the peace ship was probably confused. Since the outbreak of the war Schwimmer had been urging formation of a neutral conference. It seems impossible, therefore, that Schwimmer actually proposed to lead her pacifists to the capitals of the warring nations. At any rate, the urgent call for a meeting of the International Congress of Women at the Hague had come on March 24, 1915, and that assembly had, for several months, taken precedence over everything else.[71]

Now that it was clear that Woodrow Wilson would not call a neutral conference, Henry Ford became the great hope for Rosika Schwimmer and other pacifist leaders. In the course of Rosika's converstaion with Ford concerning a neutral conference for continuous mediation, the earlier peace ship plan must have been mentioned. Henry Ford decided that he would host a party of neutrals who would go to Europe and form a conference. His plan to charter a ship to carry American delegates to the proposed conference was announced on November 24, and was possibly intended to influence President Wilson.[72] Two days later Schwimmer saw the president and, although Wilson was "stirred deeply," he made no promises.[73]

Mrs. Ford, meanwhile, had been so impressed with the conference proposal that, in her first public act, she gave $10,000 to the Woman's Peace Party to pay for telegrams to organizations throughout the country urging their membership to petition President Wilson for a neutral conference.[74] Mrs. Ford's attitude was to change later, and Rosika Schwimmer would come to regard her as an evil influence on Mr. Ford.[75] But in 1915 she was a Schwimmer partisan. In an interview with the Brooklyn *Eagle* reporter, Cabell O'Neill, she said, just before the peace ship sailed, "I wish Henry had met you earlier, for you are fresh from the horrors 'over there' and you would strengthen his faith in Mrs. Schwimmer which certain of the party have tried to weaken."[76]

Since Henry Ford chartered the peace ship and planned to finance the neutral conference, he naturally issued the invitations to those who were to sail on the mission of peace. Apparently Mrs. Schwimmer had nothing to do with the selection of participants.[77] The group was hastily chosen and ill-assorted. Many of the large company of journalists that came aboard had previously unused press credentials. Although all of the other members of the party were genuinely interested in stopping the war, they were not in agreement on the role the United States should play in the effort. They were divided, for example, on the issue of American military preparedness. Some refused to sign a manifesto endorsed by Ford which condemned the military buildup called for by President Wilson.[78]

Ridicule of Ford's "jitney diplomacy" began immediately after the mission was announced and continued until the conference in Stockham withered and died. Only a few days after the peace ship sailed, word of the disagreements among the mission's complement reached New York, and, from that time on, the "war among the peace party" was a popular topic for the American press. This mission was also handicapped by Allied suggestions that the neutral conference party was instigated by the Germans to keep the United States out of the war.[79] The "enemy alien" Rosika Schwimmer found herself a target of suspicion even though she had worked consistently for the pacifist cause long before the war began. When Henry Ford abruptly left the ship on Christmas Eve without even saying farewell to his guests, the reason for his departure was left open to speculation and the mission was exposed to the centrifugal force of factionalism. Although Rosika Schwimmer had been named "expert adviser" for the party, others actually took charge.[80]

Since so much that has been written about the Ford expedition is derogatory, one might conclude that Rosika Schwimmer's influence on the American pacifist cause was negative from the time the ship departed. However, several points seem relevant to any final assessment of her importance in this period. First, to Schwimmer the neutral conference was what mattered: Ford's chartered ship was merely transportation. The party of delegates he invited was to be only the nucleus of a group representing all the neutral countries, which would be collected as the ship stopped in each country on the way to its final destination, the Hague. Thus, she was understandably impatient with the frivolous attitude of some members of the group who seemed to regard the whole trip as some sort of outing. They, in turn, viewed her efforts to organize them as highhanded, pushy, and "foreign."

A second point to be considered in assessing Schwimmer's real influence is that the press reports of strife within the peace party and mockery of it at home do not show the complete picture. Throughout the voyage and the subsequent informal neutral conference, which actually convened first in Stockholm rather than the Hague, there were many members of the party who remained firm supporters of Schwimmer and her consistent efforts to achieve practical results. Furthermore, the expedition itself was not so completely condemned by public opinion in America or the neutral European countries as the large eastern papers implied.

Ellis O. Jones wrote to his wife from the ship on December 17 that the party was more united than ever, and, from Stockholm ten days later, that the organization was better since Ford had left.[81] George F. Milton, editor of the Chatttanooga *News*, described the party's reception in Stockholm and Copenhagen as positive, in Norway cool. Ford's departure from Christiana (later Oslo) caused doubts of success there, and it was never adequately explained. Perhaps Ford had tired of this new "hobby," or had business reasons for returning suddenly to the United States—or really was ill. Perhaps he simply organized and launched the project and left it to be completed by people he considered trustworthy, as was his usual method.[82]

Rosika Schwimmer had received a warm welcome from the press in Copenhagen. They remembered her "brilliant and inspiring lecture" on the way to the Hague conference in April, which had ended with Suttner's slogan, "Die Waffen Nieder!"[83] But after Ford's puzzling departure remained unexplained, the Scandinavian press changed its tone toward Schwimmer. Hesitating to attack Ford directly, they dismissed him with faint praise and concentrated on the more vulnerable target.[84] The American press had already taken up the anti-Schwimmer theme. The Mobile, Alabama, *Item* of December 20 carried her picture with the caption, "Austrian Woman Who is Blamed for Troubles of Ford Peace Party," and said she was "even accused by Norwegian papers of being a paid agent of the Teuton governments." Two days later the Altoona, Pennsylvania, *Times*, was saying: "Hungarian Women [*sic*] in Ford Peace Party Alienates Norway's Interest"—without making clear just what interest was meant. The Boston *Globe* on the same day, December 22, 1915, said: "Norse Papers Assail Mme. Schwimmer," for having fooled Ford. The third paragraph got down to what was probably the genuine complaint against her, however: "The plain truth is that Mme. Schwimmer has been so 'bossy,' so exclusive and lofty in her tone, that her presence has gone far to render hopeless an expedition that was hopeless enough already."

Rosika Schwimmer's nationality certainly was not helpful to her peace efforts at this point. The United States was growing more and more incensed at German and Austrian submarine attacks since the sinking of the *Lusitania* on May 7, 1915. Although most attacks were made by German submarines, one ship, the *Ancona*, was sunk in the Mediterranean on November 10 by an Austrian submarine. This incident caused tension between the United States and Austria and must have been still fresh in the minds of Americans when, on December 30, 1915,

Germany sank the *Persia*, killing an American consular officer. That same day Louis Lochner of the peace expedition defended Schwimmer thus: "We cannot consider Mme. Schwimmer an enemy alien. It is too well known that she is a friend of peace."[85]

Although Schwimmer had offered to resign her advisory position when Ford left the peace ship, and had been refused,[86] the idea persisted that she was somehow duping Ford out of large sums of money. Actually Ford himself said shortly after his return to America that she took "not a cent" from him.[87] Other attacks against Schwimmer had a whiff of antifeminism about them as well as the predictable xenophobia. The New York *World* predicted that Schwimmer would be "deposed from her well-paid and luxurious job" and replaced with "some good strong man from the United States."[88] Her formal connection with the Ford group ended about March 1, and she was never to see Ford again. Although Schwimmer never ceased her work for peace, the war continued, and the United States was drawn into it in 1917.

Rosika Schwimmer later returned to Hungary. She was appointed ambassador to Switzerland by the brief Karolyi government, then persecuted by both the Bela Kun communist and the subsequent rightist regimes. She escaped to Vienna and then returned to the United States. Her application for United States citizenship was denied in 1929 because of her refusal to promise to bear arms. As war again approached, her lifetime efforts were recognized by the International Committee for World Peace with their Prize Award in 1937. On the eve of the Second World War even the Ford expedition received a favorable reinterpretation—which was small comfort to Schwimmer.[89] She remained in the United States as a resident alien until her death in 1948.

The efforts of Bertha von Suttner and Rosika Schwimmer, along with the work of their fellow pacifists all over the world, failed to prevent the first of the twentieth-century upheavals. Viewed from the perspective of more than a half century, their chances for success appear to have been slim at best. However, the influence that these two women from the Dual Monarchy wielded in the United States was widespread. They were both excellent speakers, and thus able to move large audiences to favor their plans for peace. The hearty reception given to Suttner's lectures in 1912 suggests that the current of peace sentiment was quite strong in the United States. Given the American penchant for titled Europeans plus the Nobel Prize, Baroness Suttner's tour added dignity and respectability to the movement. Suttner was received by Presidents Roosevelt and Taft and Schwimmer by Wilson, as serious leaders of an international movement that could not be ignored. The attention that they attracted to the cause of peace helped to show that there was a possible alternative when war came in 1914. The work of both women was, of course, much broader than the scope of this article. Since their influence contributed to the extra three years of peace enjoyed by the United States while Europe struggled, their work in America was certainly a significant part of their total effort. Conrad von Hötzendorf and the other Austro-Hungarian leaders who were eager for war represented only part of the picture. Bertha von Suttner and Rosika Schwimmer were also valid representatives of the Dual Monarchy.

Appendix

APPENDIX

English and Irish Claims
Against Flanders
1274-1275*

Editorial Note

The editorial process was intended to provide the reader with a fully expanded text which follows as closely as possible the original intention of the scribe. Obvious mistakes in writing have been corrected and noted, but deviant spellings of the same word (e.g. *arrest* and *arest*), and apparent inconsistencies in the use of possessives, have been left without comment. Modern punctuation has been added to the extent that it facilitates reading.

The document itself is a roll consisting of seven membranes sewn head to foot. It is, with a few minor exceptions, in a good state of preservation. The outer inscription on the roll, in a later hand, mistakenly attributes the document to the reign of Edward III, and this mistake is perpetuated in the *Lists and Indexes*. An effort has been made to define commercial terms and identify place names. This information is contained in a glossary and list of places at the end of the text. The document is the property of the Public Record Office. I am grateful to the keeper and the staff of that department for their assistance and for permission to publish this material.

*Great Britain, Public Record Office document number E 163/5/17.

Cest cil ki de Londres.

Cest li prisie des laines et des autres biens de cuas de Londres sai est faite et passee par les viij homes.[1]

Watiers Aubrekin — iij sas de laine del hospital de Jerusalem, le prise dou sac viij lb.; v sas, xxij claus de Codeswaus, le prise viij marcs le sac; j sac lokes del hospital devant dit, del pris de iij marcs et si a xx claus de cruture, j sac de scote — a tout le cruture, xiij marcs.

> Some de le value de le laine
> et des crutures lxiiij lb.
> xiiij s. vj. d.

Mourisses de Wateham — xij sas ke tienent xiij sas, le pris dou sac vj lb. et ij sas ki tienent iij sas, le pris dou sac vj marcs. Item ij sas d'agnelins ke font iij sas, le pris dou sac vij marcs.

> Some toute cx lb.

Henris de Coventree — xix sarpeillieres ke tienent[2] xxiiij sas d'aisles-bires pris en le maison seu hoste a Brughes, le pris dou sac viij marcs.

> Some toute vj^{xx}viij lb.

Charles de [. . . .] ome[3] de Londres avoit en le maison Pieron Ravelot de Brughes [. . . .][4] sarpellieres ke tienent viij sas, le pris del sac viij marcs.

> Some toute xlij lb. xiij s.
> iiij d.

Robers de Basinghes eut arestei a Brughes si fu amenei de le mue par le comant Philippe de Bourbourch[5] a le maison Jak' le Noir Chevalier xxxj sas[6] ki firent a tout les crutures xxxiij sas, le pris dou sac viij marcs et demi.[7]

> Some toute c iiij^{xx} vij lb.

Martins de Levesham avoit a le maison Pietre Ravelot de Brughes xxij lb. en deniers contaus et iij sas de laine de crois roies,[8] le pris dou sac c s.

> Some toute xxxvij lb. en
> deniers et laines.

---

[1] The four English and four Flemish merchants chosen to certify the value of English losses in Flanders. See page 47.

[2] MS teneient.

[3] Hole in MS.

[4] Hole in MS.

[5] Philippe de Bourbourch was the castellan of Bruges.

[6] MS sac.

[7] MS "s" for semi. The scribe consistently used the abbreviation "s" for semi, or half. I have expanded it in the more common form, demi.

[8] Laine de crois roies was wool in a sack that bore the red cross seal affixed in English ports to attest that the wool was shipped under proper export license and that the custom was paid.

Grigores de Rokelee eut en une nef de Sanwich[9] devant Sanwich arestei et pris xiij sas de laine ke font xvij sas cest asavoir ij sas de boine laine brise de Godesfort et de Wesdon et une poise de cruture, le pris dou sac xij marcs. Item iij sas de laine brise de Gowteham, une poise de cruture, le pris dou sac ix marcs. Item viij sas de laine d'okeborne, iij sas de cruture, pris dou sac viij marcs. Item iiij poids de fromage, pris de le poids xj s. Un lit et menus harnas dou pris de xx s.

Some toute cij lb. xvij s.

iiij d.

Et ce prisent: Jehans Grosseteste, Willames ses freres de Huge esclus et le menerent a Huge esclus et iloet prist Watiers Ruffins une partie de cel avoir et l'autre delivra a Jehans et Willames ses frere devant dis et mena Watiers Ruffins ce kil en prest a Gant.

Thumas de Basinghes eut a Brughes ke Crestiens le Grans eut xxxj sas[10] et une poke de laine dont le pris fu fais par les viij homes defenre dis cest asavoir viij sas de boine laine del abie de Notelee, pris dou sac xij marcs; v sas et demi et le quarte d'un sac de moine laine celi maison, pris dou sac vij marcs. Item ij sas de lokes xxv claus de grose laine de celi maison, pris dou sac vij marcs. Item viij sas de boine laine del abie[11] de Flexelee, pris dou sac xv marcs. Item j sac de moine laine de celi maison, pris dou sac viiij marcs. Item ij sas de boine lokes de celi maison, pris dou sas viiij marcs et demi. Item ij sas de secondes lokes et vij claus, pris dou sac vij marcs. Item j sac de coilette, pris dou sac v marcs.

Some toute ccxxvij lbs. xvj d.

Jehans Durans de Donestaple avoit en une nef a le mue xxiiij sas ke font xxx de le coilette de Donestaple, le pris dou sac viij marcs et demi. Item en cel [nef?] meisme viij sas ki font x sas d'agnelins[12] del pais meisme, pris dou sac vij marcs. Item iloet ij sas et demi de grose laine de celui pais, pris dou sac vj marcs. Item iloet j sac de noire laine et xx claus de cruture, pris dou sac lxxviij s. Item j sac de lokes xv claus de celui pais, pris del sac iiij marcs.

Some toute la cruture ccxxxv lb.

Willames le Pissoners de Donestaple eut a le mue xxvij sas, le pris dou sac viij marcs x1 d. Item la meisme vij sas agnelin ki font viiij sas, pris dou sac vij marcs.

Some toute ccviiij lb.

[9] *MS* Samwic.
[10] *MS* sac.
[11] *MS* abeie.
[12] agnelins *interlineated above a caret.*

Nicholes de Hice eut arestei a le mue viij sas ke font viiij sas de laine del terroir de Hice, le pris dou sac viij marcs et demi; j sac d'agnelins a tout la cruture, c s.

Some toute lvj lb.

[End of membrane one]

Some m iiij^c xix lb. vj s. iij d.[13]

Cest le prisie de caus d'isrelande de laine et d'autres biens ki est faite et passee par les viij homes.

Bernars dou Mont d'isrelande avoit a Brughes si kil dist en le maison Crestien le Grant j toursiel de dras roies et de colours, le pris xxiiij lb. vij s. Item au Dam a le maison Pietre Bonnin en deniers contaus viiij^{xx} lb. ke Philippe de Bourbourch recut de Adam Wisdon sue vallet dont il a cartre partie par eschievinage de Brughes. Item a Brughes iiij^{xx} [lb. ?][14] ke Jehans Roese de Brughes le devoit et les recut Philippe de Bourbourch. Item [x ?][15] sas de laine d'isrelande pris dou sac viiij marcs si a en sac iiij poises [et] j quarte mains. Some des x sas, lx lb. Item vij sas d'agnelins, le pris dou sac viiij marcs. Some xliiij lb. vj s. viij d. Item j sac noire laine vij claus et demi de cruture, le pris dou sac viiij marcs. Some avent le cruture vj lb. viij s. ij d. Toute cest laine fu prise a le maison Pietre Raelot de Brughes.

Some toute ccc iiij^{xx} xvij lb.

xxij d.

Willames Lambert de Corch d'isrelande demande cxvj lb. ke Philippe de Bourbourch prist donit il a cartre partie par eschievinage de Brughes.

Et Philippes Seis de Corch d'isrelande demande en teil maniere xxiiij lb.

Et Ris Hanedon de Hoskene d'isrelande demande in teil maniere iiij^{xx} xviij lb. par eschievinage de Brughes dont on a cartre partie.

Nicholes Morin de Corch avoit a Brughes a le maison Renier le Recepere xxxvij sas, le pris dou sac vj lb. vj s. et ij sas d'agnelins, le pris dou sac vj lb. vj s. viij d. Et tient cascuns sas iiij poises [et] j quarte mains.

Some toute de ceste laine

xj^{xx} xiiij lb. xiij s. iiij d.

Et Philippe de Bourbourch avoit

certe laine.

Rogers Courtois d'isrelande[16] dist kil eut arrestei a le mue xxij dras

---

[13] *In a small hand at the head of the second membrane. The second membrane is stitched to the foot of the first.*

[14] *Hole in MS.*

[15] *Hole in MS.*

[16] *MS d'isretande.*

roies et de couleurs, le pris de xxij dras xliij lb.

Summa eadem.

Jehans Gosselins d'isrelande eut arrestei a Brughes a le maison Pietre Bonin lxxvj lb. en deniers contaus et ce prisent Philippe de Bourbourch et se garantit.

Summa eadem.

Denises Tiocles d'isrelande eut a le maison Pieron Bonnin xx lb. de sterlings et les prist Philippe de Bourbourch devant dis. Item a Brughes a le maison Henri Alverdon xv lb. ke cuils Henri retient por l'ocoison de arrest.

Some toute xxxv lb.

Robers Courtle de Bristan eut en une nef au port de le mue viij sas de laine del teroir d'isrelande del pois de iiij poises et iij quartes le sac, le pris dou sac vj lb. Some xlviij lb.

Summa eadem.

Watiers de Bercham de Bristan eut en celier Henri Alverdon de Brughes v poises de cire, prise de le poise lxviij s.

Some xlvij lb. x s.

[List of Irish merchants ends here]

Henris Prious de Wincester eut arrestei en le maison Liegart a Brughes viij sas ke font viiij sas, le pris dou sac c s.

Some xlvij lb. x s.

Leurens Denne de Wincester eut arrestei a le maison Gill' Doppe a Brughes xxj^m de fier, pris dou millier xx s. Item ij bales de poivre ke tienent iiij^c libvres, pris dou c iiij lb. x d. Item alun dels kerkes de glace ki costerent vj lb. viiij s. Item ij bales de poivre ke tienent iiij^c [libvres?], le pris dou cent iiij lb. Item xv^c xli libvres d'amands, le pris del cent xj s. vj d. Item viiij^c libvres de ris, pris dou cent v s. ij d. Item ij touniels d'ole, pris dou touniel iiij lb. xvj s. Item ij bales de laine de Spainge, le pris de le bale xij s. vij d. Item vij^c lxx libvres d'amands, le pris dou cent xj s. vj d. Item viiij sas de laine ke font xj sas et demi poise de coilette de Wincester, pris dou sac[17] c s. Item iij sas ke font iij sas [et] demi de celui meisme, pris dou sac c s. Item une dousaine[18] de cauces xj s. Item liiij pieces de cire ke posent xxxix poises, pris le poise lxvj s. viij d.

Some cciiij^{xx}xvij lb. xv s.
vj d. ob.

[17] *MS* sas.
[18] *MS* desaine.

Willames de Merewere de Wincester avoit a le maison Jak'Alverdon a Brughes xvj sas[19] de laine de coilette de Wincester, pris dou sac c s. Some iiij^{xx} lb. Item xij pieces de cire ke poisent ix poises v claus, pris xxxj lb. iij s. iij d.

Alexandres de Merewelle aresteis en deniers contaus en Cordeway et Tornes lxx s.

Summa patet.

Some m vj^c liij lb. xiij s. xj d. ob.

[End of membrane two]

Hues de . . . .[20] Posterne xxxviij sas de laine de Merselande, pris dou sac viij marcs et demi. Item ij sas et demi d'agnelins, pris dou sac c s.; j sac de grose laine dou pais, pris dou sac vij marcs.

Some toute ij^c xxxij lb. x s.

Jehans Chate merchans Henre Cade de Donestaple eut en une nef a le mue xiij sas et demi le quarte part d'un sac de abie St. Alban, pris dou sac xj marcs et demi. Item a Brughes a le maison Pietre Ravelot xij sas de laine, pris dou sac vj lb. Item a Tourouch en le maison Watiers de le Capiele xj sas de laine del hospital de la Grave, le pris del sac vj lb. Item en une nef a le mue v sas d'agnelins del pais Donestaple, pris del sac c s. Item en celi[21] nef del pois iij poises ij pokes de noire laine, le pris des iij poises vj lb. xiij s. iiij d. Item ij pokes de grose laine ki font iij poises, le pris vj lb. xiij s. iiij d. Item en celi nef vij sas de boine laine de Bianlin, le pris dou sac vj lb. Item iloet j sac de lokes de celui pais, le pris dou sac lxvj s. viij d.

Some toute ccc xxiij lb. xx d.

Thumas Helric de Ludenoe eut a le maison Gill' Bonin a Brughes j sac et demi d'agnelins del pais de Ludenoe en une sarpeilliere, le pris vj lb. xl s.

Summa eadem.

Thumas de Langefort de Ludenoe eut en celi maison j sac de noire laine, le pris de iiij lb.

Summa eadem.

Thumas de Mulcedoeure avoit et Jehans Quich donerent en heres por cire a Willame Tegart bourgeois de Brughes xx lb. sterling ke Philippe de Bourbourch prist. Item encore donerent Thumas et Jehans devant dis a Pieron le Jui de Brughes en here por cire x lb. Item il donerent au vallet Lambert Dunekin de Brughes en here por cire xx lb. ke Philippe prist toute.[22] Item il avoient en le maison Gill' Dope iij^m des chienium, pris

---

[19] vij claus *cancelled by lining out.*

[20] *covered by previous membrane.*

[21] *MS* cele.

[22] *MS* tout.

dou millier l s.; une fourrure de popes, xv s. dousaine[23] et demi de
cauces de saie, le pris xviij s. et ce prist toute Philippe de Bourbourch.

Some toute lviiij lb. iij s.

Rogiers de Donestaple de Wincester eut arrertei a le mue en une nef v
sas et demi et j quarte de laine de coilette de Wincester, pris c s. Item la
meisme xx dras roies et de coulours, pris xl lb. Item une dousaine de
cauces, pris xj s. Item sarpeillieres et cordes, pris xx s. Item a Brughes en
deniers contaus[24] a le maison Gill' Doppe liiij lb. ke Philippe de Bourbourch retint[25]

Some c xxiij lbs. vj s.

Willames de Donestaple de Wincester et Willames le Taintern ses
compains eurent a Brughes en le maison Gill' Dop xvj dras roies et de
coulours, pris xxxiiij lb. Item vj poises de demi de cire et viiij claus, le
pris de le cire xxiiij lb. Item ke Jehans Derriere le Hale li dont xxv s.

Some toute lviiij lb. v s.

Jehans Scelde Dandoevre eut arrestei a Brughes en une maison au
pont Saint Jehan vj sas de laine de cruture de le contei Dorset de pris dou
viij marcs. Item xiij sas de le coilette dou pais, pris dou sac c s. Item j sac
iiij lbs.

Some toute iiij^{xx}xvj lbs.

Nicholes de Ludenowe eut[26] en l'arest de Brughes ij^{c}iiij^{xx}xvij sas de
laine ke font ccc xxx sas xlvj claus. Le pris de toute le laine devant dite
monte par le prisie des viij homes defente dis.

Some toute m viij^{c}xxviij lb.
xj s. v d.

Rogiers Prende de Soberi eut en le maison Gill' Bonnin de Brughes xvj
sas de laine ki font xvij sas et demi et demi poise de laine brise de le
priorie de Wanelake, le pris dou sac xj marcs. Item iij sas ki font iij sas et
demi et viij pierres de noire laine de celi maison, pris dou sac viiij marcs;
une sarpeilliere de laine de celi maison ke fait iij poises, pris de la
sarpeilliere viiij lb. Item iiij sas ke font v [sas] de le coilette de Seloberi, le
pris dou sac c s. Item ij sas ki font ij sas et demi de lokes de le maison de
Wanelake,[27] pris dou sac iiij marcs [et] demi. Item iij sas et demi de le

[23] *MS* xij aine.
[24] *MS* conteis.
[25] *MS* retut.
[26] *MS* heut.
[27] *MS* Wanlake.

coilette de Seloberi, pris dou sac vij marcs.

> Some toute cc lb. lxviiij s.
> iiij d.

Hues Goldinch eut a Brughes xix sas et demi de laine, pris dou sac vj marcs.

> Some toute lxxviij lb.

Robers Stille de Donewis eut a Brughes xxvj sas de laine ki font xxviij sas, pris dou sac vj marcs.

> Some toute cxij lb. *[sic]*

Some m cc xxix lb. xvij s. iiij d.

[End of membrane three]

Jehans de Tangle Dandoevre eut a Brughes arestei iiij sas de laine ke font v [sas], pris dou sac iiij lb. Item en deniers de contaus lx s.

> Some toute xxiij lb.

Jehans le Mausuers Dandoevre eut en l'arest viij sas de laine del pais Dandoevre, pris dou sac c s. Item ij pieces de cire, le pris vj lb. Item en deniers xxij lb. Item j drap xxxv s.

> Some toute lxviiij lb. xv s.

Alexandres le Riches Dandoevre eut arrestei xvj sas de laine ke font xx sas et vij claus dou pais de Credelade, le pris dou sac viij marcs et demi. Item vj sas de le coilette de Somesete, le pris dou sac vj marcs. Item ke Watiers Godrich de Brughes li devoit ki sont[28] arrestei xj lb.

> Some toute c xlix lb. x d.

Dame Denise de Pevenesee eut en l'arest xx sas de laine, le pris dou sac viij marcs. Item xxxvj poises de fromage, le pris de le poise x s.

> Some toute vj^xx iiij lb. xiij s.
> iiij d.

Richart le Blont de la Rie avoit en deniers contaus en se nef au Dam xlij lb.

> Summa eadem.

Willames de Regate de Wincester eut arrestei a le mue viij poises de cire [et] v claus mains, le pris de le poise lxix s. Item demi bale de poivre, pris de le bale xij d. Item ij^c et demi d'amand, pris dou cent xj s. xxv libvres de comin le pris dou cent iiij s. vj d.

> Some toute xxxiiij lb.

Nicholes de le Pole de Andoevre demande de retief et dist ke Clais le Lons, Willames ses freres et Hanekin de Noeport et si compagnon arresterent le xx isime jour devant le Nativite Saint Jehan[29] l'an millier

---

[28] *MS* sunt.
[29] *June 4.*

cc lxxiiij une sui nef atout les atuils, dou pris de lx marcs. Si avoit en celi nef xxvj homes ke fuerent mis hors de le nef et mis en une autre: si eut ens lxxiij pois perkeretes dou pris de xxxvj lb. x s. Item seil de Poitau c x quartruns, pris xij lb. x s. — cest cascun quartrun ij s. iiij d. Item de froment et autre vitaille a le value viij lb. Item ij touniels de vin de Gasconigne, pris v marcs. Item xix hughes dou pris de xxviij s. vj d., le pris de cascune xviij d. Item xxv lis, le pris lxxv s., pris dou lit iij s. Item vij batiel et un corde, pris de xxx s. et salmon xiij s. et iiij d. Item robes fremans aniaus d'or et d'argent le value iiij lb. et est li nef a Noefport et vint la si cum cuils Nicholes dist et les choses prisent si cum il dist devant dites.

Some toute c xij lb. xiij s.
vj d.

Jehans Lonsomier de Wesmue et Willames de Gernemue se plaingnet de Willame le Lonc et Clai le Lonc sue frere ki li colirent un nef dou pris de xxx marcs atout l'atil. Item iiij^{xx}x quartruns de seil de Poitau, le pris dou quartrun iij s. Item viij quarturns de frine de froment, pris de quartrun demi marc. Item j touniel de vin, pris xxx s. et xviij fares de ris,[30] pris del far j marc et xl s.; de sterlings en deniers contaus et huges, lis et dras, pris iiij marcs et disent ke devant dit sont de Noeport et present les choses devant dites si kil dient.

Some toute xlix lb. xvj s.
viij d.

Richars de L'angelo de Colecestre demande ke Philippe de Bourbourch prist en une nef con apiele Sainte Marie Holt xxvj lb. de sterlings.

Summa eadem.

Philippe de Maldone eut a Brughes xxiiij sas de laine agnelines, le pris dou sac c s. de laine d'exesse et en deniers contaus xix lb. xix d. ob.

Some c xxxiij lb. xix d. ob.

Adam de Messingeham de Nichole eut a Brughes xxx sas de laine de Lindeseia, le pris sou sac xj marcs et demi. Item la meismes viij sas xxiiij pieres de moiene [laine] de Lindeseia, le pris dou sac vj lb. x s.

Some toute cc iiij^{xx}vij lb.
xij s.

Watiers Danne de Wincester eut a Brughes xv sas de laine de le priorie de Wincester, le pris dou sac c s. et some de le laine lxv lb. Item viij pieces de cire del pois vj poises, pris de le poise v marcs. Item ij kerkes d'amandes, pris de le kerke xxiiij s. Item j bale comin, pris xiij s. et ce fu pris a le maison Gill' Dope de Brughes.

Some toute iiij^{xx}xviij lb.
xij d.

---

[30] *MS* reis.

Jehans Dalerons de Wincester eut arrestei a Brughes xxxiij dras de Poperinghs, le pris lj lb. x s. Item por canevach, fentres et cordes x s.

Some toute lj lb. x s.

Some mcc lb. ij lb. [sic] iiij s. xj d. ob.

[End of membrane four]

Simons Baras et Robers Berengers de Bandoch eurent arrestei en une nef a le mue xviij sas ki font xx sas et demi de boine laine brise del pais de Bandoch, le pris dou sac vij lb. Item viiij sas de laine brise de celui pais en viij sarpeillieres, le pris dou sac vj lb. Item j sac de pelis et demi et le quarte partie d'un sac, le pris dou sac vj lb. Item ij sas ki font iiij de noire laine de celui pais, le pris dou sac viiij marcs et demi. Item v sas de lokes de celui pais, pris dou sac iiij lb. Item demi sac de lokes avent les cruture, le pris toute iiij marcs.

Some toute ij^{c}xlix lb. xiij s.
iiij d.

Jehans le Parmentis de Baldoch en une nef a le mue iij sas xviij claus de laine brise del pais de Bandoc, le pris dou sac vij lb. Item iij sas et le quarte d'un sac de celui pais de coilette, le pris dou sac viij marcs. Item j sac de moine laine del pais, le pris a tout le cruture vij marcs. Item ij sas de lokes, dou sac o les crutrues iiij lb. Et xxxiiij claus de noire laine, le pris lxviij s.

Some toute lvj lb. xvj s. iiij d.

Willames Goldinch de Lenne eut arestei a Brughes en le maison Watiers de le Posterne xvj sas de laine ki font xvij sas de Merseland et de Norewich, le pris dou sac viij marcs.

Some toute iiij^{xx}xvj lb. vj s.
viij d.

Simons li Cornewalois de Wincester eut arestei a Brughes en le maison Gill' Dope iiij dras de coulours, le pris de le piece iij marcs. Item vj dras et une piece de diversses coulous, le pris viiij lb. vj s. viij d. Item iiij^c et demi de cire, le pris dou cent xliiij s. Item foureures de grise oevre, pris lx s. Item, en canevac et autres menues choses x s.

Some toute xxxij lb. xxv d.

Nicholes Horsnemain de Wincester eut arestei a Brughes a le maison Gill' Dope ij pieces de cire de Poulane, le pris c iiij s.; en deniers contaus xxviiij s. vj d.

Some vj lb. xiij s. vj d.

Jehans Consaus de Wincester eut arrestei[31] a Brughes a le maison Gill' Dope en cire, en fier et amandes le value de xvij lb. x s.

---

[31] *MS* arreste.

Richars Phelippe de Wincester eut arrester[32] a le maison Gill' Dope ij dras ki estoient en tourseil Rogers de Donestaple viij marcs.

Watiers Gavelars de Wincester eut arrestei a le maison Gill' Dope de Brughes laine de Spaingne, piaus de kieure et dras d'islande et piaus d'aginaus a le value de viij lb.; viiij s.

Willames Thomas de Soushamptone avoit a le maison Gill' Dope xj pieces de cire ki costerem xxx lb.; viij dras et demi dou pris de xiiij lb. vj s. Item j tourseil de menues robes, le value d'un marc.

Some xlv lb.

Robers Poteriaus de Wincester eut en le maison Gill' Dope arrestei demi drap de mourei del pris de xl s. Item iij dousaine de cord et j fourrure de menu vair, le pris xl s.; une lanterne de pris vj d. ob.

Some iiij lb. vj d. ob.

Nicholes de le Pole Dandoevre et Thumas Danne ses companis eut arrestei a le maison Jehans Tumberman de Burghes lxxv sas de laine ke font c sas de laine del Estoe, Burefort, Farendone, Sileterste, Saluberi, Lacot, Tekeberi, Trente, Monketone, pris del sac viij marcs. Item fromage kil racaterent de Philippe de Pole et de Philippe Bourbourch de xxv lb.

Some toute v^clviij lb. vj s. viij d.

Willames Adegier de Wincester eut arrestei a le mue vj dras d'ypre, le pris dou drap l s. et une piece de drap d'ipre, le pris xxxvij s. vj d. Item xj dras roies, pris dou drap xxx s. Item pro cire, canevac, fier et autres choses le value de xviij lb. xiij lb. xiij s. iiij d. ob. Et ce fu tout aportei a Brughes a Philippe de Bourbourch.

Some toute lij lb. x d. ob.

Gilbers de Multone de Lenne avoit a Brughes a le maison Jehans Daniel lxxv sas de laine cest a savoir xxxiiij sas del terrior d'aplebi en le contei de Westmorelande, le pris dou sac vj lb. Item vj sas des partie Saint Boutoulf, pris dou sac vj. lb. vj s. viij d. Item vj sas et demi de pelis de Spaldinghs, pris dou sac viij marcs et demi. Item xxviij sas de laine brise de Spaldinghs, pris dou sac viiij marcs.

Some toute iiij^cl lbs.

Gilbers Pouke avoit a Brughes ke Daniel le Riches et Willames li Engles li donient de laine et de fromage con lora retenu viij lb. xj s.

Some m v^c iiij^{xx}x lb. xv s. xj d.

Some toute viij^m viij^cx lb. xv s. x d.

[End of membrane five]

[32] *Ibid.*

Jehans Spaldine de Lenne eut a Brughes iiij sas de laine de Lindesie, le pris dou sac vj lb. Item vj sas v pieres d'autre laine, pris dou sac viij marcs et demi.

Some toute lix lb.

Thumas Valles [et] Willames l'espissier d'exenefort eut arrestei a Touront en le maison Gill' de Bodingeh' iiij sas de laine de Codeswal dou pris de xxxvj marcs.

Some xxiiij lb.

Leurens Denne eut encore arrestei a Burghes xxxix poises de cire j claus et demi mains, le pris ke le poise v marcs. Si eut liiij pieces de cire — some xj^{xx}ix lb. xvj s. viij d.

Some vj^{xx} ix lb. xvj s. viij d.

Richars de le Haie de Noecastiel eut arrestei a Brughes xxxvij sas de laine de Norhomberlande et d'aplebi, pris dou sac viiij marcs et demi.

Some cc xxxiiij lb. vj s. viij d.

Thumas de Cardoel eut arrestei a Brughes en le maison Jak' de Herteberge par Philippe de Bourbourch xxxvj lb.

Summa eadem.

Jehans de Orlentone de le francise le veske de Duriaume eut en l'arest de Brughes ix pieces de cire de Poulane et j bale de cire de Spainge, pris de xxiij lb. vj s. viij d.; alun, viij lb. Item por ij dras de Tournai, lx s. Item cl quartruns de froment, xviij lb.

Some lij lb. vj s. viij d.

Jehans Sanssons de celi veske eut en arrest a Brughes iiij pieces de cire, pris xj lb. Item alun, viij lb. Item en bliet c mesures con claime heut vj li. Item j touniel d'ole iij lb. xv s. Item oint lx s. et iiij^c libvres de ris, pris xx s.

Some xxxij lb. xv s.

Willames d'Alverdon de celi veske eut en arrest ole d'olive et alun, pris de vj lb. vij s.

Summa eadem.

Hues Goldine eut en arrest xix sas de laine.[33]

Summa eadem.

Thumas d'Andoevre de Soushampton eut en arrest a Brughes ix pieces de cire de Poulane, le pris xxiiij lb.

Summa eadem.

Robers le Merciers de Soushampton eut en arrest iiij pieces de cire, le pris de le cire x lb.

Summa eadem.

Richart Seleit de Soushampton eut en arrest ij pieces de cire, pris c s. Item ij matelas, pris v s.

Some cv s.

[33] *Entry cancelled.*

Rauols de Flouflanc et Hues ses freres — xvij pieces de cire del pois de xiiij poises vj claus, le pris de le poise lxvij s. vj d.

Some xlvij lb. xviij s. vj d.

Henris de Bertone eut arrestei a Brughes en le maison Gill' Dop viij pieces de cire ke poisent vj poises et iiij claus, le pris de le poise iij lb. vij s. Item fier iiij milliers et demi, le pris dou millier xx s. Item alun de glace j kerke, lx s. Item j kerke de comin, xviij s. Item amand j kerke, xl s.

Some xxx lb. xix s.

Bertremins Bourdon de Penecestre eut arrestei une nef o l'atil in le Suine [?] par Ernaut Muske bailli le contesse dou pris xv marcs. Por le pris de l s. ensi li doit on vij lb. x s. Some x lb. de con a il recut por le[34] nef nue.

Some vij lb. x s.

Richars de Cerfent d'Orefort dist ke Jehans d'Alverdonig de Brughes li retient xlvij lb. de sterlings por xiiij sas de laine agnelines kil li vende.

Summa eadem.

Mikins de Ricefort dist ke Henris Clais, Hanins Crestiens, Alanis de Vincelesiel, Jehans Stach d'isre et Honekins fils Jehans de Bere d'isre prisent de lui en le mer pres d'isre millier vj^{cc} de dur pisson de cabeill', pris dou cent xx s.

Some xvj lb.

Watiers le Paumiers de Wincester avoit en le maison Gill' Dope de Brughes c libvres de poivre, le pris c s. Item ij pieces de cire del pois de poise et demi et vj claus, pris de le poise v marcs.

Some toute x lb. xiij s. vj d.

Thumas de Bambourch et Jehans Bate de Pontefrei eurent arrestei par Philippe de Bourbourch en une nef a le mulker c quartruns de froment et de segle meslei, le pris del quartrun v s. Item un touniel de raisins, pris iiij lb. Item ij camelins de Gant, pris vj marcs. Item j drap de Stanfort roie, pris ij marcs. Item xl fais de vignor [?], pris j marc. Item xl fais d'aus, pris j marc. Item frait de le nef, xl s.

Some xxxvij lb. xiij s. iiij d.

Toute some viij^c xj lb. xj s. iiij d.

[End of membrane six]

Gerars de Eleghetone dist ke Katerine dou Dam arresta se nef en Normendei; le nef o l'apareil valut xxij lb. ij s. iij d. et dist ke por celi ocoison kele l'aresta puis le pais de Mosteroel[35] il eut damage x lb.

Some xxxij lb. ij s. iiij d.

Rauols de le Cambre de Soushampton dist kil eut arrestei en le maison Gill' Doup de Brughes une piece de drap caperet, le pris ij marcs.

[34] *MS* la.

[35] *The Peace of Montreuil-sur-mer ended hostilities between England and Flanders. It was proclaimed on July 28, 1274.*

Some xxvj s. viij d.

Hendich de le Noevehede dist ke Ernaut Muske bailli le contesse une nefo l'atil, pris iiij lb. en le suine [?] li arresta.

Some iiij lb.

Alains de Castiel et Sandre de Watelei dient con lot arresta a Trehout viij sarpeillieres de laine ki tienent x sas en le maison Watiers de le Capiele, pris del sac viij marcs.

Some liij lb. vj s. viij d.

Robers le Fierour de Sanwich dist con li arresta a Brughes en le maison Robers Ravelot et en celier Colart d'Averdonig xv sarpeilleres ki tienent xvij sas de laine agnelines del teroir de Sanwich, pris del sac vij marcs. Item en deniers contaus xlix lb. iiij s. de sterlings ke Bonin Cam li retient. Item viij peices de cire ke poisent xj et demi poises et xij claus et demi[36] achattees a Lambin Lovin, pris de le poise lxviij s. j d. ob. Item cire de Spaingne vij poises xij claus, pris xxvj lb. xviij s. v d. Item vij cuiltes et v kentil, pris iiij lb. vj s. ij d. ob. Item j drap de soie, pris viij s. Item xxv et demi libvres de cotton, pris xij s.

Some ij^{c}iiij lb. vij s. ix d. ob.

Simons Wibers de Sanwich eut arrestei a Brughes xxv sas de laine agnelines de Sanwich, pris del sac vij marcs.

Some c xvj lb. xiij s. iiij d.

Stienenes Setenai de Sanwis dist kil eut arrestei a Brughes en le maison Jehans Alverdon xiiij sas et demi et ij pieres de laine, pris del sac agnelines vij marcs. Item vij dras de Gant roies, pris dou drap xxxj s.

Some lxxviij lb. xvij s.[37]

Mahius au Pont de Ailleford dist ke Arnaut Maxele bailli la contesse de Flandre prest de lui en le suine [?] tout l'atil d'une nef dou pris de xl s.

Some xl s.

Annond le Porriere de Sanwis dist kil eut arrestei[38] a Brughes en le maison Basile dou Bogart xv sas [et] demi poise de laine agnelines de kent, pris dou sac vij marcs.

Some lxxj lb. lx d.

Stienenes de Sanwis dist kil eut arrestei a Brughes en celier Jehans d'Alverdonig xj sarpeillieres ke tienent xiiij sas et demi poise et ij claus de laine agnelines de kent, pris del sac vij marcs. Item vj dras roies de Gant, pris del drap xxxj s. v d.; une saie de Brughes, pris xxxj s. v d.

Some lxxvij lb. xiij s. iij d.

Alixandres de Groeton dist kil eut arrestei a Brughes en celier Colart Alverdon viij sarpeillieres ke tienent viiij sas iiij claus de laine agnelines de kent, pris de sac vij marcs.

Some xlij lb. vj s. viij d.

[36] et xij claus et demi *interlineated over a caret.*

[37] *The entire entry beginning with Stienenes is cancelled.*

[38] *MS* arreste.

Leurence Pores de Sanwis dist kil eut arrestei a Brughes en le maison Watiers de le Posterne xxviij sas et demi de laine agnelines de kent, pris del sac des xxvj sas et demi vij marcs et des ij sas xj marcs v s. iiij d.[39] Item li cir Roberts le Chevalier [de] Brughes le retienent por le contesse de laine kil li vendi xx lb.

Some vij^{xx}xj lb. xj s. iiij d.

Thumas de Basinghs demande de Gilebert de le Court de Gant lxvij lb. de sterlings kil prest de Hobekin sue noven ken deniers ken un sac de laine de Flexellee et ken plate d'argent.

Some lxvij lb.

Some viij^{c}xx lb. xv s. iij d. ob.[40]

Some de toute cest brief x^{m}vj^{c}xxvij lb. x s. ij d. ob.

[End of membrane seven]
Bonorum Angl' arr' in Fland'.

---

[39] et des ij sas xj marcs v s. iij d. *interlineated.*
[40] *Written in margin.*

List of Places

FLANDERS

Cordeway: Courtrai.
Dam: Damme.
Gant: Ghent.
Huge esclus: Sluys?
Isre: Yser in Belgium?
Poperinghs: Popheringhe.
Tornes: Tournai.
Tourouch: Thorout.
Ypre: Ypres.

Glossary

agnelins, agnelines: lamb's wool.

alun: alum.

alun de glace: roche alum, alum that was first melted and made into flakes like ice.

amands: almonds.

atils, atiuls: equipment or gear.

batiel: a small boat.

bleit: grain, especially wheat.

camelins de gant: a cloth of oriental design once said to have been made from camel's hair and silk, but later made from goat's hair and silk or some other combination.

canevach, canevac: canvas.

carte partie: probably a notarial document of obligation between two parties which was authorized and enforced by the éschevins of the city.

cauces: hose or britches.

claus: a clove, or nail, which was a measure of weight equivalent to seven pounds used in London and the southern ports.

comin: cumin, a condiment.

cruture: usage is not clear but it probably refers to undressed or unprepared wool.

cuiltes: quilts, mattresses, or bolsters.

drap caperet: a kind of silk?

drap de mourei: murrey cloth, a mulberry-colored cloth.

drap de soie: silk cloth.

drap de stanfort roie: red Stamford cloth, a cloth of combed wool yarn that was usually used in making expensive outer garments.

fais: a fardel, a bundle or pack.

fares: probably a bundle or package.

fourrure, foureures: furs.

fourrure de grise oevre: furs with gray work.

fourrure de menu vair: ermine or other light gray or white fur.

fourrure de popes: summer fur of squirrels.

frine: flour.

froment, forment: wheat.

grose laine: wool of inferior quality.

heres: earnest money.

huges: small casks or chests.

kentil: probably a patchwork quilt.

kerke: a common weight or measure, usually 400 pounds.

laine brise: wool that was 'broken' or 'pressed' as part of the process of dressing and packing.

lokes: small pieces of dirty wool clipped from the sheep before shearing.

matelas: a mattress.

noven: a servant or apprentice.

oint: grease or oil.

pelis: woolfells, sheep hides with the wool still attached.

perkerets: probably a kind of fish.

piaus d'aginaus: lamb skins.

piaus de kieure: goat skins.

piere, pierre: stone, an English weight of fourteen pounds.

poise: poke, a bag of wool less than an official sack. Also a wey, which was usually 182 pounds for wool and 224 pounds for cheese.

quartrun: a measure of grain. The quarter of London was equivalent to 8 bushels.

ris: rice.

sais: says?; a word of diverse meaning. It was sometimes used for silk *(soie)*, but more commonly it described a sort of weave, perhaps twilling as in serges in either wool or linen.

sarpeilliere: sarpler, a large bag of wool weighing more than an official sack.

sas: sack, a quantity of wool weighing 364 English pounds.

schienium: a kind of fish.

scote: cot wool, matted wool in the fleece.

segle meslei: the better or best grade of rye.

seil: rye.

touniel: tun, a large cask for liquids usually equivalent to 252 gallons.

vignour, vingnour: ?

Works consulted in preparing this glossary include Frederic Godefroy, *Dictionnaire L'Ancienne Langue Française*; DuCange, *Glossarium Mediae et Infirmae Latinitatis*; Randle Cotgrave, *A Dictionarie of the French and English Tongues*; Pegolotti, *La Practica Della Mercatura*; R. E. Latham, *Revised Medieval Latin Word-List*; and Florence Edler, *Glossary of Mediaeval Terms of Business: Italian Series, 1200-1600*.

NOTES

Demographic Aspects of the Norman Conquest

JOSIAH C. RUSSELL

1. The triumph of Hardrada would probably have encouraged the urbanization of England since the Northmen liked cities. H. L. Turner, *Town Defenses in England and Wales* (London, 1970), p. 20.

2. A few remarks upon population change were made by C. T. Chevallier, in *The Norman Conquest of England: Its Setting and Impact*, ed. D. Whitelock (New York, 1966), p. 2n. to be discussed later.

3. A good introduction to study on towns is in Henry Loyn. "Towns in Late Anglo-Saxon England: the Evidence and Some Possible Lines of Enquiry." *England before the Conquest*, ed. P. Clemoes and K. Hughes (Cambridge, 1971), pp. 115-28.

4. Arnold K. Price, "Differential Germanic Social Structures," *Vierteljahrschrift für Social-und Wirtschaftsgeschichte* 55 (1969), 433-48 and "Die Nibelungen als kriegischer Weihebund," *Vierteljahrschrift für Social-und Wirtschaftsgeschichte* 61 (1974), 199-211.

5. J. C. Russell, "The Earlier Medieval Plague in the British Isles," *Viator* 7 (1976), 65-78. Population rise, Russell, *Late Ancient and Medieval Population*, pp. 97-98. The surplus males are evident before and after the plague in my collection of cemetery data for the period.

6. Translated conveniently in J. F. Benton, *Town Origins. The Evidence from Medieval England* (Boston, 1968), pp. 48-50. The arrangements of places geographically in Anglo-Saxon documents is discussed in J. C. Russell, "The Tribal Hidage," *Traditio* 5 (1947), 197. See also for the document Loyn, "Towns," pp. 117-18.

7. Benton, *Town Origins*, p. 48, notes 1-5.

8. Benton, *Town Origins*, pp. 48, 71; Katherine Hume, "The Concept of the Hall in Old British Poetry," *Anglo-Saxon England* 3 (1974), 67-74.

9. F. W. Maitland, *Domesday Book and Beyond* (Cambridge, 1897), pp. 192-93; C. W. Hollister, *Anglo-Saxon Military Institutions* (Oxford, 1962), p. 80.

10. Explained in J. C. Russell, *Medieval Regions and their Cities* (Newton Abbot, 1972), pp. 34-38. The idea is well expressed by James Tait, "Such administrative and ecclesiastical centers naturally attract settlers to supply their wants." *The Medieval Borough* (Manchester, 1936), p. 6.

11. Whitelock, *The Norman Conquest*, p. 3. For other examples, J. C. Russell, "Quantitative Approach to Medieval Population Change," *The Journal of Economic History* 24 (1964), 5.

12. On civic population density, J. C. Russell, *Late Ancient and Medieval Population, Transactions of the American Philosophical Society* 48, pt. 3 (Philadelphia, 1958), 60-63.

13. A. P. R. Finberg, *The Formation of England* (London, 1974), p. 119; Maitland, *Domesday Book and Beyond*, p. 199.

14. Maitland, *Domesday Book and Beyond*, pp. 124, 185; Tait, *Medieval English Borough*, p. 209.

15. Benton, *Town Origins*, pp. 56-60; map p. 58; H. B. Petersen, *Anglo-Saxon Currency* (Lund, 1969); various works of R. H. M. Dolley, as for example his, "The Mint of Chester," *Journal of the Chester Archaeological and Historical Society* 42 (1955), 1-20.

16. Eric John, *Land Tenure in Early England* (Leicester, 1961), p. 120 for the naval circuit of England. For English economic life of the period, E. M. Carus-Wilson in A. L. Poole, *Medieval England*, 1:221-60. P. H. Sawyer, "The Wealth of England in the Eleventh Century," *Transactions of the Royal Historical Society*, 5th ser. 15 (1965), 145-64.

17. A. Ballard, *The Domesday Boroughs* (Oxford, 1904), pp. 39-40; F. Barlow, *The Feudal Kingdom of England*, p. 25; Benton, *Town Origins*, pp. 68-74; Darby (see under various boroughs); F. M. Stenton, *Anglo-Saxon England* (Oxford, 1943), p. 530; Carl Stephenson, *Borough and Town* (Cambridge, Mass., 1933), p. 221; Tait, *Medieval English Borough*, p. 76.

18. V. H. Galbraith, *Domesday Book: its Place in Administrative History* (Oxford, 1974). On the compiler of Domesday, V. H. Galbraith, "Notes on the Career of Samson, Bishop of Worcester, "*English Historical Review* 82 (1967), 86-101, esp. p. 94 for signs of haste. As probable chief clerk, F. Lieberburg, *Ungedruckte Anglo-Normannische Geschichtsquellen* (Strassburg, 1879), p. 266; J. F. R. Walmsley, "Another Domesday Text." *Medieval Studies* 39 (1977), 109-20: more pre-Domesday data.

19. Russell, *Late Ancient and Medieval Population*, p. 18.

20. J. C. Russell, *British Medieval Population* (Albuquerque, 1948), pp. 26-32.

21. J. C. Russell, "The Preplague Population of England," *The Journal of British Studies* 5 (1966), 1-21, esp. 12-14.

22. P. V. Addyman, "The Anglo-Saxon House: a New Review," *Anglo-Saxon England* 1 (1972), 273-303. Other data in *Medieval Archaeology*.

23. *Florentii Wigorniensis Monachi Chronicon ex Chronicis*, ed. Benjamin Thorpe, 2 vols. (London, 1849), 2:77-133. John of Worcester's continuation begins for 1118 (cf. 2:71).

24. Sawyer, "Wealth of England," pp. 145-64, esp. p. 153 n.14; Benton, *Town Origins*, p. 68; Russell, *British Medieval Population*, p. 47. For evidence of the plots or housing, Maitland, *Domesday Book and Beyond*, p. 100; Tait, *The Medieval English Borough*, p. 90.

25. For Ipswich and Gloucester, Russell, *British Medieval Population*, pp. 46, 286. For Cambridge, *Atlas of Historic Towns*, vol. 2, *Cambridge*, p. 4. The average number to church or priest ran about 255, Russell, *British Medieval Population*, p. 43.

26. Russell, *Medieval Regions and their Cities*, pp. 23-30.

27. H. C. Darby and I. S. Maxwell, *The Domesday Geography of Northern England* (Cambridge, 1962), pp. 155-58. To 1718 1/2 houses, persons, etc. are added 200 for the bishop's and canons' areas.

28. *Atlas of Historic Towns*, ed. M. D. Lobel, vol. 2, *Norwich*, map. 7. The churches are Giles, Peter Mancroft, John the Baptist Timberhill, Michael at Thorn, Peter Parmentergate, George Tombland, Benedict, Swithin, Margaret, Lawrence, Gregory, John Maddermarket, Andrew, Michael at Plea, Peter Hungate, Mary Coslany, Michael Coslany, George Colgate, Clement, Simon and Jude, Edmund, and Martin at Palace (?). The others were not so certain: Martin (with Michael at Thorn); John the Evangelist: Michael in Conesford, and Vedast to Peter Parmentergate; Cuthbert and Mary the Less to George Tombland; Crouche to John Maddermarket; Cristopher to Michael at Plea; Martin to Mary Coslany (?); John (Colgate); Margaret Newbridge; Olave to George Colgate. For map see also C. Stephenson, *Borough and Town*, p. 199.

29. H. C. Darby, *The Domesday Geography of Eastern England* (Cambridge, 1952), pp. 111, 139-140 (Hereafter cited as Darby, *DG* and region).

30. Martin Biddle, "Excavations at Winchester, 1971, Tenth and Final Interim Report," *Antiquaries Journal* 55 (1975), 334 for map. Estimate of inhabited area is mine.

31. Darby, *DG of Eastern England*, pp. 51, 78; Stephenson, *Borough and Town*, p. 192; J. W. F. Hill, *Medieval Lincoln* (Cambridge, 1948), p. 57.

32. Darby, *DG of Southeast England*, p. 205; H. E. Salter, *The Historic Names of the Streets and Lanes of Oxford intra Muros* (Oxford, 1921), esp. map at end.

33. Darby, *DG of Eastern England*, p. 111; Stephenson, *Borough and Town*, p. 201; *Medieval Archaeology*, 2 (1967), 197. About 2,000 by 4,000 feet.

34. Darby and I. R. Terrett, *DG of Midland England*, p. 19; Benton, *Town Origins*, p. 71.

35. Darby, *DG of Eastern England*, pp. 169, 194.

36. Darby, *DG of Southeast England*, pp. 274-75; *Medieval Archaeology* 10 (1966), 168; 11 (1967), 262, about 2,100 feet on each side.

37. Darby, *DG of Eastern England*, pp. 51-80; C. M. Mabany, *The Archaeology of Stamford* (Stamford, 1969), map on p. 5. Five wards in Lincolnshire and one in Northamptonshire.

38. Darby, *DG of Southeast England*, pp. 513, 548 (should be 499 instead of 599); W. Viry, *Canterbury under the Angevin Kings* (London, 1967), map 1.

39. Darby, *DG of Northern England*, pp. 340, 378.

40. Russell, *British Medieval Population*, p. 54.

41. For a comparison with various regions of the later Middle Ages, see Russell, *Medieval Regions and their Cities*, pp. 238-41.

42. Russell, *British Medieval Population*, pp. 142, 146.

43. Cf. note 2.

44. Benton, *Town Origins*, pp. 68-72; Cecily Clark, "Women's Names in Post-Conquest England," *Speculum* 53 (1978), 240-41.

45. 4,000 is preferred by D. M. Stenton, *English Society in the Middle Ages* (Baltimore, 1951), p. 64.

46. J. B. Given, *Society and Homicide in Thirteenth Century England* (Stanford, 1977), esp. pp. 33-40.

47. Clark, "Women's Names," pp. 223-51, esp. pp. 236-50. The position of women seems to have declined also. D. Whitelock, *The Norman Conquest*, p. 141.

48. Stephenson, *Borough and Town*, p. 152.

49. A. H. Inman, *Domesday and Feudal Statistics* (1900; repr., New York, 1970), p. 30. Landlords, mostly thegns (1066) 13,000; (1086) 9,271. The various volumes of Darby and others on Domesday geography also show the great loss of thegns.

50. J. Shepard, "The English and Byzantium: A Study of Their Role in the Byzantine Army in the late Eleventh Century," *Traditio* 29 (1973), 53-92, esp. pp. 66-70, 80-89. F. M. Stenton, "English Families and the Norman Conquest," *Transactions of the Royal Historical Society*, 4th ser. 36 (1944), 1-12.

51. That William had a papal banner or even papal approval is denied by Catherine Morton, "Pope Alexander II and the Norman Conquest," *Latomus* 34 (1975), 363-83, esp. pp. 381-82.

52. June A. Sheppard, "Medieval Village Planning in Northern England: Some Evidence for Yorkshire," *Journal of Historical Geography* 2 (1967), 3-20.

53. That is, from earlier standards. Cf. R. H. M. Dolley and D. M. Metcalf, "The Reform of the English Coinage under Edgar," in *Anglo-Saxon Coins*, ed. R. H. M. Dolley (London, 1961), pp. 136-68.

54. Ella S. Armitage, "The Early Norman Castles in England," *English Historical Review* 19 (1904), 209-45, 417-55. H. L. Turner, *Town Defenses in England* (London, 1970): Loyn, "Towns in late Anglo-Saxon England," p. 20.

55. Russell, "The Early Schools of Oxford and Cambridge," *The Historian* 5 (1943), 61-76, esp. pp. 69-72.

56. Robert Hughill, *Borderland Castles and Peles* (Newcastle upon Tyne, 1970).

57. *Atlas of Historic Towns*, vol. 2, Bristol, pp. 1-6.

58. S. D. Packard, "The Norman Communes under Richard I," *Haskins Anniversary Essays*, ed. C. H. Tayler (Boston, 1929), p. 321.

59. Armitage, "Early Norman Castles," pp. 42, 423; *Domesday Book*, 1: 181, 269a.

60. Mary Bateson, "The Laws of Breteuil," *English Historical Review* 15 (1900) and 16 (1901).

61. Stenton, *Anglo-Saxon England*, p. 672.
62. J. C. Russell, "The Triumph of Dignity over Order in England," *The Historian* 9 (1947), 137-50.
63. J. C. Russell, "Early Parliamentary Organization," *American Historical Review* 43 (1937-38), 121.
64. Russell, "The Canonization of Opposition to the King in Angevin England," *Haskins Anniversary Essays*, pp. 279-90.
65. Stenton, *Anglo-Saxon England*, pp. 584-85.

English Merchants
and the Anglo-Flemish Economic War

RICHARD H. BOWERS

1. P.R.O. Exchequer Miscellanea, E 163/5/17 m. 1-end (printed in appendix). *De antiquis legibus liber. Chronica maiorum et vicecomitum Londoniarum*, ed. Thomas Stapleton, Camden Society, Old Ser. 34 (1846), 126-27. The study of this significant Anglo-Flemish conflict was neglected by both British and American historians until the recent work by T. H. Lloyd which appears in *The English Wool Trade in the Middle Ages* (Cambridge, 1977). Continental scholars, on the other hand, have given considerable attention to the conflict, especially to the economic aspects of the confrontation. The better studies include those of H. Berben, "Une Guerre Économique au Moyen Âge,"*Études d'Histoire Dédidés a la Memorie de Henri Pirenne* (Brussels, 1937); Adolphe Schaube, "Die Woolausfuhr Englands vom Jahre 1273," *Vierteljahrschrift für Sozial und Wirtschaftsgeschichte* 6 (1908), 39-72, 159-85; and Schaube's critic, E. von Roon-Basserman, "Die Handelsperre Englands gegen Flandern," *Vierteljahrschrift für Sozial und Wirtschaftsgeschichte* 39 (1952), 72-82.
2. The Barons' War had plunged England into violence and confusion in 1264 and 1265. Commerce was interrupted and royal finances reduced to a chaotic state. Even after the royalist triumph over Simon de Montfort and the rebel barons at Evesham in 1265, scattered bands of die-hard rebels continued to disturb the realm for another two years. For the war and its impact see Maurice Powicke, *The Thirteenth Century*(Oxford, 1962); E. F. Jacob, *Studies in the Period of Baronial Reform and Rebellion, 1258-1267, Oxford Studies in Social and Legal History* (Oxford, 1925); Mable Mills, "Adventus Vicecomitum, 1258-1272," *The English Historical Review* 36 (1921), 481-96; and Berben, "Guerre Économique," pp. 2-7.
3. The annuity in question had probably been in arrears since at least 1260. In November 1265 Henry promised the countess payment from fines levied on the rebellious Cinque Ports, but nothing indicates that she ever actually received the money. *Calendar of Patent Rolls, 1258-66*, p. 509 (hereafter cited as *CPR*); *Calendar of Liberate Rolls, 1260-67*, p. 2 (hereafter cited as *CLR*); Berben, "Guerre Économique," pp. 6-7. For the financing of the Lord Edward's crusade see Powicke, *Thirteenth Century*, pp. 221-24.
4. *CPR, 1258-66*, pp. 575-76; Norman Scott Brian Gras, *The Early English Customs System: A Documentary Study of the Institutional and Economic History of Customs from the Fifteenth to the Sixteenth Century* (Cambridge, Mass., 1918), pp. 53-58.
5. *CPR, 1266-72*, p. 141; Gras, *English Customs*, p. 55.
6. *CPR, 1266-72*, p. 420; Berben, "Guerre Économique,"*p. 4*.
7. *CPR, 1266-72*, pp. 420, 456, 534.
8. Ibid., p. 420.

9. *Foedera, Conventions, Litterae, et Cujuscunque,* ed. Thomas Rymer, 10 vols. (The Hague, 1739-45), 1: pt. 2, p. 106. Ephriam Lipson, *The Economic History of England*, 12th ed., vol. 1: *The Middle Ages* (1959; repr., London, 1966), pp. 535-36.

10. *CPR, 1266-72*, pp. 5, 20, 23. Lübeck had received its first grant of privileges in 1257. Lipson, *Economic History*, p. 536.

11. Eileen Power, *The Wool Trade in English Medieval History* (Oxford, 1941), pp. 15, 53-55; Richard H. Kaeuper, *Bankers to the Crown: The Riccardi of Lucca and Edward I* (Princeton, 1973), pp. 35-36, 75-79. Italian involvement in England was greatly stimulated during the years from 1255 to 1258 when King Henry borrowed at least £54,000 from Florentine and Sienese bankers to pay part of the cost of acquiring from the papacy the kingdom of Sicily for his son Edmund. To secure these loans Henry pledged the property of the English religious houses and made each monastery responsible for repayment of an assessed portion of the debt. Thus every monastery in England found itself, usually without its knowledge or consent, indebted to Italian merchant bankers in amounts that ranged from 75 to 750 marks. William E. Lunt, *Financial Relations of the Papacy with England to 1327* (Cambridge, Mass., 1939), pp. 599-603.

12. For debts owed Flemish merchants see *CLR, 1267-72*, pp., 72, 96-97, 105-107. That royal debts owed Flemish merchants were an issue is established by the countess of Flanders' demand, after the rupture of relations in 1270, that Henry commit himself to pay all outstanding debts owed her merchants as one of the Flemish conditions for a settlement. *De antiquis legibus,* p. 144.

13. *Select Cases Concerning the Law Merchant,* ed. Charles Gross and Hubert Hall, Selden Society Publications 23, 46; 49 (London, 1908-32), 23:8-9; P.R.O. Ancient Correspondence, SC 1/3/118.

14. *CPR, 1266-1272,* pp. 456-57.

15. *De antiquis legibus,* pp. 126-27.

16. Lloyd, *English Wood Trade,* p. 28.

17. *De antiquis legibus,* pp. 137-40, 142.

18. P.R.O. Exchequer Miscellanea, E 163/5/17.

19. Ibid.

20. Ibid.; *De antiquis legibus,* pp. 144-45.

21. E 163/5/17.

22. Ibid.; *De antiquis legibus,* p. 142.

23. E 163/5/17; P.R.O. Ancient Correspondence SC 1/12/23.

24. E 163/5/17.

25. *De antiquis legibus,* p. 127.

26. Ibid. The first licenses were issued in March 1272. *CPR, 1266-72*, pp. 593-95.

27. *CPR, 1266-72,* p. 486.

28. Ponce de Mora's letter of commission ordered the bailiffs of Boston and Hull to assist him in every way and to assemble local juries to assist in the investigation if necessary. *CPR, 1266-72*, pp. 599-600. In July 1272 Nicholas Adele, Alexander le Riche, Roger of Dunstable and two clerks, John de Gernemuth and Walter of Andover, received new letters of commission assigning them additional responsibilities and specifying that their authority extended into private liberties of the lay ecclesiastical magnates. Ibid., p. 706.

29. *De antiquis legibus,* p. 142.

30. As late as July 1275 only £5,871 13s. 2 1/2d. of the estimated £8,000 in Flemish assets actually had been collected. *Calendar of Close Rolls, Edward I, 1272-79,* pp. 198-99 (hereafter cited as *CCR*).

31. *CPR, 1266-72,* pp. 687-88. Thomas of Windsor died before the commission completed its work, and Roger de la Legh, a baron of the Exchequer, began working with Master William de la Corner as early as April 1272 probably because failing health

incapacitated Thomas. *CCR, 1272-79*, p. 56; *CPR, 1266-72*, pp. 644-45.

32. *CPR, 1266-72*, pp. 648, 697, 700, 709, 717.

33. *Historical Letters and Papers from the Northern Registers*, ed. James Raine, Rolls Series (London, 1873), p. 41. There appear to have been two men named John de Castello who were known to English officials. One was a Flemish merchant from Ypres, but it appears more likely that Archbishop Giffard was referring to another John de Castello, who was a German knight and a pensioner of the king of England. *CLR, 1267-72*, pp. 35, 60, 72. The German knight had served as envoy from John de Avesnes, Countess Margaret's younger son, and had been entrusted with a diplomatic mission to Germany for King Henry. *Index to the Ancient Correspondence of the Chancery and Exchequer*, Lists and Indexes of the Public Record Office, Suplementary Series, no. 15, 2 vols. (1902; repr. New York, 1969), 1: 232, *CLR, 1251-60*, p. 345. The latter Castello was in England in 1271 seeking a settlement for the arrears of his own pension. *CPS, 1266-72*, p. 582.

34. *CPR, 1266-72*, p. 520; *De antiquis legibus*, pp. 137-140.

35. Rotuli Hundredorum temp. Henr. III et Edw. I in turr' Lond' et curia receptae scaccarii West. asservati, ed. W. Illingworth, 2 vols. (London, 1812-18), 1:403, 407, 409-425; 430-31.

36. Ibid., 1:403.

37. As early as May 1, 1272, the abbot of Newminster, the prior of Alvingham, and four others received letters patent acknowledging that they had surrendered to the "use of merchants of England" who had sustained losses in Flanders, money that they owed Flemish merchants. *CPR, 1266-72*, p. 648.

38. *Close Rolls, Henry III, 1268-72*, p. 439 (hereafter cited as *CR*).

39. *CPR, 1266-72*, p. 625; Lloyd, *Wood Trade*, p. 30.

40. *CCR, 1272-79*, p. 338.

41. *CPR, 1266-72*, pp. 593-95; *De antiquis legibus*, p. 127. Nicholas de Lyuns was one of the king's creditors and enjoyed the special protection of Queen Eleanor and of Walter Giffard, archbishop of York. *CPR, 1266-72*, pp. 393, 395, 462, 529, 531.

42. *CPR, 1266-72*, pp. 553-57.

43. Ibid., 698-99.

44. *CPR, 1272-81*, pp. 13-27; *De antiquis legibus*, pp. 144-45.

45. The count of Ponthieu, the lord of Abbeville, had requested King Henry to establish a staple in his town. *CCR, 1272-79*, p. 32. However, testimony preserved in the *Hundred Rolls* indicates that English merchants later took their wool to St. Omer. *Rotuli Hundredorum*, 1: 276, 290, 414. Lloyd, *Wool Trade*, pp. 36, 101.

46. Collection of the "new aid" was first farmed to an anonymous Florentine syndicate in 1267. *De antiquis legibus*, p.109. In 1270 the farm was granted to a Florentine consortium headed by Deutayutus Willelmi, a denizen of London, and Hugh Pape. *CPR, 1266-72*, p. 442. However, Prince Edward ordered the revocation of this grant in September 1270 and assigned the collection of the custom to a Cahorsin syndicate organized by Peter and William Bernaldi. Ibid., p. 463. In December 1271 Walter Giffard, archbishop of York, Roger Mortimer, and Robert Burnell, acting for the council of regents again granted the farm of the "new aid" to Willelmi and Pape until Christmas 1272. Ibid., p. 617.

47. Schaube, "Die Woolausfuhr Englands," pp. 39-72; 159-85.

48. Lloyd, *Wool Trade*, pp. 32-33, 40-59; von Roon-Basserman, "Die Handelsperre Englands gegen Flandern," pp. 71-82.

49. Lloyd, *Wool Trade*, pp. 33, 50. For the effect of the scab see N. Denholm-Young, *Seignorial Administration in England* (1937; repr., London, 1963), pp. 60-62.

50. Jurors in Lincolnshire testified that William de Lenn and several other burgesses of Louth Park bought and shipped 200 sacks of wool to Flanders. *Rotuli Hundredorum*, 1:338, 375. No license was issued to William or his associates. In August 1276 William

and fifteen of his associates obtained royal pardons for violating the embargo. *CPR, 1272-81*, p. 159. For other examples of illegal exports see *Rotuli Hundredorum*, 1: 162, 249, 321, 398, et passim.

51. Lloyd, *Wool Trade*, pp. 56-59; P.R.O. Miscellaneous Inquisitions, C145/211,7; P.R.O. Chancery Miscellanea, C47/29/File 1,5; C47/29/File 1, 4.

52. *Rotuli Hundredorum*, 1: 123, 328, 385.

53. Ibid., 1:357, 375. Jean Boinebroke, the great Douai capitalist, also referred to the export duty as a "maletote" in the statement enumerating his losses in England during the conflict. Georges Espinas, *Sire Jehan Boinebroke Patricien et Drapier Douaisien* (Lille, 1933), p. 9. It is significant, perhaps, that Magna Carta contained a provision guaranteeing all merchants the right to leave England, or come to England, and to buy and sell under "right and ancient customs" without any evil exactions (*malis toltis*—maltotes). Carl Stephenson and Frederick George Marcham, eds., *Sources of English Constitutional History* (New York, 1937), p. 121 and nn.

54. *Rotuli Hundredorum*, 1:249, 293, 381, 414; *CPR, 1272-79*, p. 50; *CCR, 1272-79*, p. 119.

55. *Rotuli Hundredorum*, 1:19, 178, 183, 225, 249, 321, 333, 370, 375, 378; 2:10, 209.

56. *CPR, 1266-72*, p. 706.

57. *CPR, 1266-72*, pp. 209, 462, 489, 523, 526, 558-59, 571, 659; *CPR, 1272-81*, p. 55.

58. *De antiquis legibus*, pp. 138-39, 144; *CPR, 1266-72*, pp. 687-88.

59. *Rotuli Hundredorum*, 1:321, 370, 375.

60. Ibid., 1:164, 343, 370.

61. Ibid., 1:105, 321; *CPR, 1272-81*, p. 112.

62. *Rotuli Hundredorum*, 1:225.

63. Ibid., 2:171.

64. Charles Gross, *The Gild Merchant*, 2 vols. (1890; repr., Oxford, 1964), 1:109.

65. *CPR, 1266-72*, pp. 548-49. Officials at Newcastle seized ninety-two sacks of wool belonging to Boinebroke. This wool was subsequently sold to a syndicate of English merchants that included Thomas of Basings of London. Thomas and his associates shipped the wool to the French port of Abbeville where it was arrested on Boinebroke's complaint and held for a time. Since the seizure in Abbeville took place in 1273, it would appear that Boinebroke had bought and lost the wool sometime after the initial arrests of 1270. *CR, 1268-72*, p. 32. Boinebroke later claimed that the loss in Newcastle totaled ninety-three sacks and two pokes. Epinas, *Sire Jehan Boinebroke*, p. 9.

66. *Rotuli Hundredorum*, 1:118, 123.

67. *De antiquis legibus*, p. 159.

68. Lloyd, *Wool Trade*, pp. 53-54. Power, *Wool Trade*, pp. 41-48.

69. Evidence of agency relationships between English merchants who traded in Flanders and their Flemish hosts is tenuous, but certainly suggestive of cooperative commercial activity. For example, in 1272 William Golding of Lynn paid Master William de la Corner £18 that he owed to Walter de Posterne of Bruges, who had been Golding's Flemish host in 1270. E 163/5/17; *CPR, 1266-72*, p. 697. Also Richard Cersent of Desford had sold fourteen sacks of wool in 1270 to Jean de Alverdon, one of the burgesses of Bruges who was a host for English merchants. E 163/5/17.

70. Espinas, *Sire Jehan Boinebroke*, p. 9.

71. *Rotuli Hundredorum*, 1:321, 398. Peter de Trois stood as a pledge for an export license that Marota received in 1271. *CPR, 1266-72*, p. 595.

72. *Rotuli Hundredorum*, 1:105.

73. Ibid., 1:321, 416-17.

74. *De antiquis legibus*, pp. 159-60.

75. Ibid., p. 161; *CPR, 1272-81*, p. 12.

76. *De antiquis legibus*, pp. 159-60. Local officials appear to have enforced the new

orders with unaccustomed vigor. Peter Bonyn of Bruges, who had previously been granted immunity from the reprisals and enjoyed the royal license to trade in England, complained that officials had arrested his goods before Christmas, 1273, the date by which he and other privileged Flemings were to have left the country. The government promptly ordered the local officials involved to restore to Peter whatever they had taken from him. *CPR, 1272-81*, p. 55.

77. *CPR, 1272-81*, p. 46.

78. Ibid., p. 50; Kaeuper, *Bankers to the Crown*, pp. 146-47.

79. *Rotuli Hundredorum*, 1: 321, ff. For fines for violations of the embargo later paid by Italian companies see P.R.O., Exchequer, Accounts Various, E 101/126/1. Luke de Lucca and the Society of the Riccardi were fined £1498 5 s. but this fine was pardoned by King Edward. *CCR, 1272-79*, pp. 532-33; *CPR, 1272-81*, p. 125.

80. *De antiquis legibus*, p. 163; E. Varenburgh, *Relations Diplomatiques entre Flandre et L'Angleterre* (Brussels, 1874), p. 139.

81. *De antiquis legibus*, p. 163; *Foedera*, 1: pt. 2, p. 140; Varenburgh, *Relationes Diplomatiques*, pp. 139-40.

82. *CPR, 1272-81*, p. 60; *Foedera*, 1:pt. 2, p. 140.

83. *Foedera*, 1:pt. 2, p. 140.

84. *CPR, 1272-81*, p. 48.

85. Ibid., pp. 91-92; *Foedera*, 1:pt. 2, p. 147.

86. *CPR, 1272-81*, pp. 115, 128.

87. Ibid.

88. M. Cam, *The Hundred and the Hundred Rolls, an Outline of Local Government in Medieval England* (New York, 1960), pp. 34-46: *Rotuli Hundredorum*, 1:321, 370, 375, et passim.

89. E 101/126/1; *CCR, 1272-79*, pp. 522-23; *CPR, 1272-81*, pp. 91-93, 125.

90. *CPR, 1272-81*, p. 108.

91. *CCR, 1272-79*, p. 286.

92. *Rotuli Hundredorum*, 1:338, 375; *CPR, 1272-79*, p. 159.

93. *CPR, 1272-81*, pp. 107, 127.

94. Ibid., pp. 106, 112.

95. Poncius de Mora, a wine merchant, rose to prominence in the late 1260's when he received the offices of purveyor of the kings' wines, gauger of wines, chamberlain of London, and ulnar of imported cloth. *CPR, 1266-72*, pp. 231, 321, 422, 670, 675, 715.

96. *CPR, 1272-81*, p. 60.

97. As late as 1282 three Irish merchants who professed that they had not heard about the proceeding in 1274 and 1275 came forward to make claims for losses totaling more than £900. SC 1/12/23.

98. *Select Cases Concerning the Law Merchant*, 2:xxxii-xxxiii and n., 18-25; Powicke, *Thirteenth Century*, pp. 623-26; *CPR, 1272-81*, p. 86. Lovel and Bek appointed two clerks, John of Yarmouth and Alan of Bissopesthrop (who was later replaced by John de Bosco), to actually receive and keep safe money raised from the liquidation of Flemish debts and other assets until the money could be apportioned among the English claimants. *CPR, 1272-81*, pp. 89, 95.

99. *CCR, 1272—1279*, pp. 198—99. E 163/5/17 m. 1-end. For some reason the claim of at least one English merchant who had already received compensation from Flemish property seized in England was not included in these totals. Simon the Draper, a Winchester wool merchant, said that he had lost sixteen sacks of wool in the Flemish arrests, and at the order of King Henry III he had received compensation from Flemish-owned merchandise arrested at Southampton. *CCR, 1272-79*, pp. 495-96. No claim from Simon the Draper is included in the document prepared by Fulk Lovel, John Bek, and the eight merchant tellers.

100. Varenburgh, *Relationes Diplomatiques*, pp. 141-44; *CPR, 1272-81*, p. 247.

101. Kaeuper, *Bankers to the Crown*, pp. 144-51; Lloyd, *Wool Trade*, p. 247.
102. *CCR, 1272-79*, p. 423.
103. Ibid., p. 337.
104. *CPR, 1272-81*, p. 247.
105. *Calendar of Various Chancery Rolls, 1277-1326* (London, 1912), pp. 1-16.
106. SC 1/11/61.
107. *Calendar of Various Chancery Rolls, 1277-1326*, p. 16.
108. *CPR, 1272-81*, p. 247.
109. Ibid., p. 330.
110. Ibid., p. 400.
111. The balance of the indemnity had been increased by claims from merchants who professed that they had not been informed of the proceedings in 1274-1275. SC 1/12/23; P.R.O. King's Remembrancer Memoranda Rolls, E 159/59/m. 23.

Canonists and Law Clerks

CHARLES E. LEWIS

1. Basic to all modern canonistic study is Stephen Kuttner, *Repertorium der Kanonistik (1140-1234), Padromus corporis glossarum I*, Studi e testi (Vatican, 1937). See also the bibliographical notes in Stephen Kuttner and Eleanor Rathbone, "Anglo-Norman Canonists of the Twelfth Century: An Introductory Study," *Traditio* 7 (1949-51), 279-80, notes 1, 2, 4; Kuttner, "Bernardus Compostellanus Antiquus," *Traditio* 1 (1943), notes, passim. The Maitland Lectures of Dr. Walter Ullman, *Medieval Papalism: the Political Theories of Medieval Canonists* (London, 1949), should be consulted, but with caution in view of the critique of Professor Alfons M. Stickler in *Traditio* 7 (1949-51), 450-63. The "Bulletin of the Institute of Medieval Canon Law [Yale]" found in recent volumes of *Traditio* is the outstanding showplace for European and American canonical researches.
2. H. Bresslau, *Handbuch der Urkundenlehre*, 2nd ed. (1912-13), and the references cited in Dahlmann-Waitz, *Quellenkunde der deutschen Geschichte*, 9th ed. (1931), p. 30.
3. Christopher R. Cheney, *English Bishops' Chanceries, 1100-1250* (Manchester, 1950), especially pp. 1-12.
4. "The 'Familia' of Archbishop Stephen Langton," *English Historical Review* 48 (1933), 529-53; *Acta Stephani Langton*, Canterbury and York Society 50 (Oxford, 1950); "Episcopal Acta in Mediaeval Capitular Archives," *Bulletin of the Institute of Historical Research* 9 (1931-32), 145-53.
5. This list is based on an as yet incomplete collection of *acta*. Not included are those clerks whose names appear only in *acta* without witness lists, thus making it difficult to place them with certainty in any category. Professor Cheney (*Chanceries*, p. 11) counted thirty-eight clerks, of whom twenty-four are masters. For a comparison with an earlier archbishop's chancery, see Avrom Saltman, *Theobald, Archbishop of Canterbury, 1139-1161* (London, 1956), pp. 214-16, where there are listed fifty-five "clerks and chaplains" of whom but thirteen are masters.
6. Henry of Châtillon, archdeacon of Canterbury; Master Richard, chancellor of the archbishop; Master Honorius, archdeacon of Richmond; and Peter of Blois, archdeacon of Bath. Evidence concerning the positions of these and other officials in the household will be presented in my essay "The Household of Archbishop Hubert Walter." The term "official" is used here in the general, rather than the more specific, sense indicated by the term *officialis*.

7. A. B. Emden, *Biographical Register of the University of Oxford to A. D. 1500,* 2 vols. (Oxford, 1957-59); Cheney, *Chanceries,* ch. 1; Kuttner and Rathbone, "Anglo-Norman Canonists," pp. 179-358. A handy guide to the references, with a valuable collation with the London *Quaestiones* (British Museum MS Royal 9 E VII, fos. 191ᵛ-198ᵛ), is to be found in James A. Brundage, "The Crusade of Richard I: Two Canonical Quaestiones," *Speculum 38 (1963), 477 n.13.* For evidence that Master Richard de Mores (*Ricardus Anglicus*) should be added to Brundage's and Emden's lists, see my remarks in this paper, below.

8. F. J. West, *The Justiciarship in England, 1066-1232* (Cambridge, 1966), pp. 78-96. A more complete study of Hubert's career prior to 1198 is contained in C. E. Lewis, "The Justiciarship of Archbishop Hubert Walter, 1194-1198" (Ph.D. dissertation, Mississippi State University, 1964).

9. These clerks will be discussed in "The Household of Hubert Walter." Some are mentioned by Cheney, *Chanceries,* pp. 17-18. The separation of chanceries postulated by Mr. H. G. Richardson, *Memoranda Roll 1 John,* Pipe Roll Society (1943), p. 1xxxiv, is most unlikely; note the evidence of Cheney, *Chanceries,* p. 19 n.1.

10. Roger of Hovden, *Chronica,* ed. W. Stubbs, 4 vols., Rolls Series (London, 1868-71), 4:48; Gervase of Canterbury, *Opera Historica,* ed. W. Stubbs, 2 vols., Rolls Series (London, 1879-80), 1:572; Thomas Rymer, ed., *Foedera, Conventiones, Litterae, etc.,* 4 vols., new ed. (London, 1816-69), 1:71.

11. *Epistolae Cantuarienses,* vol. 2 of *Chronicles and Memorials of the Reign of Richard I,* ed. W. Stubbs, 2 vols., Rolls Series (London, 1864-65), 2:391-94, 399-400.

12. That the archbishop had been keeping abreast of developments in Rome is demonstrated by his letter of June 1198 to his suffragans. *Epp. Cant.,* pp. 395-96.

13. Gerald of Wales, *Opera,* ed. J. S. Brewer et al., 8 vols., Rolls Series (London, 1861-91), 3:228.

14. Kuttner and Rathbone, "Anglo-Norman Canonists," pp. 317, 320, and App. D (pp. 347-53). The pertinent MSS are Gonville and Caius College, Cambridge, MS 676 (283), and British Museum MS Royal 9 E VII. The references to the *Quaestiones* are given by Brundage as noted above, n.7. It is notable that the latter MS originally was found in the archives of St. Augustine's, Canterbury. Moreover, the identification of John of Tynemouth with the "Jo. de Ti." of the Caius glosses was made independently by Professor Cheney (*Chanceries,* p. 13), by Dr. Kuttner, and by Dr. J. C. Russell (Kuttner and Rathbone, "Anglo-Norman Canonists," p. 317 n.4). See also Emden, *Biographical Register,* 3:1704, 1923.

15. Kuttner and Rathbone, "Anglo-Norman Canonists," p. 320 n.47; Kuttner, *Repertorium,* pp. 25, 251; Leipzig University MS 1242, cited by Kuttner in *Traditio* 4 (1948), 349 n.40.

16. Cheney, *Chanceries,* pp. 12-14; Kuttner and Rathbone, "Anglo-Norman Canonists," pp. 324-27 et passim.

17. I have followed the usual practice in the style of Simon's name. However, Emden, *Biographical Register,* 3:1704, is quite correct in noting that the canonist may have come either from Southwell, Nottinghamshire, or Sywell, Northamptonshire.

18. Caius and Gonville glosses, fo. 198, printed in Kuttner and Rathbone, "Anglo-Norman Canonists," pp. 352-53 (App. D): "Hoc capitulum (*Antiqui et sanctissimi patris*) iactat S'. de S'. se docuisse bononie. Est enim aliquantulum difficile, set Io.de Ti. intelligit de martio qui commisit adulterium incestuosum manifestum insidians personis tantum, uel etiam matrimonio, set consanguinitate longinqua."

19. Ibid., p. 348 (fo. 167): "Hinc arg(uit) S. de S. mandatum pape posse durare mortuo papa etiam se integra, et ita persuasit Precentori parisiensi."

20. Cheney, *Chanceries,* pp. 13, 79 n.2.

21. Kuttner and Rathbone, "Anglo-Norman Canonists," pp. 320-21, referring to all the canonists in the "Oxford group."

22. References for Lincoln are cited by Cheney, *Chanceries,* pp. 13, 79 n.2.

23. Simon witnessed many of the charters of Hubert's legatine period, e.g., British Museum Additional Charter 33596; Archives Office, Maidstone, Kent, Cartulary of Leeds Priory, fo. 7; Lambeth Palace MS 241 (Dover Cartulary) fo. 8. Lichfield *Magnum Registrum Album*, William Salt Archaeological Society (1924), no. 252, has been dated 1193 by the editor, H. E. Savage, and the date was accepted by Kuttner and Rathbone, "Anglo-Norman Canonists," p. 326. However, Savage's proof is unconvincing, especially when no. 753, a legatine charter (1195-1198, is taken into account. Both charters were for Bishop Hugh of Coventry (d. March 27 1198). The absence of the legatine title in no. 252 was probably an accidental omission of the cartulary copyist. Cf. Cheney, *Chanceries*, pp. 13, 35 n.3.

24. *Epp. Cant.*, p. 407. The messengers found the archbishop at Lambeth 3, May 1, 1198, and the colloquy at which appeals were prepared was held the next morning, June 1.

25. Kuttner and Rathbone, "Anglo-Norman Canonists," p. 326. The sources cited in their note 44 seem to make it plain that Simon was in England. Cheney, *Chanceries*, p. 13 used the same sources and found no indication of activities in Rome. A Leeds charter witnessed by Simon (Maidstone Archives Office, Cartulary of Leeds Priory, fo. 8) can be assigned to early 1198 by the witness of Geoffrey of Buckland as archdeacon of Norfolk and Simon fitz Robert, who became archdeacon of Wells in that year.

26. Kuttner and Rathbone, "Anglo-Norman Canonists," p. 326, citing his report to Pope Innocent (Potthast, *Regesta*, 395).

27. *The Registrum Antiquissium of the Cathedral Church of Lincoln*, ed. C. W. Foster and Kathleen Major, Lincoln Record Society, 7 vols. (1931-53), 4: no. 1385 (witness to a quitclaim document, ca. 1200).

28. Evidence for this statement will be given in my forthcoming note, "Ricardus Anglicus: A 'Familiaris' of Archbishop Hubert Walter." [This note was subsequently published in *Traditio* 22 (1966), pp. 469-71.]

29. Gerald of Wales, *Opera*, 3:203. On this occasion Simon was accompanied "cum clericorum caterva."

30. Ibid., 3:203, 216-17.

31. Cheney, *Chanceries*, p. 14; Kuttner and Rathbone, "Anglo-Norman Canonists," p. 325; Emden, *Biographical Register*, 3:1923.

32. *Select Documents of the English Lands of the Abbey of Bec*, ed. Marjorie Chibnall, Camden Society, 3rd ser. (1951), pp. 5, 13, 21; F. A. Cazel, "Norman and Wessex Charters of the Roumare Family," in *Medieval Miscellany for Doris Mary Stenton*, Pipe Roll Society (1960), p. 88. Dr. Cazel gives an account of this case, ibid., pp. 83-84, where he suggests that the several documents of the settlement "all were done between April and June when the archbishop came to England for the accession of the new king." Two of the Bec documents are originals (Archives de l'Eure, H.11), both witnessed by John of Tynemouth and dated with the phrase, "Actum anno gratie M° C° XC° IX° in presencia . . ." (followed by names of witnesses), revealing that the signatories were, in fact, the board of arbitration.

33. Cheney, *Chanceries*, p. 13; Kuttner and Rathbone, "Anglo-Norman Canonists," p. 325. John may have written a history of St. Frideswide's, Oxford: Dugdale, *Monasticon Anglicanum*, 2:143, cites a reference thus, "Ex Historia MS Johannis Tinemuthensis in Bibliotheca Bodleiana, lib. xvii. cap. 210." I have been unable to trace this document.

34. The document of 1188 cited by Cheney (*Chanceries*, n.33) was a confirmation of a decision by judges-delegate of the bishop of Lincoln. A Lincoln charter which lists John among the canons might date from as early as 1195, according to Canon Foster and Miss Major, *Registrum Antiquiss. Lincs.*, 3:no. 687 and note. Cf. Cheney, *Chanceries*, p. 14.

35. Kuttner and Rathbone, "Anglo-Norman Canonists," p. 317 passim.

36. Ibid., App. D passim.

37. Gerald of Wales, *Opera*, 3:203, 216, 218.

38. Ibid., 3:265-66, 273-74, 277, 281, 298, 323.

39. Ibid., 3:291-97, 307; Cheney, *Chanceries*, p. 14. The full account of the episode was given by J. S. Brewer in his preface to Gerald of Wales, *Opera*, 1:1xxxii-1xxxiv.

40. Kuttner and Rathbone, "Anglo-Norman Canonists," p. 305, estimate that Honorius was at Oxford ca. 1185-95 and cite a document that proves he was there in 1192.

41. Ibid., pp. 306-08, and, for other sources, p. 305 n.5.

42. Migne, *Patrologia Latina*, 214:1023. Pope Innocent, in a letter dated June 1, 1202, wrote that "venerabilis frater noster, Cantuariensis archiepiscopus, tunc apostolicae sedis legatus in Anglia, communicato multorum coepiscoporum et aliorum prudentium virorum consilio, pronuntiavit te [Honorio] hujusmodi sententia non teneri, sicut rescripto litterarum ipsius legati ostendere satagebas." The times of Honorius' appointment and the termination of Hubert's legatine commission establish that the archbishop took a hand in the case in 1198.

43. Ibid., 214:1026-29; Cheney, *Chanceries*, p. 12.

44. *Chronicon Abbatiae de Evesham*, ed. W. D. Macray, Rolls Series (London, 1863), p. 126.

45. Kuttner, "Bernardus Compostellanus Antiqua," p. 323 n.18. Kuttner and Rathbone, "Anglo-Norman Canonists," p. 304. See ibid., pp. 309-16, for an analysis of the treatise.

46. *Acta Stephani Langton*, p. 50. The *actum* was cited by Kuttner and Rathbone "Anglo-Norman Canonists," p. 338 n.76, without drawing the conclusion reached here. Hubert's charter appears in an original *inspeximus* by Langton, dated 1231-1215 by Miss Major. Since several of Hubert's clerks were serving in Langton's *familia* at that time (*English Historical Review* 48:530-31, adding the name of Roger of Pont-Audemer), the accuracy of the *inspeximus* copy may be assumed.

47. The identification was first made by Professor Josiah Russell based on the incipit of Dublin, Trinity College MS 275: "Ric. de mores Summa de decreta Gratiani." *Dictionary of Writers of Thirteenth Century England* (London, 1933), pp. 111-13. Kuttner and Rathbone, "Anglo-Norman Canonists," pp. 329-33, made the identification more positive through textual criticism. For other masters with whom Ricardus Anglicus has been confused, see Russell's *Dictionary of Writers*.

48. Kuttner and Rathbone, "Anglo-Norman Canonists," p. 338; S. Kuttner, "Ricardus Anglicus (Richard de Mores ou de Morins)," *Dictionnaire de droit canonique* (1960), 7:676-81.

49. Kuttner and Rathbone, "Anglo-Norman Canonists," p. 291; Kuttner, *Repertorium*, pp. 222 ff., 417 ff.; Kuttner, "Bernardus Compostellanus Antiquus," pp. 299, 312, 321n. 4, 323-24 notes; Russell, *Dictionary*, pp. 111-12. Master Richard later wrote the greater part of the Dunstable Annals in *Annales Monastici*, ed. H. R. Luard, Rolls Series, 5 vols. (London, 1864-69), 3:3-158.

50. Dr. Kuttner graciously transmitted this information to me [in] a recent letter. For a more complete discussion of Richard's service as a *familiaris*, see my forthcoming note. (See n. 28 above.)

51. Gerald of Wales, *Opera*, 3:292.

52. Ibid., 3:218. Master William sat as one of the judges of the commission at Brackley (1202), but Simon and John were specified as the archbishop's proctors. In 1199, William was one of a group sent by Hubert to suspend contumacious clerks serving the Lambeth chapel (*Epp. Cant.*, p. 467).

53. Lambeth Palace MS 242, fo. 59b. I can date the inquisition 1193-1195. Later, Master William was a royal official (Cheney, *Chanceries*, p. 17).

54. British Museum, Harleian Charter 43 G 25 (1198-1204); Additional Charter 33596 (1195-1198). The dates assigned these charters are my own. See also, Kuttner, *Repertorium*, p. 221, and Cheney, *Chanceries*, p. 11).

55. *Acta Stephani Langton,* pp. xxxvii, 19, 47; Kuttner and Rathbone, "Anglo-Norman Canonists," p. 320.

56. In addition to the references cited by Kuttner and Rathbone, "Anglo-Norman Canonists," p. 320 n. 43, see Canterbury Cathedral Library Register A, fo. 147; *Cartulary of St. Gregory's, Canterbury,* ed. Audrey M. Woodcock, Camden Society, 3rd ser. (1956), no. 8; British Museum Harleian Charter 84 C. 42; *Monasticon Anglicanum,* 6:565 (reprinted in *Acta Stephani* Langton, pp. 45-47). Cf. S. Kuttner, "Pierre de Roissy and Robert of Flamborough," *Traditio* 2 (1944), 494 n.9; Russell, *Dictionary,* p. 59; and Emden, *Biographical Register,* 2:1037.

57. Lambeth Palace MS 241, fo. 8; MS 1212, fo. 118; Mansi, *Concilia,* 22:666. These documents place Master William's association with the archbishop in the period 1195-1198. For many cases of "Providees and Italians in English benefices," see C. R. Cheney, *From Becket to Langton* (Manchester, 1956), pp. 178-81.

58. Gervase of Canterbury, *Opera,* 2:406.

59. Note that this claim has been made for the household of Archbishop Theobald.

60. P. Gerbenzon, "Bertram of Metz the Author of 'Elegantius in jure diuino' (*Summa Coloniensis*)?," *Traditio* 21 (1965), 510-11; Kuttner and Rathbone, "Anglo-Norman Canonists," pp. 296 ff. I hasten to point out that there is no hint that Gerald Pucelle's traffic with the German schismatics had any influence at Oxford or at Canterbury.

61. Cheney, *From Becket to Langton,* p. 41.

The Making of An Archbishop

LEE WYATT

1. Edward Foss, *The Judges of England with Sketches of Their Lives,* 9 vols. (London, 1848-64), 2:78. Dugdale argues that Walter's parents were Henry and Isolda de Gray of Thurrock since Walter's uncle was surnamed John and there would not have been two Johns in the same family in the same generation. This, however, was not unusual, and most existing records indicate that the first lineage is correct. W. H. Dixon, *Fasti Eboracenses: Lives of the Archbishops of York,* ed. J. Raine (London, 1863), p. 280 n. Also Ivor J. Sanders, *English Baronies: A Study of Their Descent, 1086-1327* (Oxford, 1963), p. 36.

2. *Dictionary of National Biography,* ed. Leslie Stephen and Sidney Lee, 21 vols. (London, 1937-38), 8:651.

3. Dixon, *Fasti Eboracenses,* pp. 280-81.

4. *The Great Roll of the Pipe,* 4 John, Pipe Roll Society (London, 1937), p. 216 (hereafter cited as *Pipe Roll*): Roger of Wendover, *Flores Historiarum ab Anno Domini MCLIV Annoque Henrici Anglorum Regis Secundi Primo,* ed. Henry G. Hewlett, 3 vols., Rolls Series (London, 1886-89), 2:56; Radulphus de Coggeshall, *Chronicon Anglicanum,* ed. J. Stevenson, Rolls Series (London, 1875), p. 43; William Dugdale, *Monasticon Anglicanum,* 6 vols. (London, 1817-30), 4:2.

5. Sidney Painter, *The Reign of King John* (Baltimore, 1949), p. 155.

6. Ibid.

7. *Foedera, Conventiones, Litterae,* ed. Thomas Rymer, 10 vols. (The Hague, 1739-45), 1:93; T. F. Tout, *Chapters in the Administrative History of Medieval England,* 6 vols. (Manchester, 1937), 1:185.

8. Painter, *King John,* pp. 64-65.

9. Ibid., pp. 79-80.

10. J. Solloway, "Walter de Gray," *York Minster Historical Tracts* 11 (London,

1927), pp. 1-2; *Calendar Rotulorum Patentium in Turri Londinensi*, Record Commission (London, 1802), p. 81 (hereafter cited as *Cal. Rot. Pat.*); Francis Blomefield, *An Essay towards a Topographical History of the County of Norfolk*, 11 vols. (London, 1805-10), 2:417.

11.   *Selected Letters of Innocent III Concerning England*, ed. C. R. Cheney and W. H. Semple (New York, 1953), pp. 115-16 and nn.

12.   *Cal. Rot. Pat.*, p. 103; *Pipe Rolls, 12 John*, p. 177; *Letters of Innocent III*, p. 125n.

13.   Painter, *King John*, p. 65. Pandulph is said to have set aside the elections of Gray and Prior Josbert. *Letters of Innocent III*, p. 125n.

14.   *Letters of Innocent III*, p. 123 and n.

15.   Painter, *King John*, pp. 184-85.

16.   Rymer, *Foedera*, 1:111; *Pipe Roll, 16 John*, p. 145; *Rotuli Literarum Clausarum*, ed. Thomas Hardy, 2 vols., Record Commission (London, 1833-44), 1:145, 156, 160, 206 (hereafter cited as *Rot. Lit. Claus*).

17.   *Rot. Lit. Claus.*, 1:160, 162.

18.   *Annals of Worcester* in vol. 4 of *Annales Monastici*, ed. H. R. Luard, 5 vols., Rolls Series (London, 1864-69), p. 403; *The Victoria History of the County of Worcester*, ed. J. W. Willis-Bund and William Page, 4 vols. (London, 1906), 2:98-99 (hereafter cited as *VCH, Worcester*).

19.   Dugdale, *Monasticon Anglicanum*, 1:573.

20.   *VCH, Worcester*, 3:312; *The Cartulary of Worcester Cathedral Priory Register I* ed. R. R. Darlington, Pipe Roll Society (London, 1968), pp. 57, 121-22.

21.   *Cartulary of Worcester*, p. 100n.

22.   *Pipe Roll, 16 John*, p. 156. No reason is given for his resignation. One explanation could be that he was leaving the realm at a time when the king was in the midst of the difficult and abrasive business of raising a feudal army for an overseas campaign, and John may not have wanted anyone to use the absence of the chancellor as an excuse to question the summonses issued by Peter des Roches. According to Wendover, Walter de Gray was still chancellor in the summer of 1215. Wendover, *Flores Historiarum*, 2:136.

23.   Wendover, *Flores Historiarum*, 2:118-19, 136.

24.   Ibid., pp. 146-48; Painter, *King John*, pp. 360-61.

25.   Painter, *King John*, p. 362.

26.   Gervase of Canterbury, *Opera Historica*, ed. William Stubbs, 2 vols., Rolls Series (London, 1879-80), 2:101-03; *Patrologia cursus completus, Series Latina*, ed. Jacques Paul Migne, 221 vols. (Paris 1844-82), 215: 1528-79.

27.   *Letters of Innocent III*, pp. 166-67 and nn.

28.   *Rot. Lit. Pat.*, p. 109; *Letters of Innocent III*, p. 211 n.3.

29.   *Rotuli Chartarum in Turri Londinensi asservati, 1199-1216*, ed. T. D. Hardy, (London, 1837), p. 207; *Letters of Innocent III*, p. 211 n.4; Painter assumed that the letter referred to Simon Langton. Painter, *King John*, p. 200.

30.   *Letters of Innocent III*, p. 211 n.4; *Rot. Lit. Pat.*, pp. 141, 143.

31.   Wendover, *Flores Historiarum*, 2:153.

32.   Frederick Maurice Powicke, *Stephen Langton* (Oxford, 1928), p. 134.

33.   Painter, *King John*, p. 200; *Letters of Innocent III*, p. 211.

34.   Wendover, *Flores Historiarum*, 2:153.

35.   It is significant that Innocent quashed the election of Simon Langton only four days before he condemned the Great Charter, whose principal architect was Stephen Langton, archbishop of Canterbury. *Letters of Innocent III*, pp. 210-15.

36.   Ibid., pp. 210-11.

37.   Wendover, *Flores Historiarum*, 2:159-60. Pope Innocent confirmed the legate Pandulph's suspension of Stephen Langton on November 4, 1215. *Letters of Innocent III*, p. 220.

38. Wendover, *Flores Historiarum*, 2:160-61; *The Register and Rolls of Walter de Gray, Lord Archbishop of York*, ed. James Raine, Surtees Society 56 (1872), p. xxxvii; Raine, *Fasti Eboracenses*, p. 283n.

39. William F. Lunt, *Financial Relations of the Papacy with England to 1327* (Cambridge, Mass., 1939), p. 462.

40. *Rot. Lit. Claus.*, 2:248; *Register and Rolls of Walter de Gray*, p. xxxvii.

Peter Chaceporc

JOHN E. DAVIS

1. F. M. Powicke, *King Henry III and the Lord Edward: The Community of the Realm in the Thirteenth Century*, 2 vols. (Oxford, 1947), 1:296n. *Calendar of Patent Rolls, 1232-47*, p. 502 (hereafter cited as *CPR*).

2. W. Dugdale, *Monasticon Anglicanum*, 6 vols. in 8 parts (London, 1817-30), 6:498. Dugdale incorrectly transcribed from the charter rolls the name of the uncle as Hugh de Vynon. He should have read Hugh de Vyvon. See P.R.O., Charter Rolls, C 53/46A/m. 4.

3. T. F. Tout, *Chapters in the Administrative History of Medieval England*, 6 vols. (Manchester, 1920-33), 6: passim.

4. Ibid., 1:191-95.

5. Ibid., 1:260-78.

6. John E. Davis, "The Wardrobe of Henry III of England, 1234-1272" (Ph.D. dissertation, Mississippi State University, 1970), passim.

7. Ibid.

8. *CPR, 1232-47*, pp. 275, 285, 287, 312, 314, 367, 452, 457.

9. Ibid., p. 268. *Calendar of Liberate Rolls, 1240-45*, p. 95 (hereafter cited as *CLR*); F. M. Powicke, *The Thirteenth Century* (Oxford, 1962), pp. 102-03.

10. *CPR, 1232-47*, pp. 348, 362.

11. Ibid., pp., 401-02. *Foedera, Conventiones, Litterae et cuiuscunque*, ed. Thomas Rymer, 10 vols. (The Hague, 1739-45), 1:pt. 1, p. 146.

12. *CPR, 1232-47*, p. 481. Isabella of Angoulême died in 1246. James's ancestors had been counts of Provence, and he was the titular overlord of Carcassonne and Bziers and still held Montpellier and many other fiefs in southern France. Powicke, *Thirteenth Century*, pp. 99-103.

13. *CPR, 1247-58*, p. 52. Henry took the cross in March 1250. Powicke, *Thirteenth Century*, p. 106.

14. Aymer was elected bishop of Winchester on November 4, 1250. Harold S. Snellgrove, *The Lusignans in England, 1247-1258* (Albuquerque, 1950), p. 59. Peter Chaceporc received his commission to treat with the pope about the postulation to Winchester in November 1251. *CLR, 1245-51*, p. 313.

15. Matthew Paris, *Chronica Majora*, ed. H. R. Luard, 7 vols., Rolls Series (London, 1872-83), 5:335. King Louis IX was absent on crusade in Syria and Egypt.

16. Snellgrove, *Lusignans*, pp. 58-59.

17. *Close Rolls, 1251-53*, pp. 203-05 (hereafter cited as *CR*); Powicke, *Thirteenth Century*, p. 113n.

18. *CPR, 1247-58*, p. 38; *CR, 1247-51*, pp. 157, 325.

19. For King Henry's attempt to secure Durham for his half brother see Snellgrove, *Lusignans*, pp. 57-58.

20. *CPR, 1247-58*, p. 13; *CR, 1247-51* p. 43.

21. *CR, 1242-47*, pp. 328, 419, 523; *CR, 1251—53*, pp. 5, 136, passim.

22.   On March 11, 1241, King Henry granted Peter an annual stipend of 50 marks until he could give him a benefice of equal value or more. *CPR, 1232-47, p. 247*.

23.   *CPR, 1232-47*, pp. 246, 249, 257.

24.   *CR, 1242-47*, p. 59.

25.   *CPR, 1232-47*, pp. 423, 448.

26.   *CR, 1242-47*, p. 290; *CPR, 1247—58*, p. 79.

27.   *CPR, 1247-58*, pp. 226, 241, 251, 366; *Rôles Gascons*, ed. F. Michel and C. Bêmont, 3 vols., Collection de Documents inedits sur l'histoire de France (Paris, 1885-1906), 1:279.

28.   Tout, *Chapters*, 1:266.

29.   Paris, *Chronica Majora*, 5:484.

30.   *CPR, 1247-58*, p. 388.

31.   Dugdale, *Monasticon*, 4:497-98; *Calendar of Charter Rolls, 1226-57*, p. 447; *CR, 1268-72*, p. 370.

Henry III, Westminster Abbey, and the Court School of Illumination

R. KENT LANCASTER

1.   For a brief survey of the extent of Henry's patronage, see my "Artists, Suppliers and Clerks: The Human Factors in the Art Patronage of Henry III," *Journal of the Warburg and Courtauld Institutes* 35 (1972), 81-82.

2.   George Henderson, "Studies in English Manuscript Illumination," *Journal of the Warburg and Courtauld Institutes* 30 (1967), 71-137; 31 (1968), 103-47. See also Peter Brieger, *English Art, 1216-1307* (Oxford, 1957), p. 154; E. W. Tristram, *English Medieval Wall Painting: the Thirteenth Century* (New York, 1950), pp. 155-56, 445, 449; Francis Wormald, "Paintings in Westminster Abbey and Contemporary Paintings," *Proceedings of the British Academy* 34 (1949), 161, 163, 165; W. R. Lethaby, "Medieval Paintings at Westminster Abbey," *Proceedings of the British Academy* 13 (1927), 151.

3.   Henderson, "Studies," 30: 71-75.

4.   Ibid., pp. 84-85, 112-14, 126, 128; Henderson, "Studies," 31:103.

5.   *Calendar of Liberate Rolls*, 6 vols. (London, 1916-66), passim (hereafter cited as *CLR*); *Close Rolls of the Reign of Henry III*, 14 vols. (London, 1902-38), passim (hereafter cited as *CR*). The writs cited are *CR, 1242-47*, p. 201; *CLR, 1226-40*, p. 321.

6.   *CR, 1242-47*, p. 283; *CLR, 1226-40*, p. 288.

7.   See, for examples in a single volume *CLR, 1245-51*, pp. 30, 45, 65, 73, 106, 137, 162, 190, 200, 237, 381.

8.   For Windsor and Woodstock, see *CLR, 1240-45*, p. 47; *CLR, 1245-51*, p. 200; *CR, 1247-51*, pp. 162, 447; *CR, 1256-59*, p. 114. On the orders for Margaret's wedding, see *CLR, 1251-60, pp. 8, 10, 14-15, 28-29, 40, 55*.

9.   Tristram, *Wall Painting*, pp. 94, 448, 461; *CR, 1251-53*, p. 57.

10.   *CR, 1251-53*, p. 407.

11.   *CR, 1242-47*, pp. 430, 465; *CR, 1247-51*, p. 521; *CR, 1251-53*, p. 57. Dungan's career can be traced through the indices of the Close, Liberate, and Patent Rolls and in documents from St. Paul's, London, where he was a canon. See W. Sparrow Simpson, ed. *Documents Illustrating the History of St. Paul's Cathedral*, Camden Society, n. s. (London, 1880), pp. 42, 97-98.

12.   For examples of their purchases, see *CLR, 1251-60*, pp. 54, 108, 112, 121.

13. *CR, 1242-47*, pp. 153, 201, 331; *CR, 1247-51*, pp. 70, 238, 422; *CR, 1254-56*, pp. 59, 238, 314; *CR, 1256-59*, pp. 362, 377; *CLR, 1226-40*, p. 501; *CLR, 1240-45*, p. 205; *Calendar of Patent Rolls, 1266-72*, pp. 52, 64-65, 134-40.

14. Brieger, *English Art*, p. 172; Wormald, "Paintings in Westminster," p. 162; Albert Hollaender, "The Pictorial Work in the 'Flores Historiarum' of the so-called Matthew of Westminster," *Bulletin of the John Rylands Library* 28 (1944), 377; Margaret Rickert, *Painting in Britain: the Middle Ages* (London, 1954), p. 107.

15. J. Wickham Legg, "On an Inventory of the Vestry in Westminster Abbey taken in 1388," *Archaeologia* 52 (1890), pt. 1, pp. 233-234; M. R. James, "The Drawings of Matthew Paris," Walpole Society 14 (1925-26), 2.

16. James, "Drawings," p. 2; T. S. R. Boase, (*English Art, 1100-1216* Oxford, 1953), p. 286; Hollaender, "Pictorial Work," pp. 361, 377; Eric G. Millar, *English Illuminated Manuscripts from the Xth to the XIIIth Century* (Paris, 1926), p. 117; N. R. Ker, *Medieval Libraries of Great Britain* (London, 1941), p. 109; Wormald, "Painting in Westminster," p. 162; O. Elfrida Saunders, *English Illumination*, 2 vols. (Paris, 1928), 1:52.

17. For the range of opinion, see James, "Drawings," pp. 2, 26; Richard Vaughan, *Matthew Paris* (Cambridge, 1958), p. 222; Hollaender, "Pictorial Work," p. 377; Wormald, "Paintings in Westminster," p. 163; Rickert, *Painting in Britain*, p. 120; Brieger, *English Art*, p. 138n.; Tristram, *Wall Painting*, pp. 154-56; Henderson, "Studies," 30:85.

18. Wormald, "Paintings in Westminster," p. 165; Henderson, "Studies," 30:85.

19. Tristram, *Wall Painting*, pp. 449-50, states that William must have become a master painter after he became a monk at Westminster, but he offers no evidence.

20. Brieger, *English Art*, pp. 132-33, 138; Tristram, *Wall Painting*, pp. 94, 155-56; Lethaby, "Medieval Paintings," pp. 133-34.

21. *Customary of the Benedictine Monasteries of St. Augustine's, Canterbury, and St. Peter's, Westminster*, ed. E. M. Thompson, 2 vols., Henry Bradshaw Society, nos. 23 (1902) and 28 (1904); and see Wormald, "Paintings in Westminster," p. 161-62.

22. See David Knowles, *The Religious Orders in England*, 3 vols. (Cambridge, 1948-59), 1:13; J. Armitage Robinson, "The Benedictine Abbey of Westminster," *Church Quarterly Review* 59 (1907), 74; Barbara F. Harvey, *Documents Illustrating the Rule of Walter de Wenlock, Abbot of Westminster, 1283-1307*, 2 vols., Camden Society, 4th ser. (London, 1965), 2:5, 9; *Customary*, 1: Introduction.

23. *Customary*, 2: 36, 97, 161, 165. I have translated *infra* in passage 2 as "below." Its exact meaning here is not clear in relation to Westminster Abbey nor is there precise information about the extent of the abbey walls in the thirteenth century.

24. For the parallel passages, see *Customary*, 1:96, 206-07, 211; 2:36, 161, 165. On the Bermondsey Statute, see Matthew Paris, *Chronica Majora*, 7 vols., ed. H. R. Luard, Rolls Series (London, 1872-84), 6:179; *Chapters of the Black Monks*, ed. W. A. Pantin, Camden Society, 3rd ser. (London, 1931), p. 38.

25. See, for examples, Francis Bond, *Westminster Abbey* (Oxford, 1909), p. 282; Brieger, *English Art*, p. 154n.; Wormald, "Paintings in Westminster," pp. 161-62.

26. *Customary*, 2:xviii, 36, 96; H. F. Westlake, *Westminster Abbey, the Church of St. Peter*, 2 vols. (London, 1923) 2:415; T. F. Tout, *Chapters in the Administrative History of Medieval England*, 6 vols. (Manchester, 1920-33), 1:131-32, 134.

27. Bond, *Westminster Abbey*, p. xv; and see note 22 above.

28. G. Nilolaus Pevsner, *The Cities of London and Westminster*, 2 vols., The Buildings of England (London, 1957), 1:402; G. Gilbert Scott, *Gleanings from Westminster Abbey* (Oxford, 1863), pp. 31, 37; J. T. Mickelthwaite, "Further Notes on the Abbey Buildings at Westminster," *Archaelogical Journal* 51 (1894), 24; Bond, *Westminster Abbey*, p. 279; Brieger, *English Art*, p. 113.

Medieval Academe:
The Medical Masters of Montpellier

HOWELL H. GWIN, JR.

. Some of the better historical studies of the medical university at Montpellier are Stephen d'Irsay, *Histoire des Universités Françaises et Étrangeres des Origins à Nos Jours* 2 vols. (Paris, 1933-35); P. Pansier, "Les Maîtres de la Faculté de Medécine de Montpellier au Moyen-age," *Janus* 9 (1904), continued in 10 (1905); Vern L. Bullough, "The Development of the Medical University of Montpellier to the End of the Fourteenth Century," *Bulletin of the History of Medicine* 30 (1956); Richard Kohn, *L'Influence des Juifs à l'Origine de la Faculté de Medécine de Montpellier* (Paris, 1913); and Frédéric Fabrège, *Histoire de Maguelone*, 3 vols. (Montpellier, 1894-1911).

. Marcel Fournier, *Les Statuts et Priviléges des Universités Françaises depuis Leur Fondation Jusqu'en 1789*, 3 vols. (Paris, 1890-92), 2:78, 151-52.

. Ibid., 2:25-26, 37, 83.

. Ibid., 2:30, 98.

. *Cartulaire de l'Université de Montpellier*, 2 vols. (Montpellier, 1890-1912), 1:454; Pansier, "Les Maîtres," 9:540.

. Fournier, *Statuts*, 2:23, 37-39.

. Ibid., 2:74.

. Pansier, "Les Maîtres," 9:448.

. *Cartulaire*, 1:226-27.

. Ibid., 1:278.

. Fournier, *Statuts*, 2:68.

. Bullough, "Medical University," p. 217.

. Fournier, *Statuts*, 2:234, 268-69.

. Ibid., 2:68.

. Pansier, "Les Maîtres," 10, 117; Fournier, *Statuts*, 2:20-21.

. Fournier, *Statuts*, 2:21.

. Ibid., 2:69.

. Ibid., 2:70.

. Ibid., 2:69, 71.

. Alexandre-Charles Germain, *La Médecine Arabe et la Médecine Grèque à Montpellier* (Montpellier, 1879), p. 23.

. Fournier, *Statuts*, 2:69.

. Ibid., 2:26, 68, 86, 234.

. Ibid., 2:70.

. Quoted in Fabrège, *Histoire de Maguelone*, 3:344-45.

. Fournier, *Statuts*, 2:7.

. Lowrie J. Daly, *The Medieval University, 1200-1400* (New York, 1961), p. 109.

. Fournier, *Statuts*, 2:69.

. Pansier, "Les Maîtres," 9:449.

. Fournier, *Statuts*, 2:68.

. Ibid., 2:135.

. Alexandre-Charles Germain, *Les Maîtres Chirurgiens et l'École de Chirurgie de Montpellier* (Montpellier, 1880), p. 5.

. Fournier, *Statuts*, 2:170, 235.

. P. Pansier, "Les Medécins des Papes d'Avignon," *Janus* 14 (1909), 406.

. Theodor Puschmann, *A History of Medical Education from the Most Remote to the Most Recent Times*, tr. Evan H. Hare (London, 1891), p. 248.

. Fournier, *Statuts*, 2:67.

. Ibid., 2:69.

. Ibid., 2:5, 67, 103.

38. Ibid., 2:67.
39. Ibid., 2:66.
40. Ibid., 2:8, 14-16.
41. Ibid., 2:67.
42. Ibid., 2:68.
43. Pansier, "Les Maîtres," 9:508.
44. Ibid., 10:9; Pansier, "Les Medécins," p. 405.
45. Jean Imbert, *Les Hopitaux en Droit Canonique* (Paris, 1947), p. 167.

Eleanor of Provence

MARTHA BILES

1. *Foedera, Conventiones, Litterae*, ed. Thomas Rymer, 20 vols. (London, 1727), 1:346.
2. Matthew Paris, *Chronica Majora*, 7 vols., Rolls Series (London, 1876), 3:336.
3. *Calendar of the Patent Rolls, 1247-58*, pp. 200, 209 (hereafter cited as *CPR*).
4. J. H. Ramsay, *The Dawn of the Constitution, or the Reigns of Henry III and Edward I, 1216-1307* (New York, 1908), p. 281.
5. *Royal and Other Historical Letters Illustrative of the Reign of Henry III*, ed. W. W. Shirley, 2 vols., Rolls Series (London, 1866), 1:99 (hereafter cited as *Royal Letters*).
6. *Close Rolls of the Reign of Henry III, 1251-53*, pp. 334, 381 (hereafter cited as *CR*).
7. Michael R. Powicke, "Distraint of Knighthood and Military Obligation under Henry III," *Speculum* 25 (1950), p. 463.
8. John Campbell, *Lives of the Lord Chancellors of England*, 7 vols. (London, 1856), 1:144.
9. Powicke, "Distraint of Knighthood," p. 463.
10. Campbell, *Lives of the Lord Chancellors*, 1:144,
11. Paris, *Chronica Majora*, 6:282-88; *CR, 1253-54*, pp. 107, 111-12.
12. *Select Charters and Other Illustrations of English Constitutional History*, ed. William Stubbs (Oxford, 1890), pp. 366-67.
13. Ibid.
14. *Chronica Johannis de Oxenedes*, ed. H. Ellis, Rolls Series (London, 1859), p. 179.
15. *CPR, 1247-58*, pp. 400-01; *Calendar of Liberate Rolls, 1251-60*, p. 157.
16. Paris, *Chronica Majora*, 5:284-86.
17. *CPR, 1247-58*, p. 368.
18. Paris, *Chronica Majora*, 5:284-86.
19. M. le Marquis de Villeneuve-Trans, *Histoire de Saint Louis, Roi de France*, 3 vols. (Paris, 1839), 3:8.
20. Ramsay, *Dawn of the Constitution*, p. 150.
21. Agnes Strickland, "Eleanora of Provence, Surnamed La Belle, Queen of Henry III," *Lives of the Queens of England from the Norman Conquest*, 8 vols. (London, 1857), 1:386.
22. *Royal Letters*, passim; M. Champollion-Figeac, *Lettres des Rois et des Reines d'Angleterre*, 2 vols. (Paris, 1847), passim.
23. Paris, *Chronica Majora*, 3:362.
24. Reginald F. Treharne, *The Baronial Plan of Reform, 1258-1263* (Manchester, 1932), pp. 67-79.
25. Charles Bémont, *Simon de Montfort*, trans. E. F. Jacob (Oxford, 1930), pp. 152-55; Frederick M. Powicke, *King Henry III and the Lord Edward: The Community of*

the Realm in the Thirteenth Century 1947; repr. Oxford, 1966, pp. 374-79.

26. Harold S. Snellgrove, *The Lusignans in England, 1247-1258* (Albuquerque, 1950), pp. 84-86.

27. Paris, *Chronica Majora*, 4:703: Edward Jenks, *Edward Plantagenet, the English Justinian or the Making of the Common Law* (New York, 1902), p. 114.

28. M. Gavrilovitch, *Étude sur le traité de Paris de 1259* (Paris, 1899), pp. 54-66; Frederick M. Powicke, *The Thirteenth Century, 1216-1307* (Oxford, 1962), pp. 123-28.

29. *Royal Letters*, 2:168-71.

30. Powicke, *Thirteenth Century*, p. 168.

31. Bémont, *Simon de Montfort*, pp. 192-94.

32. William de Rishanger, *The Chronicle of the Barons' War*, ed. James O. Halliwell, Camden Society (London, 1840), p. 118.

33. *Annals of Dunstable* in vol. 3 of *Annales Monastici*, ed. H. R. Luard, 4 vols. Rolls Series (London, 1864), p. 223.

34. Bémont, *Simon de Montfort*, p. 201.

35. Powicke, *Thirteenth Century*, pp. 178-80.

36. Ibid., p. 180; *Calendar of Entries in the Papal Registers relating to Great Britain and Ireland: Papal Letters*, ed. W. H. Bliss, 4 vols. (London, 1893), 1:396-97 (hereafter cited as *Papal Letters*).

37. Bémont, *Simon de Montfort*, pp. 205-08.

38. Riśhanger, *Chronica*, p. 123.

39. Powicke, *Henry III*, pp. 459-68.

40. Gavrilovitch, *Étude sur le traité de Paris*, pp. 120-21.

41. Reinhold Pauli, *Simon de Montfort, Earl of Leicester, the Creator of the House of Commons* (London, 1876), p. 164; *Chronicon Thomae Wykes*, in vol. 4, *Annales Monastici*, ed. H. R. Luard, 5 vols., Rolls Series (London, 1864-69), p. 155 (hereafter cited as *Wykes*).

42. *Foedera*, 1:800.

43. Powicke, *Thirteenth Century*, pp. 199, 207n.; *Papal Letters*, 1:420.

44. *Wykes*, 162-64; *CPR, 1258-66*, p. 423; *Royal Letters*, 2:228; Rishanger, *Chronicle of the Barons' War*, pp. 44-47.

45. Ramsay, *Dawn of the Constitution*, p. 249; Walter Besant, *Medieval London*, 6 vols. (London, 1908-09), 1:33; Bémont, *Simon de Montfort*, p. 250 and n.3.

46. Bémont, *Simon de Montfort*, p. 251; George W. Prothero, *Simon de Montfort*, (London, 1877), p. 364. Eleanor de Montfort never came back to England. She died in 1274 at the Dominican convent of Montargis in France.

47. *CPR, 1266-72*, p. 715.

48. Henry made the original assignment of Eleanor's dower in October 1262 while the royal family was in Paris. The king and many members of his entourage were struck down during an epidemic, and several prominent nobles, including the young earl of Devon, Baldwin de Reviers, died. Even though Henry recovered, the careful arrangements he made for Eleanor's dower show that he must have been very near death. *CPR, 1268-72*, pp. 736-37. The dower she actually received in August 1273 had apparently not been altered since Henry's assignment in 1262. *CPR, 1272-81*, pp. 27-28.

49. *CPR, 1272-81*, pp. 76-77.

50. *Annals of Waverly*, in vol. 2 of *Annales Monastici*, ed. H. R. Luard, 4 vols., Rolls Series (London, 1864-69), p. 404.

51. *CPR, 1272-81*, p. 76.

52. *Annals of Waverly*, p. 409.

53. Ibid.; Powicke, *Henry III and the Lord Edward*, pp. 732-33.

54. *Annals of Waverly*, p. 410; Powicke, *Henry III and the Lord Edward*, pp. 733-35. *Annals of Oseney*, in vol. 4 of *Annals Monastici*, ed. H. R. Luard, Rolls Series (London, 1864-69); pp. 329-31.

55. The ceremony is described in British Museum Additional MSS 24686.

Josefa Amar y Borbón

CARMEN CHAVES MCCLENDON

1. Twentieth-century scholars have shown interest in the Spanish Enlightenment. Recent studies which provide new information as well as extensive bibliographies include: J. L. Alborg, *Historia de la literatura española*, 3 vols. (Madrid, 1975); Paula Demerson, *María Francisca de Sales Porto-carrero; Condesa del Montijo: Una figura de le ilustración* (Madrid, 1975); Carmen Martín Gaite, *Usos amorosos del dieciocho en españa* (Madrid, 1973); Joel Saugnieux, *Le Jansenisme Espagnol de XVIIIe Siecle: Ses Composants et Ses Sources* (Oviedo, 1975); Richard Her, *The Eighteenth Century Revolution in Spain* (Princeton, 1969); and Jean Sarrailh, *L'Espagne éclairée de la seconde moitie de XVIIIe* (Paris, 1964).

2. Biographical information about Josefa Amar is scarce. What has been included has come from Felix Latassa y Ortís, *Biblioteca nueva de los escritores aragoneses* (Zaragoza, 1793), part 4, p. 25; Federico Carlos Sainz de Robles, *Ensayo de un diccionario de mujeres célebres (Madrid, 1959)*; Rufino Blanco y Sanchez, *Bibliografia general de la educacion fisica* (Madrid, 1927), p. 10; as well as papers found at the Parroquia de San Miguel de los Navarros in Saragossa, Spain, and at the Archivo Histórico Nacional (Sección de Estado, Legajo, 3224) in Madrid.

3. Nigel Glendinning, *A Literary History of Spain: The Eighteenth Century* (New York, 1972), pp. 129-36.

4. The creation of the *Junta de damas* in Madrid was the culmination of about ten years of controversy about whether or not women should be allowed to attend meetings of the Economic Societies. The debate involved Campomanes, one of the government ministers; Cabarrús, an important banker; Jovellanos; Josefa Amar; and López de Ayala. Paula Demerson outines the controversy in her study of the countess of Montijo. The minutes of the thirteen years of meetings of the Junta are kept in the Archives of the Economic Society in Madrid.

5. E. García-Pandevenes, ed., *El Censor, 1781-1787* (Barcelona, 1972), pp. 124-25.

6. Jovellañós is recognized as the best example of Spain's enlightened elite. The most recent study of his career is Gaspar Gómez de la Serna, *Jovellanos el español perdido*, 2 vols. (Madrid, 1975).

7. Josefa's publications during the 1780s include: *Discurso del problema de si corresponde a los párrocos y curas de las aldeas, el instruir a los cobradores en los buenos elementos de la economía campestre* (Zaragoza, 1783); *Estado de la eloqüencia española en 1783* (Zaragoza, 1783); *Importancia de la instruccion que conviene dar a las mugeres* (Zaragoza, 1784); *Ramillete de escogidos eonsejos que la muger debe tener presentes en la vida del matrimonio* (Zaragoza, 1784); "Discurso en defensa del talento de las mugeres y de su aptitud para el gobierno," in *Memorial literario instructivo y curioso de la corte de Madrid* (August, 1786); *Memorias literarias de varios escritores de la corte* (Zaragoza, 1787). For a discussion of Amar y Borbón's essays, see Eva M. Kahiluoto Rudat, "La mujer ilustrada," *Letras femeninas* 2, no. 1 (1976), p. 20-32; see also Carmen C. McClendon, "Josefa Amar y Borbón y la educación femenina," *Letras femeninas* 4, no. 2 (1978), 3-11 and Josefa Amar y Borbón: Essayist, *Dieciocho*, 3:2 (1980), 138-43.

8. Josefa Amar y Borbón, *Discurso sobre la educacion fisica y moral de las mugeres* (Madrid, 1790).

9. Ibid., p. 16.

10. Ibid., p. xxvi.

11. Ibid., p. xxv.

12. Ibid., p. 340. In her annotated bibliographical information Josefa recommends reading M. de Leveson's *Émile Chretien, ou de l'education*.

13. Ibid., p. 13.

14. Ibid., p. 111.

15. Ibid., p. 108.
16. Ibid., p. 125.
17. Ibid., p. 128.
18. Ibid., p. 131.
19. Ibid., p. 136.
20. Ibid., p. 20.
21. Ibid., p. 21.
22. Ibid., p. 22.
23. Ibid., p. 197.
24. See Alice S. Rossi, *The Feminist Papers* (New York, 1974).

Bertha von Suttner and Rosika Schwimmer

REBECCA S. STOCKWELL

1. Mississippi University for Women supported this work with a faculty research grant.

2. Tolstoy to Suttner, October 10/12, 1891, Library of the United Nations, Geneva, Peace Archives, collection Suttner-Fried (Du 9), cited in Beatrix Kempf, *Woman for Peace* (Park Ridge, N.J., 1973), p. 27. Suttner was born in 1843 the daughter of Count Franz Joseph Kinsky and his wife Sophia Wilhelmine. She married Baron Artur Gundaccar von Suttner in 1876.

3. Suttner to Leopold Katscher, December 15 and 25, 1896, Schwimmer-Lloyd Collection R47, New York Public Library, Manuscripts and Archives Division (hereafter cited as S-L).

4. Suttner to Katscher, January 8, 1897, S-L R47.

5. S—L R42-47.

6. Suttner to Katscher, January 2 and 24, 1895, S-L R46.

7. Ibid., March 22 and November 29, 1896, S-L R47.

8. Ibid., April 23, 1900, S-L R42. It was 10 years later that Carnegie established the Endowment for International Peace, and 1913 when the Carnegie Foundation granted Suttner a monthly stipend.

9. Bertha von Suttner, *Memoirs of Bertha von Suttner: The Records of an Eventful Life*, 2 vols. (Boston, 1910), 2:393.

10. Ibid., 2: 419.

11. Edwin D. Mead, "Erinnerungen an Bertha von Suttner," *Die Friedens-Warte* 16, no. 7 (July 1914), 257, S-L R44.

12. Suttner to Katscher, Vienna, December 14, 1904, S-L R43, tells of receiving the contribution. Her luncheon with the Pulitzer family is described in her *Memoirs*, 2:425.

13. Suttner, *Memoirs*, 2:428-29.

14. *The Nation* 82 (April 12, 1906), 299.

15. New York *Evening World*, June 18, 1912, cited in Kempf, *Woman for Peace*, p. 116.

16. Marie L. Walton, "Lesson of the Last Biennial," *Overland Monthly* 61 (January 1913), 21.

17. Theodor Herzl, *The Complete Diaries of Theodor Herzl*, 5 vols. (New York & London, 1960), 4: 1496-1497.

18. Ibid., 3:837, 843.

19. Suttner, *Memoirs*, 2:430.

20. Hayne Davis, "The Baroness von Suttner," *Outlook* 82 (January 27, 1906), 213.

21. Ibid., p. 214.

22. Ellen Maury Slayden, *Washington Wife: Journal of Ellen Maury Slayden from 1897-1919* (New York, 1962), p. 190.

23. Suttner to Katscher, Vienna, December 19, 1910, S-L R43.

24. Ibid., November 24, 1906; see also the letter of October 7, 1908.

25. Ibid., November 7, 1911.

26. Kempf *Woman for Peace*, p. 115.

27. New York *Times*, May 30, 1912, p. 4. The reporter said she made an "eloquent address."

28. Kempf, *Woman for Peace*, p. 118.

29. Andrea Hofer-Proudfoot to Rosika Schwimmer, July 20, 1913, S-L R44, note.

30. Suttner to Katscher, April 29, 1912, S-L R43.

31. Kempf, *Woman for Peace*, p. 114.

32. Bertha von Suttner, *Der Kampf um die Vermeidung des Weltkriegs*, ed. Alfred H. Fried, 2 vols. (Zurich, 1917), 2:444, 455.

33. *Die Friedensbewegung* 7 (June 15, 1914), 290, in S-L N110.

34. San Francisco *Chronicle*, July 3, 1912.

35. Ibid.

36. Suttner, *Kampf*, p. 445.

37. New York *Times*, December 10, 1912. The *Times* account would place the incident in November.

38. Suttner, *Kampf*, p. 445.

39. San Francisco *Chronicle*, July 3, 1912.

40. *Die Friedensbewegung* (June 15, 1914), 290, S-L N110.

41. Suttner mentioned the meeting in her letter from St. Louis on October 20 in Suttner, *Kampf*, p. 442, and in a talk at the Hotel Astor on December 9, New York *Times*, December 10, 1912, p. 8; however, she did not state the exact date on which it took place.

42. Suttner, *Kampf*, p. 437.

43. San Francisco *Chronicle*, July 5, 1912.

44. Suttner, *Kampf*, p. 447.

45. Leopold Katscher, "Eine Philosophin des Mitleids," *Am hauslichen Herd* 16 (June 1913), 268-71, S-L N110.

46. Baltimore *Sun*, December 6, 1912.

47. Ibid. Suttner to Alfred Fried, Chicago, November 11, 1912, S-L R44. As far as practical results were concerned, she helped to form the Missouri and Wisconsin peace societies during the tour. Edson L. Whitney, *The American Peace Society: A Centennial History* (Washington, D.C., 1928), p. 273.

48. Fanny Hertz, "A Palm of Peace from German Soil," *International Journal of Ethics* 2, (January 1892), 202.

49. *The Outlook* 82 (March 3, 1906), 521.

50. *Review of Reviews* 43 (January 1911), 124.

51. Slaydon, *Washington Wife*, p. 190.

52. David Lloyd George, *War Memoirs*, 6 vols. (Boston, 1933-37), 1:50. Sutherland Denlinger, "If War Comes," New York *World Telegram*, March 25, 1935. Lola Maverick Lloyd to Schwimmer, Geneva, December 19, 1926, S-L A77.

53. Andrea Hofer-Proudfoot was the other. Hofer-Proudfoot to Schwimmer, July 20, 1913, S-L R44.

54. "A Page of Wilsoniana," p. 2, S-L A44.

55. International Committee for World Peace Award, *Rosika Schwimmer: World Patriot* (New York, 1937), p. 5.

56. London *Peace News*, January 31, 1941, S-L A77.

57. S-L A44.

58. S-L A45, A46, A47, M2, contain numerous press clippings and letters citing endorsement of Schwimmer's proposal wherever she spoke. Among those who approved her plan was Charlotte Perkins Gilman. Gilman to Schwimmer, New York, October 28, 1914, S-L A47.

59. Dayton, (Ohio) *Daily News*, October 19, 1914.

60. John Palmer Gavit, "A Woman Without a Country," *Survey Graphic* (September 1937), p. 487. Lola Maverick Lloyd to Schwimmer, Winnetka, Illinois, January 23, 1915, S-L A78, M3.

61. Chicago *Sunday Tribune*, December 20, 1914.

62. International Congress of Women, The Hague, 28th April-May 1st 1915, *Report* (Amsterdam, 1915), p. xlvii.

63. S-L A77.

64. Chicago *Daily Tribune*, July 22, 1915, S-L M36.

65. International Congress, *Report*, p. 154.

66. Jane Addams to Paul Kellogg, Hull's Cove, Maine, September 24, 1915, S-L A78. Addams wrote: "Mme. Schwimmer and Miss MacMillan . . . have made me see that if I came out conspicuously for any other plan than that adopted by the Hague Congress, . . . it would make great confusion in the continuity of our propaganda."

67. Chicago *Evening Post*, September 29, 1915; Lexington, Kentucky *Herald*, November 10, 1915; International Peace Congress, San Francisco and Berkeley, October 10-13, 1915, *Program*, S-L M3.

68. Louis Lochner, "Statement of Plans of the Henry Ford Expedition," S-L E4.

69. Alice Henry, "War and Its Fruits," *Life and Labor*, December 1914, discussed Schwimmer's work and then queried: "Why Not a Peace Ship?" S-L M2. The Brooklyn *Eagle*, December 5, 1915, said Schwimmer first proposed the "peace ship" a year earlier, S-L M3. A number of papers carried the story March 7-15, 1915, S-L M35.

70. Boston *Record*, March 13, 1915 and New York *Sun*, March 13, 1915 (the latter mentions negotiations with the Holland-American Line), S-L M35.

71. New York *Times*, March 24, 1915; New York *Tribune*, April 7, 1915, S-L M36. Most of the delegates did travel together on a Dutch ship, although Schwimmer sailed on the Scandinavian liner *Frederick VIII.*

72. Pittsburgh Press, November 24, 1915. The Meadville (Pennsylvania) *Tribune-Republican*, November 20, 1915, in an article datelined Detroit, said Ford had announced after his meeting with Schwimmer that he would see Wilson for peace, S-L M3.

73. New York *World*, November 27, 1915, S-L M3.

74. New York *Times*, November 23, 1915, S-L M3.

75. Schwimmer to Jane Addams, New York, August 19, 1916, S-L E40.

76. Jean Cabel O'Neill statement in S-L A78.

77. Ibid. In O'Neill's opinion, "Mr. Ford failed in that he did not let her have *some authority* in selection of those making up the party."

78. Lella Secor, *A Diary in Letters, 1915-1922*, ed. Barbara Moench Florence (New York, 1978), pp. 5, 11. Lella Secor was herself a young but experienced reporter incited at the last minute because of her acquaintance with another member of the party, Rebecca Shelly. She was very critical of the behavior of some of her colleagues, pp. 11n., 31, 277-78.

79. Waterbury (Connecticut) *American*, November 26, 1915: "Peacettes Fail to Move Wilson," "No Government Official to Go on the Ford Junket." Rochester (New York) *Union and Advertiser*, December 7, 1915: "All Is Not Peace on the Peace Ship Says Wireless." Detroit *Free Press*, November 26, 1915, reported that London, Ontario, clubwomen were unsympathetic to the peace mission, saying, "it is quite possible that Mrs. Schwimmer is an envoy of the central powers." London (Ontario) *Free Press*, November 26, 1915: "Windsor Women Take No Stock in Mrs. Schwimmer: Believe She Is Simply a Peace Emissary of the Huns." Providence (Rhode Island) *Journal*, December

4, 1915: "Entente Suspects Teuton Hand in Ford Undertaking." S-L M3.

80. Gaston Plantiff, "To the Members of the Ford Peace Expedition," December 23-24, 1915, S-L E5. Plantiff, who was left as business manager, explained Ford's departure as the result of illness.

81. S-L E5.

82. S-L M8. The last explanation was attributed to Gaston Plaintiff by John Ennis Jones, who was with the party.

83. Copenhagen *Pax*, January 1, 1916, S-L M6.

84. Elin Wagner typescript, January 1916, S-L M6.

85. Pottsville (Pennsylvania) *Chronicle*, December 30, 1915, S-L M5.

86. Florence L. Lattimore, "Jitney Diplomacy," *The Survey* 35 (February 12, 1916), 580.

87. *Pipp's Weekly* 4, no. 21 (September 15, 1923), 4-5. The Omaha *Bee*, December 26, 1915, S-L M37, defended Schwimmer.

88. New York *World*, February 26, 1916, S-L M6. Actually, she resigned two days later (S-L E5) and received her "formal release" on March 8 (S-L E57). Her male "replacement," Frederick H. Holt, did prefer to dismiss all the women delegates (S-L E18). Ford, too, was said to have thought "it was better that women did not have much to do with this." Katherine Leckie to Lewis Maverick, New York, October 16, 1916, S-L E10.

89. Schwimmer to Lewis Maverick, March 3, 1938, S-L E7.

CONTRIBUTORS

Martha Biles is professor of history at Delta State University, Cleveland, Mississippi.

Richard H. Bowers is honors professor of history at the University of Southern Mississippi, Hattiesburg, and has published articles on medieval history in *Speculum* and *The Southern Quarterly*.

John E. Davis is professor of history at Radford University, Radford, Virginia.

Howell H. Gwin, Jr. is professor of history and director of graduate studies at Lamar University, Beaumont, Texas.

R. Kent Lancaster is associate professor of history at Goucher College, Towson, Maryland.

Charles E. Lewis was associate professor of history at Mississippi State University, Starkville, until his death in 1975. He published articles in *Colloquia Germanica* and *Traditio*.

Carmen Chaves McClendon is director of honors and associate professor of foreign languages at Mississippi State University, Starkville. She is co-editor of *Dissertations in Hispanic Languages and Literatures, 1967-76,* (University Press of Kentucky), and has had articles published in *Letras Femeninas, Comparative Literature Studies,* and other journals.

Glover Moore is professor emeritus at Mississippi State University, Starkville. He is the author of *The Missouri Controversy,* (University Press of Kentucky), and several other books and articles.

Josiah C. Russell is professor emeritus at the University of New Mexico, Albuquerque. He is the author of nearly fifty books and articles including *Writers of Thirteenth Century England,* (Institute of Historical Research, London), *British Medieval Population,* (University of New Mexico Press), *Late Ancient and Medieval Populations,* (American Philosophical Society).

Rebecca S. Stockwell is professor of history at Mississippi University for Women, Columbus, and is co-author of *German Minorities and the Third Reich,* (Holmes and Meier).

Lee Wyatt is a captain in the United States Army and has taught at the United States Military Academy, West Point, New York. He is presently assigned to the Pentagon.

INDEX

Abingdon, St. Edmund of, 65
Addams, Jane, 149-50
Aldham, church of (Essex), 80
Alexander III, king of Scotland, 115
Alfred, king of England, 4
Almonds, 162, 165-67, 170
Alphonse, king of Castile, 115, 118-19.
Alum, 162, 169-70
Amar, Dr. José, 133
Amar y Borbón, Josefa: education of, 133-34; and the Junta de damas of the Madrid Economic Society, 135; publications of, 135-36; on the education of children, 136-37; on the education of women, 137-38; on the health of mothers and children, 138-39
American Federation of Women's Clubs, 146
Andover, 29, 164
Anglo-Saxons, size of families, 9. *See also* Thegns *and* Towns
Antifeminism, 155
Aubusson, Peter of, 75
Austrian Peace Society, 142

Baldock, 167
Balliol, John, 117
Banbury, church of (Lincs.), 80
Barri, Gerald du, 58
Beatrice of Provence, countess of Anjou, 119
Bek, John, king's clerk, 47, 50-51
Berwick, 43
Bigod, Hugh, justiciar of England, 126
Bigod, Roger, earl of Norfolk and marshal of England, 42, 49-50, 117
Blanche of Castile, queen of France, 77-78
Boston, 40
Bourbourch, Philippe de, castellan of Bruges, 21, 30, 159-70 *passim*
Boves, Hugh, 68, 70
Brewer, William, 70
Broughton, Ralph, justice, 48
Bristol, 49
Brittany, John of, earl of Richmond, 42
Bruges, 21, 29-30, 159, 161-72
Bryan, William Jennings, U. S. secretary of state, 148
Burghal Hidage, demographic information in, 4
Burh. *See* Towns
Burian, Count Stephan, Austro-Hungarian foreign minister, 150

Calais, 29
Cambridge, 10

Canonists, individuals cited: Balbus, Master Robert, 62; Blois, Master Peter of, 62; Calne, Master William of, 62; Honorius, Master, archdeacon of Richmond, 61; Mores, Master Richard de (also Anglicus, Ricardus), 61-62; Necton, Master William of, 62; Southwell, Master Simon of, 58-60; Tynemouth, Master John of, 58, 60
Canterbury, 6, 12; monks of, 58, 66
Cantilupe, William de, royal steward, 70
Carnegie, Andrew, 145
—Foundation, 145
—Peace Endowment, 145
Casalbon, Don Rafael, 133
Castello, John de, German knight, 33
Catt, Carrie Chapman, 148
Celestine III, pope, 58
Chaceporc, Hugh, 75
—Peter, keeper of the king's wardrobe, 75-81: and wardrobe administration, 75-76; diplomatic missions of, 77-78; episcopal election at Winchester, 78; constable of St. Briavel's, 79; benefices held by, 80; death of, 80
Charles III, king of Spain, 134
Chauliac, Guy, 106
Cheese, 160, 165, 168
Chester, 6, 12
Chichester, 49
—cathedral, 80
Cinque Ports, 45
Clare, Gilbert de, earl of Gloucester and Hertford, 32, 127-30
Clement IV, pope, 127
Clement V, pope, 99, 101
Cloth, 161-62, 164-65, 167-71; assize of, 24
Comnenus, Alexius, emperor of Byzantium, 16
Cork, 160
Corner, Master William de la, justice and bishop of Salisbury, 33, 43
Cossey, church of (Norfolk), 67
Cotswolds, 159
Cotton, 171
Court School of Illumination, 85-95; works attributed to, 86
Courtrai, 163
Croyden, church of (Surrey), 80

Damme, 161, 165
—Catherine of, 29, 170
Dampierre, Guy de, count of Flanders, 46-47, 50, 53
Dean, forest of, 79
Dixmude, 52